D0927275

TensorFlow®

by Matthew Scarpino

A Wiley Brand

TensorFlow® For Dummies®

Published by: **John Wiley & Sons, Inc.,** 111 River Street, Hoboken, NJ 07030-5774, www.wiley.com

Copyright © 2018 by John Wiley & Sons, Inc., Hoboken, New Jersey

Published simultaneously in Canada

For general information on our other products and services, please contact our Customer Care Department within the U.S. at 877-762-2974, outside the U.S. at 317-572-3993, or fax 317-572-4002. For technical support, please visit https://hub.wiley.com/community/support/dummies.

Wiley publishes in a variety of print and electronic formats and by print-on-demand. Some material included with standard print versions of this book may not be included in e-books or in print-on-demand. If this book refers to media such as a CD or DVD that is not included in the version you purchased, you may download this material at http://booksupport.wiley.com. For more information about Wiley products, visit www.wiley.com.

Library of Congress Control Number: 2018933981

ISBN 978-1-119-46621-5 (pbk); ISBN 978-1-119-46619-2 (ePub); 978-1-119-46620-8 (ePDF)

Manufactured in the United States of America

10 9 8 7 6 5 4 3 2 1

Contents at a Glance

Table of Contents

Introduction

Machine learning is one of the most fascinating and most important fields in modern technology. As I write this book, NASA has discovered faraway planets by using machine learning to analyze telescope images. After only three days of training, Google's AlphaGo program learned the complex game of Go and defeated the world's foremost master.

Despite the power of machine learning, few programmers know how to take advantage of it. Part of the problem is that writing machine learning applications requires a different mindset than regular programming. The goal isn't to solve a specific problem, but to write a general application capable of solving many unknown problems.

Machine learning draws from many different branches of mathematics, including statistics, calculus, linear algebra, and optimization theory. Unfortunately, the real world doesn't feel any obligation to behave mathematically. Even if you use the best mathematical models, you can still end up with lousy results. I've encountered this frustration on many occasions, and I've referred to neural networks more than once as "high-tech snake oil."

TensorFlow won't give you the ideal model for analyzing a system, but it will reduce the time and frustration involved in machine learning development. Instead of coding activation functions and normalization routines from scratch, you can access the many built-in features of the framework. *TensorFlow For Dummies* explains how to access these features and put them to use.

About This Book

TensorFlow is a difficult subject to write about. Not only does the toolset contain thousands of classes, but many of them perform similar roles. Furthermore, some classes are deprecated, while others are simply "not recommended for use."

Despite the vast number of classes, there are three classes that every TensorFlow developer should be familiar with: `Tensor`, `Graph`, and `Session`. The chapters in the first part of this book discuss these classes in detail and present many examples of their usage.

The chapters in Part 2 explain how you can use TensorFlow in practical machine learning tasks. I start with statistical methods, including linear regression, polynomial regression, and logistic regression. Then I delve into the fascinating topic of neural networks. I explore the operation of basic neural networks, and then I present convolutional neural networks (CNNs) and recurrent neural networks (RNNs).

The chapters in Part 3 present high-level TensorFlow classes that you can use to simplify and accelerate your applications. Of the many topics discussed, the most important is the Estimator API, which allows you to implement powerful machine learning algorithms with minimal code. I explain how to code estimators and execute them at high speed using the Google Cloud Platform (GCP).

Foolish Assumptions

In essence, this book covers two topics: the theory of machine learning and the implementation of the theory using TensorFlow. With regard to theory, I make few assumptions. I expect you to know the basics of linear algebra, but I don't expect you to know anything about machine learning. I also don't expect you to know about statistical regression or neural networks, so I provide a thorough introduction to these and other concepts.

With regard to TensorFlow development, I made assumptions related to your programming background. TensorFlow supports a handful of programming languages, but the central language is Python. For this reason, this book is Python-centric, and I provide all of the example code in Python modules. I explain how to install TensorFlow and access its modules and classes, but I don't explain what modules and classes are.

Icons Used in this Book

To help you navigate through the text, I inserted icons in the book's margin. Here's what they mean:

TIP

This icon indicates that the text contains suggestions for developing machine learning applications.

TECHNICAL STUFF

This icon precedes content that delves into the technical theory of machine learning. Many readers may find this theory helpful, but you don't need to know all the gritty details.

REMEMBER

As much as I love TensorFlow, I admit that it isn't simple to use or understand. There are many critical points to be familiar with, and in many cases, I use this icon to emphasize concepts that are particularly important.

Beyond the Book

This book covers a great deal of the TensorFlow API, but there's still a lot more to learn. The first place to look is the official documentation, which you can find at www.tensorflow.org. If you're interested in TensorFlow's functions and data structures, the best place to look is www.tensorflow.org/api_docs.

If you have a problem that you can't solve using this book or the official documentation, a great resource is StackOverflow. This site enables programmers to present questions and receive answers, and in my career, I've provided plenty of both. For TensorFlow-specific questions, I recommend visiting www.stackoverflow.com/questions/tagged/tensorflow.

In addition to what you're reading right now, this product also comes with a free access-anywhere Cheat Sheet that gives you some pointers on using TensorFlow. To get this Cheat Sheet, simply go to www.dummies.com and search for "TensorFlow For Dummies Cheat Sheet" in the Search box.

I also provide a great deal of example code that demonstrates how to put the theory into practice. Here's how to download the tfbook.zip file for this book.

1. On www.dummies.com, search for *TensorFlow For Dummies* or the book's ISBN.
2. When the book comes up, click on the More about this book link.

   You are taken to the book's product page, and the code should be on the Downloads tab.

After decompressing the archive, you'll find a series of folders named after chapters of this book. The example code for Chapter 3 is in the ch3 folder, the code for Chapter 6 is in ch6, and so on.

Where to Go from Here

The material in this book proceeds from the simple to the complex and from the general to the recondite. If you're already a TensorFlow expert, feel free to skip any chapters you're already familiar with. But if you're new to the toolset, I strongly recommend starting with Chapter 1 and proceeding linearly through Chapters 2, 3, 4, and so on.

I've certainly enjoyed writing this book, and I hope you enjoy the journey of discovery. *Bon voyage!*

1

Getting to Know TensorFlow

Explore the fascinating field of machine learning and discover why TensorFlow is so vital to machine learning development.

Download the TensorFlow package to your computer and install the complete toolkit.

Discover the fundamental data types of TensorFlow and the many operations that you can perform on tensors.

Understand how tensors and operations are stored in graphs and how graphs can be executed in sessions.

Investigate the process of TensorFlow training, which minimizes the disparity between a mathematical model and a real-world system.

Chapter **1**

Introducing Machine Learning with TensorFlow

TensorFlow is Google's powerful framework for developing applications that perform machine learning. Much of this book delves into the gritty details of coding TensorFlow modules, but this chapter provides a gentle introduction. I provide an overview of the subject and then discuss the developments that led to the creation of TensorFlow and similar machine learning frameworks.

Understanding Machine Learning

Like most normal, well-adjusted people, I consider *The Terminator* to be one of the finest films ever made. I first saw it at a birthday party when I was 13, and though most of the story went over my head, one scene affected me deeply: The heroine calls her mother and thinks she's having a warm conversation, but she's really talking to an evil robot from the future!

The robot wasn't programmed in advance with the mother's voice or the right sequence of phrases. It had to figure these things out on its own. That is, it had to analyze the voice of the real mother, examine the rules of English grammar, and generate acceptable sentences for the conversation. When a computer obtains information from data without receiving precise instructions, it's performing *machine learning*.

The Terminator served as my first exposure to machine learning, but it wouldn't be my last. As I write this book, machine learning is everywhere. My email provider knows that messages involving an "online pharmacy" are spam, but messages about "cheap mescaline" are important. Google Maps always provides the best route to my local Elvis cult, and Amazon.com always knows when I need a new horse head mask. Is it magic? No, it's machine learning!

Machine learning applications achieve this power by discovering patterns in vast amounts of data. Unlike regular programs, machine learning applications deal with uncertainties and probabilities. It should come as no surprise that the process of coding a machine learning application is completely different than that of coding a regular application. Developers need to be familiar with an entirely new set of concepts and data structures.

Thankfully, many frameworks have been developed to simplify development. At the time of this writing, the most popular is TensorFlow, an open-source toolset released by Google. In writing this book, my goal is to show you how to harness TensorFlow to develop your own machine learning applications.

Although this book doesn't cover the topic of ethics, I feel compelled to remind readers that programming evil robots is wrong. Yes, you'll impress your professor, and it will look great on a resume. But society frowns on such behavior, and your friends will shun you. Still, if you absolutely have to program an evil robot, TensorFlow is the framework to use.

The Development of Machine Learning

In my opinion, machine learning is the most exciting topic in modern software development, and TensorFlow is the best framework to use. To convince you of TensorFlow's greatness, I'd like to present some of the developments that led to its creation. Figure 1-1 presents an abbreviated timeline of machine learning and related software development.

FIGURE 1-1:
Developments in
machine learning
extend from
academia to
corporations.

1894	Francis Galton uses statistical regression to study inherited traits
1943	McCulloch and Pitts devise the first artificial neuron
1957	Frank Rosenblatt invents the perceptron
1963	Vapnik and Chervonenkis invent the Support Vector Machine algorithm
1974	Paul Werbos uses backpropagation to train a neural network
1982	John Hopfield demonstrates the Hopfield network
1998	Yann LeCunn trains a convolutional neural network to recognize digits
2002	Collobert, Kavukcuoglu, and Farabet release the Torch framework
2006	Netflix offers $1M for assistance with movie recommendations
2014	Ian Goodfellow et al invent generative adversarial networks
2015	Francois Chollet releases Keras for developing deep neural networks
2015	The Google Brain team releases TensorFlow 1.0

Once you understand why researchers and corporations have spent so much time developing the technology, you'll better appreciate why studying TensorFlow is worth your own time.

Statistical regression

Just as petroleum companies drill into the ground to obtain oil, machine learning applications analyze data to obtain information and insight. The formal term for this process is *statistical inference,* and its first historical record comes from ancient Greece. But for this purpose, the story begins with a nineteenth-century scientist named Francis Galton. Though his primary interest was anthropology, he devised many of the concepts and tools used by modern statisticians and machine learning applications.

Galton was obsessed with inherited traits, and while studying dogs, he noticed that the offspring of exceptional dogs tend to acquire average characteristics over time. He referred to this as the *regression to mediocrity.* Galton observed this phenomenon in humans and sweet peas, and while analyzing his data, he employed modern statistical concepts like the normal curve, correlation, variance, and standard deviation.

To illustrate the relationship between a child's height and the average height of the parents, Galton developed a method for determining which line best fits a series of data points. Figure 1-2 shows what this looks like. (Galton's data is provided by the University of Alabama.)

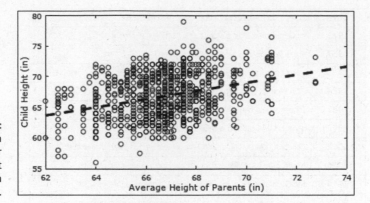

FIGURE 1-2:
Linear regression
identifies a clear
trend amidst
unclear data
points.

Galton's technique for fitting lines to data became known as *linear regression*, and the term *regression* has come to be used for a variety of statistical methods. Regression plays a critical role in machine learning, and Chapter 6 discusses the topic in detail.

Reverse engineering the brain

In 1905, Ramón y Cajal examined tissue from a chicken's brain and studied the interconnections between the cells, later called *neurons*. Cajal's findings fascinated scientists throughout the world, and in 1943, Warren McCulloch and Walter Pitts devised a mathematical model for the neuron. They demonstrated that their artificial neurons could implement the common Boolean AND and OR operations.

While researching statistics, a psychologist named Frank Rosenblatt developed another model for a neuron that expanded on the work of McCulloch and Pitts. He called his model the *perceptron,* and by connecting perceptrons into layers, he created a circuit capable of recognizing images. These interconnections of perceptrons became known as *neural networks.*

Rosenblatt followed his demonstrations with grand predictions about the future of perceptron computing. His predictions deeply influenced the Office of Naval Research, which funded the development of a custom computer based on perceptrons. This computer was called the Mark 1 Perceptron, and Figure 1-3 shows what it looks like.

The future of perceptron-based computing seemed bright, but in 1969, calamity struck. Marvin Minsky and Seymour Papert presented a deeply critical view of Rosenblatt's technology in their book, *Perceptrons* (MIT Press). They mathematically proved many limitations of two-layer feed-forward neural networks, such as the inability to learn nonlinear functions or implement the Boolean Exclusive OR (XOR) operation.

FIGURE 1-3:
The Mark 1
Perceptron was
the first
computer created
for machine
learning.

Credit: Cornell Aeronautical Laboratory.

Neural networks have progressed dramatically since the 1960s, and in hindsight, modern readers can see how narrow-minded Minsky and Papert were in their research. But at the time, their findings caused many, including the Navy and other large organizations, to lose interest in neural networks.

Steady progress

Despite the loss of popular acclaim, researchers and academics continued to investigate machine learning. Their work led to many crucial developments, including the following:

>> In 1965, Ivakhnenko and Lapa demonstrated multilayer perceptrons with nonlinear activation functions.

>> In 1974, Paul Werbos used backpropagation to train a neural network.

>> In 1980, Kunihiko Fukushima proposed the neocognitron, a multilayer neural network for image recognition.

>> In 1982, John Hopfield developed a type of recurrent neural network known as the Hopfield network.

>> In 1986, Sejnowski and Rosenberg developed NETtalk, a neural network that learned how to pronounce words.

These developments expanded the breadth and capabilities of machine learning, but none of them excited the world's imagination. The problem was that computers lacked the speed and memory needed to perform real-world machine learning in a reasonable amount of time. That was about to change.

The computing revolution

As the 1980s progressed into the 1990s, improved semiconductor designs led to dramatic leaps in computing power. Researchers harnessed this new power to execute machine learning routines. Finally, machine learning could tackle real-world problems instead of simple proofs of concept.

As the Cold War intensified, military experts grew interested in recognizing targets automatically. Inspired by Fukushima's neocognitron, researchers focused on neural networks specially designed for image recognition, called *convolutional neural networks* (CNNs). One major step forward took place in 1994, when Yann LeCunn successfully demonstrated handwriting recognition with his CNN-based LeNet5 architecture.

But there was a problem. Researchers used similar theories in their applications, but they wrote all their code from scratch. This meant researchers couldn't reproduce the results of their peers, and they couldn't re-use one another's code. If a researcher's funding ran out, it was likely that the entire codebase would vanish.

In the late 1990s, my job involved programming convolutional neural networks to recognize faces. I loved the theory behind neural networks, but I found them deeply frustrating in practice. Machine learning applications require careful tuning and tweaking to get acceptable results. But each change to the code required a new training run, and training a CNN could take *days*. Even then, I still didn't have enough training data to ensure accurate recognition.

One problem facing me and other researchers was that, while machine learning theory was mature, the process of software development was still in its infancy. Programmers needed frameworks and standard libraries so that they weren't coding everything by themselves. Also, despite Intel's best efforts, practical machine learning still required faster processors that could access larger amounts of data.

The rise of big data and deep learning

As the 21st century dawned, the Internet's popularity skyrocketed, and the price of data storage plummeted. Large corporations could now access terabytes of data about potential consumers. These corporations developed improved tools for analyzing their data, and this revolution in data storage and analysis has become known as the *big data revolution*.

Now CEOs were faced with a difficult question: How could they use their wealth of data to create wealth for their corporations? One major priority was advertising — companies make more money if they know which advertisements to show to their customers. But there were no clear rules for associating customers with products.

Many corporations launched in-house research initiatives to determine how best to analyze their data. But in 2006, Netflix tried something different. They released a large part of their database online and offered one million dollars to whoever developed the best recommendation engine. The winner, BellKor's Pragmatic Chaos, combined a number of machine learning algorithms to improve Netflix's algorithm by 10 percent.

Netflix wasn't the only high-profile corporation using machine learning. Google's AdSense used machine learning to determine which advertisements to display on its search engine. Google and Tesla demonstrated self-driving cars that used machine learning to follow roads and join traffic.

Across the world, large organizations sat up and paid notice. Machine learning had left the realm of wooly-headed science fiction and had become a practical business tool. Entrepreneurs continue to wonder what other benefits can be gained by applying machine learning to big data.

Researchers paid notice as well. A major priority involved distinguishing modern machine learning, with its high complexity and vast data processing, from earlier machine learning, which was simple and rarely effective. They agreed on the term *deep learning* for this new machine learning paradigm. Chapter 7 goes into greater detail regarding the technical meaning of deep learning.

Machine Learning Frameworks

One of the most important advances in practical machine learning involved the creation of frameworks. *Frameworks* automate many aspects of developing machine learning applications, and they allow developers to re-use code and take advantage of best practices. This discussion introduces five of the most popular frameworks: Torch, Theano, Caffe, Keras, and TensorFlow.

Torch

Torch is the first machine learning framework to attract a significant following. Originally released in 2002 by Ronan Collobert, it began as a toolset for numeric computing. Torch's computations involve multidimensional arrays called *tensors*, which can be processed with regular vector/matrix operations. Over time, Torch acquired routines for building, training, and evaluating neural networks.

Torch garnered a great deal of interest from academics and corporations like IBM and Facebook. But its adoption has been limited by its reliance on Lua as its interface language. The other frameworks in this discussion —Theano, Caffe, Keras, and TensorFlow — can be interfaced through Python, which has emerged as the language of choice in the machine learning domain.

Theano

In 2010, a machine learning group at the University of Montreal released Theano, a library for numeric computation. Like NumPy, Theano provides a wide range of Python routines for operating on multidimensional arrays. Unlike NumPy, Theano stores operations in a data structure called a *graph*, which it compiles into high-performance code. Theano also supports *symbolic differentiation*, which makes it possible to find derivatives of functions automatically.

Because of its high performance and symbolic differentiation, many machine learning developers have adopted Theano as their numeric computation toolset of choice. Developers particularly appreciate Theano's ability to execute graphs on graphics processing units (GPUs) as well as central processing units (CPUs).

Caffe

As part of his PhD dissertation at UC Berkeley, Yangqing Jia created Caffe, a framework for developing image recognition applications. As others joined in the development, Caffe expanded to support other machine learning algorithms and many different types of neural networks.

Caffe is written in C++, and like Theano, it supports GPU acceleration. This emphasis on performance has endeared Caffe to many academic and corporate developers. Facebook has become particularly interested in Caffe, and in 2007 it released a reworked version called Caffe2. This version improves Caffe's performance and makes executing applications on smartphones possible.

Keras

While other offerings focus on performance and breadth of capabilities, Keras is concerned with modularity and simplicity of development. François Chollet created Keras as an interface to other machine learning frameworks, and many developers access Theano through Keras to combine Keras's simplicity with Theano's performance.

Keras's simplicity stems from its small API and intuitive set of functions. These functions focus on accomplishing standard tasks in machine learning, which makes Keras ideal for newcomers to the field but of limited value for those who want to customize their operations.

François Chollet released Keras under the MIT License, and Google has incorporated his interface into TensorFlow. For this reason, many TensorFlow developers prefer to code their neural networks using Keras.

TensorFlow

As the title implies, this book centers on TensorFlow, Google's gift to the world of machine learning. The Google Brain team released TensorFlow 1.0 in 2015, and as of the time of this writing, the current version is 1.4. It's provided under the Apache 2.0 open source license, which means you're free to use it, modify it, and distribute your modifications.

TensorFlow's primary interface is Python, but like Caffe, its core functionality is written in C++ for improved performance. Like Theano, TensorFlow stores operations in a graph that can be deployed to a GPU, a remote system, or a network of remote systems. In addition, TensorFlow provides a utility called TensorBoard, which makes visualizing graphs and their operations possible.

Like other frameworks, TensorFlow supports execution on CPUs and GPUs. In addition, TensorFlow applications can be executed on the Google Cloud Platform (GCP). The GCP provides world-class processing power at relatively low cost, and in my opinion, GCP processing is TensorFlow's most important advantage. Chapter 13 discusses this important topic in detail.

Chapter **2**

Getting Your Feet Wet

Many chapters of this book present complex technical subjects and lengthy mathematical formulas. But not this one. This chapter is dead simple, and its goal is to walk you through the process of installing TensorFlow and running your first TensorFlow application.

A complete TensorFlow installation contains a vast number of files and directories. This chapter explores the installation and explains what the many files and folders are intended to accomplish. The discussion touches on many of Tensor-Flow's packages and the modules they contribute.

Once you've installed the TensorFlow toolset, it's easy to start coding and running applications. The end of the chapter presents a basic application that provides a cheery welcome to TensorFlow development.

Installing TensorFlow

Google provides two methods for installing TensorFlow, and the simpler option involves installing precompiled packages. This discussion presents a three-step process for installing these packages:

1. **Install Python on your development system.**

2. **Install the pip package manager.**

3. **Use pip to install TensorFlow.**

The second installation method involves compiling TensorFlow from its source code. This option takes time and effort, but you can obtain better performance because your TensorFlow package will take the fullest advantage of your processor's capabilities. Chapter 12 explains how to obtain and compile TensorFlow's source code.

Python and pip/pip3

TensorFlow supports development with Java and C++, but this book focuses on Python. I use Python 3 in the example code, but you're welcome to use Python 2. As I explain in the upcoming section "Setting the Style," TensorFlow applications should be accessible to both versions.

Python's official package manager is *pip*, which is a recursive acronym that stands for "pip installs Python." To install packages like TensorFlow, you can use pip on Python 2 systems or pip3 on Python 3 systems. Package management commands have the following format:

```
pip <command-name> <command-options>
```

pip and pip3 accept similar commands and perform similar operations. For example, executing pip list or pip3 list prints all the Python packages installed on your system. Table 2-1 lists this and five other commands.

TABLE 2-1 ## Package Management Commands

Command Name	Description
install	Installs a specified package
uninstall	Uninstalls a specified package
download	Downloads a package, but doesn't install it
list	Lists installed packages
show	Prints information about a specified package
search	Searches for a package whose name or summary contains the given text

For this discussion, the most important command to know is pip install and pip3 install. But keep in mind that pip/pip3 can perform many other operations.

TIP

If you execute a TensorFlow application using a precompiled package, you may receive messages like "The TensorFlow library wasn't compiled to use *XYZ* instructions, but these are available on your machine and could speed up CPU computations." To turn off these messages, create an environment variable named `TF_CPP_MIN_LOG_LEVEL` and set its value to 3.

Installing on Mac OS

Many versions of Mac OS have Python already installed, but I recommend obtaining and installing a new Python package. If you visit `www.python.org/downloads`, you see one button for Python 2 and another for Python 3. If you click one of these buttons, your browser downloads a PKG file that serves as the Python installer.

When you launch the installer, the Python installation dialog box appears. To install the package, follow these five steps:

1. **In the Introduction page, click the button labeled Continue.**
2. **In the Read Me page, click the button labeled Continue.**
3. **In the License page, click the button labeled Continue and then click Agree to accept the software license agreement.**
4. **In the Installation Type page, click Install to begin the installation process, entering your password, if necessary.**
5. **When the installation is complete, click Close to close the dialog box.**

If the installation completes successfully, you can run `pip` or `pip3` on a command line. You can install TensorFlow with the following command:

```
pip install tensorflow
```

This command tells the package manager to download TensorFlow, TensorBoard, and a series of dependencies. One dependency is `six`, which supports compatibility between Python 2 and 3. If the installation fails due to a preinstalled `six` package, you can fix the issue by executing the following command:

```
pip install --ignore-installed six
```

This command tells pip to install `six` on top of the existing installation. After this installation completes, you should be able to run `pip install tensorflow` without error. On my system, the installer stores the TensorFlow files in the `/Library/Frameworks/Python.framework/Versions/<ver>/lib/python<ver>/site-packages/tensorflow` directory.

Installing on Linux

Many popular distributions of Linux are based on Debian, including Ubuntu and Linux Mint. These distributions rely on the Advanced Package Tool (APT) to manage packages, which you can access on the command line by entering `apt-get`. This discussion explains how to install TensorFlow on these and similar operating systems.

Most Linux distributions already have Python installed, but it's a good idea to install the full development version and pip/pip3. The following command installs both for Python 2:

```
sudo apt-get install python-pip python-dev
```

Alternatively, the following command performs the installation for Python 3:

```
sudo apt-get install python3-pip python3-dev
```

After installation completes, you should be able to execute `pip` or `pip3` on the command line. The following command installs the TensorFlow package and its dependencies (use `pip3` for Python 3):

```
sudo pip install tensorflow
```

This command installs TensorFlow, TensorBoard, and their dependencies. On my Ubuntu system, the installer stores the files in the `/usr/local/lib/python<ver>/dist-packages/tensorflow` directory.

Installing on Windows

For Windows users, TensorFlow's documentation specifically recommends installing a 64-bit version of Python 3.5. To download the installer, visit `www.python.org/downloads/windows`, find a version of Python 3, and click the link entitled Windows x86-64 executable installer. This downloads an `*.exe` file that serves as the installer.

When you launch the installer, the Python setup dialog box appears. The following steps install Python on your system:

1. Check the checkbox for adding the Python installation directory to the PATH variable.
2. Click the link labeled Install Now.
3. When installation finishes, click the Close button to close the installer.

After you install Python, you should be able to run `pip3` on a command line. You can install TensorFlow with the following command:

```
pip3 install tensorflow
```

The package manager downloads TensorFlow, TensorBoard, and the packages' dependencies. On my Windows system, the installer stores the files to the `C:\Users\<name>\AppData\Local\Programs\Python\Python<ver>\Lib\site-packages\tensorflow` directory.

Exploring the TensorFlow Installation

Once you install TensorFlow, you have a directory named `tensorflow` that contains a wide variety of files and folders. Two top-level folders are particularly important. The `core` directory contains the TensorFlow's primary packages and modules. The `contrib` directory contains secondary packages that may later be merged into core TensorFlow.

When you write a TensorFlow application, it's important to be familiar with the different packages and the modules they provide. Table 2-2 lists the all-important `tensorflow` package and nine other packages.

TABLE 2-2   **Important TensorFlow Packages**

Package	Content
tensorflow	Central package of the TensorFlow framework, commonly accessed as `tf`
tf.train	Optimizers and other classes related to training
tf.nn	Neural network classes and related math operations
tf.layers	Functions related to multilayer neural networks
tf.contrib	Volatile or experimental code
tf.image	Image-processing functions
tf.estimator	High-level tools for training and evaluation
tf.logging	Functions that write data to a log
tf.summary	Classes needed to generate summary data
tf.metrics	Functions for measuring the outcome of machine learning

The first package, `tensorflow`, is TensorFlow's central package. Most applications import this package as `tf`, so when you see `tf` in code or an example, remember that it refers to the `tensorflow` package.

As I explain in Chapter 5, training is a crucial operation in machine learning applications. The `tf.train` package provides many of the modules and classes needed for TensorFlow training. In particular, it provides the optimizer classes that determine which algorithm should be used for training.

The `tf.nn` and `tf.layers` packages provide functions that create and configure neural networks. The two packages overlap in many respects, but the functions in `tf.layers` focus on multilayer networks, while the functions in `tf.nn` are suited toward general purpose machine learning.

Many of the packages in `tf.contrib` contain variants of core capabilities. For example, `tf.contrib.nn` contains variants of the features in `tf.nn` and `tf.contrib.layers` contains variants of the features in `tf.layers`. `tf.contrib` also provides a wealth of interesting and experimental packages, including the following:

>> `tf.contrib.keras`: Makes it possible to interface TensorFlow using the Keras interface

>> `tf.contrib.ffmpeg`: Enables audio processing through the open-source FFMPEG toolset

>> `tf.contrib.bayesflow`: Contains modules related to Bayesian learning

>> `tf.contrib.integrate`: Provides the `odeint` function, which integrates ordinary differential equations

The last three packages in Table 2-2 enable developers to analyze their applications and produce output. The functions in `tf.logging` enable logging and can be used to write messages to the log. The classes and functions in `tf.summary` generate data that can be read by TensorBoard, a utility for visualizing machine learning applications. The functions in `tf.metrics` analyze the accuracy of machine learning operations.

Running Your First Application

After you install TensorFlow, you're ready to start creating and executing applications. This section walks through the process of running an application that prints a simple message.

Exploring the example code

You can download this book's example code from www.dummies.com by searching for *TensorFlow For Dummies* and going to the Downloads tab. The archive's name is tf_dummies.zip, and if you decompress it, you see that it contains folders named after chapters (ch2, ch3, and so on).

Each chapter folder contains one or more Python files (*.py). In each case, you can execute the module by changing to the directory and running python or python3 followed by the filename.

For example, if you have Python 2 installed, you can execute the code in simple_math.py by changing to the ch3 directory and entering the following command:

```
python simple_math.py
```

The code for Chapter 13 is special because it's intended to be executed on the Google Cloud Platform, but that topic is far too exciting to be discussed here.

I haven't provided any official license for this book's example code, so you're free to use it in professional products, academic work, and morally questionable experiments. But if you use any of this code to program evil robots, I will know, and I'll be disappointed.

Launching Hello TensorFlow!

Programming books have a long tradition of introducing their topic with a simple example that prints a welcoming message. This book is no exception. If you open the ch2 directory in this book's example code, you find a module named hello_tensorflow.py. Listing 2-1 presents the code.

LISTING 2-1: **Hello TensorFlow!**

```python
"""A simple TensorFlow application"""
from __future__ import absolute_import
from __future__ import division
from __future__ import print_function
import tensorflow as tf

# Create tensor
msg = tf.string_join(["Hello ", "TensorFlow!"])

# Launch session
with tf.Session() as sess:
    print(sess.run(msg))
```

This code performs three important tasks:

1. **Creates a `Tensor` named `msg` that contains two string elements.**

2. **Creates a `Session` named `sess` and makes it the default session.**

3. **Launches the new `Session` and prints its result.**

Running the code is simple. Open a command line and change to the `ch2` directory in this book's example code. Then, if you're using Python 2, you can execute the following command:

```
python hello_tensorflow.py
```

If you're using Python 3, you can run the module with the following command:

```
python3 hello_tensorflow.py
```

As the Python interpreter does its magic, you should see the following message:

```
b'Hello TensorFlow!'
```

The welcome message is straightforward, but the application's code probably isn't as clear. A `Tensor` instance is an n-dimensional array that contains numeric or string data. Tensors play a central role in TensorFlow development, and Chapter 3 discusses them in detail.

A `Session` serves as the environment in which TensorFlow operations can be executed. All TensorFlow operations, from addition to optimization, must be executed through a session. Chapter 4 explains how you can create, configure, and execute sessions.

Setting the Style

Google provides the TensorFlow Style Guide at `www.tensorflow.org/community/style_guide`. Four of its guidelines are as follows:

>> Code in TensorFlow applications should be compatible with both Python 2 and Python 3.

>> In keeping with the first guideline, every module should have `import` statements for `absolute_import`, `division`, and `print_function`.

» Indenting should use two spaces instead of four.

» TensorFlow modules should rely on the guidelines in the PEP (Python Enhancement Proposal) 8 Style Guide except where they conflict with the TensorFlow Style Guide.

You can find the PEP8 guide at www.python.org/dev/peps/pep-0008. Its many recommendations include the use of docstrings, uppercase for class names, and lowercase for functions and modules. You can check Python code against the PEP8 by installing the pylint package and running `pylint filename.py`.

The example code in this book follows all of Google's recommendations except two. First, I use four spaces because that's the Python way. Second, I prefer to name constants with simple lowercase names, such as the `msg` constant in Listing 2-1, earlier in this chapter.

I don't blame you if you find my rebellion inexcusable. But if you send the Python police after me, they'll never take me alive.

Chapter **3**

Creating Tensors and Operations

I n grad school, I took a course on tensor mathematics that covered the usage of tensors in electromagnetism. The professor assured us that the theory was "beautiful" and "elegant," but we beleaguered students described the relativistic mathematics as "indecipherable" and "terrifying."

TensorFlow's central data type is the tensor, and happily, it has nothing to do with electromagnetism or relativity. In this book, a tensor is just a regular array. If you're familiar with Torch's Tensors or NumPy's ndarrays, you'll be glad to know that TensorFlow's tensors are similar in many respects.

Unfortunately, you can't access these tensors with regular Python routines. For this reason, the TensorFlow API provides a vast assortment of functions for creating, transforming, and operating on tensors. This chapter presents many of these functions and demonstrates how you can use them.

Creating Tensors

Just as most programs start by declaring variables, most TensorFlow applications start by creating tensors. A tensor is an array with zero or more dimensions. A zero-dimensional tensor is called a *scalar*, a one-dimensional tensor is called a *vector*, and a two-dimensional tensor is called a *matrix*. Keep in mind these three points about tensors:

>> Every tensor is an instance of the Tensor class.

>> A tensor may contain numbers, strings, or Boolean values. Every element of a tensor must have the same type.

>> Tensors can be created, transformed, and operated upon using functions of the tf package.

This discussion explains how to create tensors with known values and random values. Then I also present functions that transform a tensor's content. Once you understand these topics, you'll have no trouble coding simple routines for tensor processing.

Creating Tensors with Known Values

The tf package provides seven functions that form tensors with known values. Table 3-1 lists them and provides a description of each.

TABLE 3-1 **Creating Tensors with Known Values**

Function	Description
constant(value, dtype=None, shape = None, name = 'Const', verify_shape=False)	Returns a tensor containing the given value
zeros(shape, dtype=tf.float32, name = None)	Returns a tensor filled with zeros
ones(shape, dtype=tf.float32, name=None)	Returns a tensor filled with ones
fill(dims, value, name=None)	Returns a tensor filled with the given value
linspace(start, stop, num, name=None)	Returns a tensor containing a linear range of values
range(start, limit, delta=1, dtype=None, name='range')	Returns a tensor containing a range of values
range(limit, delta=1, dtype=None, name='range')	Returns a tensor containing a range of values

A tensor may have multiple dimensions, and the number of dimensions in a tensor is its *rank*. The lengths of a tensor's dimensions form an array called the tensor's *shape*. Many of the functions in Table 3-1 accept a shape parameter that identifies the desired shape of the new tensor. The following examples demonstrate how you can set this parameter:

» [] — The tensor contains a single value.

» [3] — The tensor is a one-dimensional array containing three values.

» [3, 4] — The tensor is a 3-x-4 matrix.

» [3, 4, 5] — The tensor is a multidimensional array whose dimensions equal 3, 4, and 5.

Most of the functions in Table 3-1 have a dtype argument that identifies the data type of the tensor's elements. The default value of dtype is float32, which indicates that, by default, tensors contain single-precision floating-point values. Table 3-2 lists float32 and other possible data types.

TABLE 3-2

Tensor Data Types

Data Type	Description
bool	Boolean values
uint8/uint16	Unsigned integers
quint8/quint16	Quantized unsigned integers
int8/int16/int32/int64	Signed integers
qint8/qint32	Quantized signed integers
float16/float32/float64	Floating-point values
complex64/complex128	Complex floating-point values
string	Strings

Each function in Table 3-1 accepts an optional name argument that serves as an identifier for the tensor. Applications can access a tensor by name through the tensor's graph. Chapter 4 discusses the topic of graphs in detail.

The constant function

The most popular function in Table 3-1 is constant. Its only required argument is the first, which defines the value or values to be stored in the tensor. You can provide these values in a list, and the following code creates a one-dimensional tensor containing three floating-point values:

```
t1 = tf.constant([1.5, 2.5, 3.5])
```

Multidimensional arrays use similar notation. The following code creates a 2-x-2 matrix and sets each of its elements to the letter b:

```
t2 = tf.constant([['b', 'b'], ['b', 'b']])
```

By default, TensorFlow won't raise an error if the function's first argument does-n't have the shape given by the shape argument. But if you set the last argument, verify_shape, to True, TensorFlow will verify that the two shapes are equal. The following code provides an example of mismatched shapes:

```
t3 = tf.constant([4, 2], tf.int16, [3], 'Const', True)
```

In this case, the given shape, [3], doesn't match the shape of the first argument, which is [2]. As a result, TensorFlow displays the following error:

```
TypeError: Expected Tensor's shape: (3,), got (2,).
```

zeros, ones, and fill

The functions zeros, ones, and fill create tensors whose elements all have the same value. For zeros and ones, the only required argument is shape, which identifies the shape of the desired tensor. As an example, the following code creates a simple 1-x-3 vector whose elements equal 0.0:

```
zero_tensor = tf.zeros([3])
```

Similarly, the following function call creates a 4-x-4 matrix whose elements equal 1.0:

```
one_tensor = tf.ones([4, 4])
```

The fill function requires a value parameter, which sets the value of the tensor's elements. The following code creates a three-dimensional tensor whose values are set to 81.0:

```
fill_tensor = tf.fill([1, 2, 3], 81.0)
```

Unlike `zeros` and `ones`, `fill` doesn't have a `dtype` argument. It can only create tensors containing 32-bit floating point values.

Creating sequences

The `linspace` and `range` functions create tensors whose elements change regularly between a start and end value. The difference between them is that `linspace` creates a tensor with a specific number of values. For example, the following code creates a 1-x-5 tensor whose elements range from 5.0 to 9.0:

```
lin_tensor = tf.linspace(5., 9., 5)
# Result: [5. 6. 7. 8. 9.]
```

Unlike `linspace`, `range` doesn't accept the number of elements in the tensor. Instead, it computes successive elements by adding a value called a `delta`. In the following code, `delta` is set to 0.5:

```
range_tensor = tf.range(3., 7., delta=0.5)
# Result: [3.0 3.5 4.0 4.5 5.0 5.5 6.0 6.5]
```

Like Python's `range` function, TensorFlow's `range` function can be called without the `start` parameter. In this case, the starting value is assumed to be 0.0. The following code demonstrates this:

```
range_tensor = tf.range(1.5, delta=0.3)
# Result: [0.0 0.3 0.6 0.9 1.2]
```

If the `delta` parameter is positive, the starting value must be less than the ending value. If `delta` is negative, the starting value must be greater than the ending value.

Creating Tensors with Random Values

Many TensorFlow applications require tensors that contain random values instead of predetermined values. The `tf` package provides many functions for creating random-valued tensors and Table 3-3 lists five of them.

The `random_normal` and `truncated_normal` functions create tensors containing normally distributed values. Their arguments determine the characterristics of the distribution. Figure 3-1 shows what a normal distribution looks like with a mean of 0.0 and a standard deviation (σ) of 1.0.

TABLE 3-3   **Creating Tensors with Random Values**

Function	Description
`random_normal(shape, mean=0.0, stddev=1.0, dtype=tf.float32, seed=None, name=None)`	Creates a tensor with normally distributed values
`truncated_normal(shape, mean=0.0, stddev=1.0, dtype=tf.float32, seed=None, name=None)`	Creates a tensor with normally distributed values excluding those lying outside two standard deviations
`random_uniform(shape, minval=0, maxval=None, dtype=tf.float32, seed=None, name=None)`	Creates a tensor with uniformly distributed values between the minimum and maximum values
`random_shuffle(tensor, seed=None, name=None)`	Shuffles a tensor along its first dimension
`set_random_seed(seed)`	Set the seed value for all random number generation in the graph

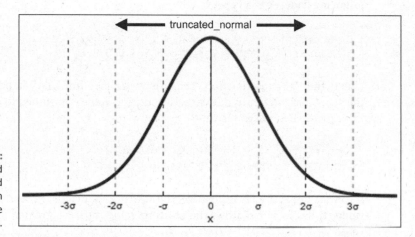

FIGURE 3-1: Values beyond three standard deviations from the mean are highly unlikely.

Standard deviation tells you how much a normally distributed variable is expected to vary from the mean. Approximately 68.2 percent of the time, a variable lies within one standard deviation from the mean, while 95.4 percent of the time, the variable lies within two standard deviations.

In the `random_normal` and `truncated_normal` functions, the default mean is 0.0, and the default standard deviation is 1.0. `random_normal` generates random values throughout the distribution, so very large and very small values are unlikely but possible. The following code calls `random_normal` to generate 20 random values:

```
rnd_ints = tf.random_normal([10], dtype=tf.float64)
```

In contrast, `truncated_normal` guarantees that the generated values lie within two standard deviations from the mean. Any value outside this range will be discarded and reselected. In this manner, `truncated_normal` ensures that the tensor won't contain any improbably large or small values.

`random_uniform` creates a tensor containing uniformly distributed values that lie between a minimum and maximum. Because the distribution is uniform, every value is equally likely.

`random_shuffle` doesn't create a new tensor, but randomly shuffles the values in an existing tensor. This shuffling is limited to the tensor's first dimension.

Each function in Table 3-3 accepts a `seed` parameter that initializes the random number generator. Setting a random seed is important to ensure that sequences aren't repeated.

You can obtain and set a seed value by calling `set_random_seed`, which accepts a floating-point value and makes the argument the seed for every operation in the current graph. Chapter 4 discusses the topic of graphs in detail.

Transforming Tensors

An application must specify the shape of each tensor to be created. The `tf` package provides functions that update tensors and their shapes after creation. Table 3-4 lists these transformation functions and provides a description of each.

TABLE 3-4   **Functions for Transforming Tensors**

Function	Description
`cast(tensor, dtype, name=None)`	Changes the tensor's data type to the given type
`reshape(tensor, shape, name=None)`	Returns a tensor with the same elements as the given tensor with the given shape
`squeeze(tensor, axis=None, name=None, squeeze_dims=None)`	Removes dimensions of size 1
`reverse(tensor, axis, name=None)`	Reverses given dimensions of the tensor
`slice(tensor, begin, size, name=None)`	Extracts a portion of a tensor
`stack(tensors, axis=0, name='stack')`	Combines a list of tensors into a tensor of greater rank
`unstack(tensor, num=None, axis=0, name='unstack')`	Splits a tensor into a list of tensors of lesser rank

Despite its name, reshape doesn't modify an existing tensor. Instead, the function returns a tensor with the same elements as the given tensor and the specified shape. For example, the following code uses reshape to convert a four-element vector into a 2-x-2 matrix:

```
vec = tf.constant([1., 2., 3., 4.])
mat = tf.reshape(vec, [2, 2])
# Result: [[1. 2.], [3. 4.]]
```

If any dimension of a tensor has a size of 1, calling squeeze will remove it from the tensor, thereby reducing the tensor's rank. If the function's axis parameter identifies one or more dimensions, only those dimensions will be affected by squeeze.

In the reverse function, the axis parameter identifies one or more dimensions to be reversed. The following code demonstrates how reverse works:

```
mat = tf.constant([[1., 2., 3.], [4., 5., 6.]])
rev_mat = tf.reverse(end, [0])
# Result: [[4. 5. 6.], [1. 2. 3.]]

rev_mat = tf.reverse(end, [1])
# Result: [[3. 2. 1.], [6. 5. 4.]]

rev_mat = tf.reverse(end, [0, 1])
# Result: [[6. 5. 4.], [3. 2. 1.]]
```

The slice function extracts subtensors from a tensor. The begin parameter identifies the index of the first element to be extracted, and size identifies the shape of the tensor to be extracted, starting from the begin location.

For example, suppose that you want to extract the lower-right 2-x-2 matrix from a 3-x-3 matrix. The index of the first extracted element is [1, 1] and the size of the desired tensor is [2, 2]. The following code uses slice to perform this extraction:

```
mat =
    tf.constant([[1., 2., 3.], [4., 5., 6.], [7., 8., 9.]])
slice_mat = tf.slice(mat, [1, 1], [2, 2])
# Result: [[5. 6.] [7. 8.]]
```

stack accepts a list of tensors of rank N and returns a single tensor of rank N+1. In addition to having the same rank, the input tensors must have the same shape.

The following code demonstrates how `stack` can be used. The function combines three one-dimensional tensors into a two-dimensional tensor:

```
t1 = tf.constant([1., 2.])
t2 = tf.constant([3., 4.])
t3 = tf.constant([5., 6.])
t4 = tf.stack([t1, t2, t3])
```

When these operations execute, t4 will equal [[1. 2.] [3. 4.] [5. 6.]]. If the `axis` parameter is set to 1, stacking will be performed along the second dimension, so t4 will set to [[1. 3. 5.] [2. 4. 6.]].

`unstack` performs the inverse operation of `stack`. That is, `unstack` accepts a tensor of rank N and returns a list of tensors of rank N-1. The `num` parameter determines how many tensors should be unpacked, and if this isn't set, `unstack` infers the number from the tensor's shape.

Creating Operations

Machine learning applications are fundamentally mathematical, and TensorFlow provides a wealth of routines for performing mathematical operations on tensors. Each routine is represented by a function of the `tf` package, and each function returns a tensor. This section presents a large portion of the operations available, but the `tensorflow` package provides many more functions than those discussed here.

To describe these functions, I use statements like "function X performs operation Y." But these statements aren't completely accurate. These functions, like the transformation functions discussed in the preceding section, don't actually perform their corresponding operations — at least, not directly.

For example, `tf.multiply` doesn't immediately multiply its arguments and return a product. Instead, it adds a multiplication operation to the current graph, and when a session executes the graph, the multiplication will be performed along with the rest of the graph's operations. This process may seem confusing, but don't be concerned. Chapter 4 looks at graphs and sessions in detail.

Basic math operations

When it comes to TensorFlow operations, its best to start simple. Table 3-5 lists 12 functions that perform basic math operations.

TABLE 3-5 **Basic Math Operations**

Function	Description
add(x, y, name=None)	Adds two tensors
subtract(x, y, name=None)	Subtracts two tensors
multiply(x, y, name=None)	Multiplies two tensors
divide(x, y, name=None)	Divides the elements of two tensors
div(x, y, name=None)	Divides the elements of two tensors
add_n(inputs, name=None)	Adds multiple tensors
scalar_mul(scalar, x)	Scales a tensor by a scalar value
mod(x, y, name=None)	Performs the modulo operation
abs(x, name=None)	Computes the absolute value
negative(x, name=None)	Negates the tensor's elements
sign(x, name=None)	Extracts the signs of the tensor's element
reciprocal(x, name=None)	Computes the reciprocals

The first four functions perform element-wise arithmetic. The following code demonstrates how they work:

```
a = tf.constant([3., 3., 3.])
b = tf.constant([2., 2., 2.])
sum = tf.add(a, b)            # [ 5. 5. 5. ]
diff = tf.subtract(a, b)      # [ 1. 1. 1. ]
prod = tf.multiply(a, b)      # [ 6. 6. 6. ]
quot = tf.divide(a, b)        # [ 1.5 1.5 1.5 ]
```

Applications can perform identical operations by using regular Python operators, such as +, -, *, /, and //. For example, the following two lines of code create the same tensor:

```
total = tf.add(a, b)          # [ 5. 5. 5. ]
total2 = a + b                # [ 5. 5. 5. ]
```

When operating on floating-point values, div and divide produce the same result. But for integer division, divide returns a floating-point result, and div returns an integer result. The following code demonstrates the difference between them:

```
a = tf.constant([3, 3, 3])
b = tf.constant([2, 2, 2])
div1 = tf.divide(a, b)          # [ 1.5 1.5 1.5 ]
div2 = a / b                    # [ 1.5 1.5 1.5 ]
div3 = tf.div(a, b)             # [ 1 1 1 ]
div4 = a // b                   # [ 1 1 1 ]
```

The div function and the / operator both perform element-wise division. In contrast, the divide function performs Python-style division.

Rounding and comparison

Most of the mathematical routines in this book accept floating-point values as input and return floating-point values as output. But many applications need to convert floating-point values into integer values. For this reason, TensorFlow provides the rounding operations listed in Table 3-6.

Table 3-6 also lists functions that perform comparisons. These functions return maximum and minimum values, both within a tensor and across two tensors.

TABLE 3-6   ## Rounding and Comparison Operations

Function	Description
round(x, name=None)	Rounds to the nearest integer, rounding up if there are two nearest integers
rint(x, name=None)	Rounds to the nearest integer, rounding to the nearest even integer if there are two nearest integers
ceil(x, name=None)	Returns the smallest integer greater than the value
floor(x, name=None)	Returns the greatest integer less than the value
maximum(x, y, name=None)	Returns a tensor containing the larger element of each input tensor
minimum(x, y, name=None)	Returns a tensor containing the smaller element of each input tensor
argmax(x, axis=None, name=None, dimension=None)	Returns the index of the greatest element in the tensor
argmin(x, axis=None, name=None, dimension=None)	Returns the index of the smallest element in the tensor

The round function examines each element of a tensor and returns the closest integer. If two closest integers are equally close, it returns the one further from zero. rint is similar, but rounds to the nearest even value. The following code demonstrates how you can use round, rint, ceil, and floor:

```
t = tf.constant([-6.5, -3.5, 3.5, 6.5])
r1 = tf.round(t)                    # [-6. -4.  4.  6.]
r2 = tf.rint(t)                     # [-6. -4.  4.  6.]
r3 = tf.ceil(t)                     # [-6. -3.  4.  7.]
r4 = tf.floor(t)                    # [-7. -4.  3.  6.]
```

The next two functions in the table, maximum and minimum, are easy to understand. maximum returns a tensor containing the larger element of each input tensor, and minimum returns a tensor containing the smaller element of each input tensor.

argmax and argmin return the index values of the largest and smallest elements of a tensor. The following code shows how you can use these functions:

```
t1 = tf.constant([0, -2, 4, 6])
t2 = tf.constant([[1, 3], [7, 2]])
r1 = tf.argmin(t1)                  # 1
r2 = tf.argmax(t2)                  # [ 1 0 ]
```

If a tensor has multiple maximum/minimum values, argmax and argmin will return the index values of the first occurring element.

Exponents and logarithms

Machine learning applications frequently need exponents and logarithms to compute errors and probability. To meet this need, TensorFlow provides many of the same functions available in NumPy. Table 3-7 lists 11 of them and provides a description of each.

TABLE 3-7 **Exponential and Logarithmic Operations**

Function	Description
square(x, name=None)	Returns the square of the argument
squared_difference(x, y, name=None)	Subtracts the first argument from the second and returns the square
sqrt(x, name=None)	Returns the square root of the argument
rsqrt(x, name=None)	Returns the reciprocal of the square root

Function	Description
pow(x, y, name=None)	Returns elements of the first tensor raised to the power of the elements of the second vector
exp(x, name=None)	Returns the exponential function of the argument
expm1(x, name=None)	Returns the exponential function of the argument minus one, exp(x) - 1
log(x, name=None)	Returns the natural logarithm of the argument
log1p(x, name=None)	Returns the natural logarithm of the argument plus 1, log(x + 1)
erf(x, name=None)	Returns the error function of the argument
erfc(x, name=None)	Returns the complementary error function of the argument

These functions are straightforward to use and understand. Each executes in an element-wise manner, and the following code demonstrates how you can call square, sqrt, and rsqrt:

```
t = tf.constant([4.])
t1 = tf.square(t)          # 16
t2 = tf.sqrt(t)            # 2
t3 = tf.rsqrt(t)           # 0.5
```

The exp function computes the exponential functions of a tensor's elements, and expm1 subtracts 1 from each exponential. If x is a value in the input tensor, the result of expm1 equals exp(x) - 1.

Similarly, the log function computes the natural logarithm of a tensor's elements. logp1 adds 1 to the value before the logarithm is computed, so if x is a value in the input tensor, the result of logp1 equals log(x + 1).

Vector and matrix operations

Machine learning applications store a great deal of data in vectors (one-dimensional tensors) and matrices (two-dimensional tensors). To process this data, TensorFlow provides many functions that operate on vectors and matrices. Table 3-8 lists these functions and provides a description of each.

TABLE 3-8   **Vector and Matrix Operations**

Function	Description
tensordot(a, b, axes, name=None)	Returns the sum of products for the elements in the given axes
cross(a, b, name=None)	Returns the element-wise cross product
diag(diagonal, name=None)	Returns a matrix with the given diagonal values, other values set to zero
trace(x, name=None)	Returns the sum of the diagonal elements
transpose(x, perm=None, name='transpose')	Switches rows and columns
eye(num_rows, num_columns=None, batch_shape=None, dtype=tf.float32, name=None)	Creates an identity matrix with the given shape and data type
matmul(a, b, transpose_a=False, transpose_b=False, adjoint_a=False, adjoint_b=False, a_is_sparse=False, b_is_sparse=False, name=None)	Returns the product of the two input matrices
norm(tensor, ord='euclidean', axis=None, keep_dims=False, name=None)	Returns the norm of the given axis of the input tensor with the specified order
matrix_solve(A, b, adjoint=None, name=None)	Returns the tensor x, such that $Ax = b$, where A is a matrix, and b is a vector

Function	Description

`qr(input, full_matrices=None,`
 	
   `name=None)`
	Returns the eigenvectors and eigenvalues of the given matrix or matrices

`svd(tensor,`
 	
   `full_matrices=False,`
 	
   `compute_uv=True,`
 	
   `name=None)`
	Factors the matrix into a unitary matrix, a diagonal matrix, and the conjugate transpose of the unitary matrix

`einsum(equation, *inputs)`	Executes a custom mathematical operation

Of these functions, the two most common are `tensordot` and `matmul`. `tensordot` returns the dot product of one or more axes of two input tensors. That is, `tensordot` multiplies the corresponding elements of both tensors' dimensions and returns the sum of the products.

The `axes` parameter tells `tensordot` which dimensions to process. If you set this parameter to a scalar, N, the function will access the last N axes of the first tensor and the first N axes of the second tensor. If you set `axes` equal to a list or tensor, the first row identifies axes of the first tensor, and the second row identifies axes of the second tensor.

I frequently call `tensordot` to compute the dot product of two one-dimensional tensors. The following code shows what this looks like:

```
t1 = tf.constant([4., 3., 2.])
t2 = tf.constant([3., 2., 1.])
dot = tf.tensordot(t1, t2, 1)
# 4*3 + 3*2 + 2*1 = 20
```

`matmul` performs traditional matrix multiplication. That is, it multiplies rows of the first tensor by columns of the second tensor and returns a matrix containing the sums. The following code shows how this can be used:

```
t1 = tf.constant([[1.0, 2.0, 3.0], [4.0, 5.0, 6.0]])
t2 = tf.constant([[1.0, 2.0], [3.0, 4.0], [5.0, 6.0]])
dot = tf.matmul(t1, t2)
# [[ 22. 28.], [ 49. 64.]]
```

My favorite function in Table 3-8 is `einsum`, which makes it possible to create and execute custom mathematical operations. The first parameter is a string that identifies the operation using a special format called the *Einstein summation convention*. This convention has a number of characteristics, including the following:

>> The operation is assumed to have one or two inputs. If you provide two inputs, you must separate them with a comma.

>> Dimensions of input and output matrices are represented by subscripts (usually i, j, and k). Input subscripts must be separated from output subscripts with the -> symbol.

>> If an input's subscript is repeated and no output subscripts are given, the operation performs addition. Therefore, `einsum('i,i', t1, t2)` computes the dot product of tensors t1 and t2.

>> If an input's subscript is repeated and output subscripts are given, the operation performs multiplication. Therefore, `einsum('i,i->i', t1, t2)` computes the element-wise product of tensors t1 and t2.

The following code calls `einsum` to transpose a matrix and multiply two matrices together:

```
m1 = tf.constant([[1, 2], [3, 4]])
m2 = tf.constant([[5, 6], [7, 8]])
e1 = tf.einsum('ij->ji', m1)         # [[1, 3], [2, 4]]
e2 = tf.einsum('ij,jk->ik', m1, m2)  # [[19, 22], [43, 50]]
```

For a more complete discussion of the Einstein summation convention, I recommend Samuel Prime's presentation at `https://samuelprime.wordpress.com/2015/03/25/einstein-summation-convention`.

Putting Theory into Practice

The code in `ch3/simple_math.py` demonstrates many of the functions presented in this chapter. Listing 3-1 presents the full application.

LISTING 3-1: **Simple Mathematics Operations**

```
# Math with constant tensors
const_a = tf.constant(3.6)
const_b = tf.constant(1.2)
total = const_a + const_b
quot = tf.div(const_a, const_b)

# Math with random tensors
rand_a = tf.random_normal([3], 2.0)
rand_b = tf.random_uniform([3], 1.0, 4.0)
diff = tf.subtract(rand_a, rand_b)

# Vector multiplication
vec_a = tf.linspace(0.0, 3.0, 4)
vec_b = tf.fill([4, 1], 2.0)
prod = tf.multiply(vec_a, vec_b)
dot = tf.tensordot(vec_a, vec_b, 1)

# Matrix multiplication
mat_a = tf.constant([[2, 3], [1, 2], [4, 5]])
mat_b = tf.constant([[6, 4, 1], [3, 7, 2]])
mat_prod = tf.matmul(mat_a, mat_b)

# Execute the operations
with tf.Session() as sess:
    print("Sum: %f" % sess.run(total))
    print("Quotient: %f" % sess.run(quot))
    print("Difference: ", sess.run(diff))
    print("Element-wise product: ", sess.run(prod))
    print("Dot product: ", sess.run(dot))
    print("Matrix product: ", sess.run(mat_prod))
```

Most of this code should look familiar. The application creates and operates on constant tensors, random tensors, vectors, and matrices. To process vectors, the application performs element-wise multiplication with tf.multiply and then computes the dot product of the two vectors with tf.tensordot.

The last portion of code deserves explanation. The application creates a Session named sess and calls its run method once for each operation to be performed. To understand what sessions are and how they work, you need to be familiar with graphs. The next chapter explores the topics of sessions and graphs.

IN THIS CHAPTER

» **Creating graphs and accessing their data**

» **Serializing data from a graph into a GraphDef**

» **Creating and launching sessions**

» **Printing messages to the log**

» **Visualizing summary data with TensorBoard**

Chapter **4**

Executing Graphs in Sessions

The preceding chapter introduced a plethora of functions that create, transform, and process tensors. Most of these functions return a tensor, and this may lead you to believe that the function performs its operation as soon as it's called. This is how Python functions usually work, but this is not how TensorFlow functions work.

When an application executes a TensorFlow function that creates, transforms, or processes a tensor, the function doesn't execute its operation. Instead, it stores its operation in a data structure called a *graph*. A graph can hold many operations, and they're not executed until the application executes the graph in a session. When a session executes a graph, it performs the graph's operations in order.

The benefit of storing operations in a graph is that the graph can be exported to a file or launched on a remote system. The drawback is that graphs tend to confuse newcomers to TensorFlow. In writing this chapter, my goal is to reduce this confusion by providing a full explanation of graphs and sessions.

Forming Graphs

If an operation returns a tensor, an operation can feed its output into another operation. To demonstrate this process, the following code feeds the result of an addition operation into a multiplication operation.

```
c = tf.add(a, b)
e = tf.multiply(c, d)
```

Figure 4-1 illustrates the relationships between these nested operations and their tensors.

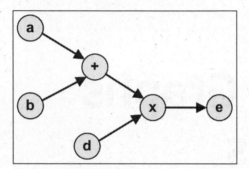

In Figure 4-1, each circle identifies a tensor or operation, and each line transfers tensor data. Mathematicians and computer scientists refer to this structure of nodes and edges as a *graph*. The graph's circles are called *nodes*, and the straight lines are called *edges*.

When an application executes a function that creates a tensor or an operation, TensorFlow adds the data structures to a container structure called a Graph. Graphs can't be nested, and only one Graph can be active at a time. An application can access its default Graph by calling get_default_graph. The following code shows how this can be used:

```
graph = tf.get_default_graph()
```

An application can create a new Graph by calling the constructor without arguments. Then the application can set the Graph as the default Graph by calling the Graph's as_default method. The following code demonstrates how this works:

```
newgraph = tf.Graph()
with newgraph.as_default():
    ...
```

After `as_default` is called, TensorFlow will add new tensors and operations to `newgraph` instead of the original `Graph`.

The `Graph` class provides many methods that access and modify the graph's contents. This discussion divides these methods into two categories:

» **Accessing graph data:** Reading a graph's containers and elements

» **Creating `GraphDefs`:** Serializing a graph into a protocol buffer

Accessing graph data

A graph stores its elements in a set of named collections. Table 4-1 presents the methods of the `Graph` class that access and update these collections.

TABLE 4-1 **Accessing Graph Data**

Method	Description
get_tensor_by_name(name)	Returns the tensor with the given name
get_operation_by_name(name)	Returns the operation with the given name
get_operations()	Returns a list containing the graph's operations
get_all_collection_keys()	Returns a list of the graph's collections
get_collection(name, scope=None)	Returns a list of values in the given collection
add_to_collection(name, value)	Adds the value to the container, can be accessed with name
add_to_collections(name, value)	Adds the value to the containers, can be accessed with name

The first three methods make it easy to access tensors and operations in the current graph. Each method returns a list containing the desired elements, and the following code demonstrates how they can be used:

```
a = tf.constant(2.5, name='first_val')
b = tf.constant(4.5, name='second_val')
sum = a + b;
print(tf.get_default_graph().get_operations())
print(tf.get_default_graph().
    get_tensor_by_name('first_val:0'))
```

The first `print` statement calls `get_operations` to obtain a list of the graph's operations. The printed result is given as follows:

```
[<tf.Operation 'first_val' type=Const>,
 <tf.Operation 'second_val' type=Const>,
 <tf.Operation 'add' type=Add>]
```

The second `print` statement accesses the first tensor using the `name:index` format. In this case, the tensor's name is `first_val`, and the index is 0. TensorFlow prints the following result:

```
("first_val:0", shape=(), dtype=float32)
```

A graph can hold more than just tensors and operations. This additional information is stored in a set of lists called the graph's *collections*. As with dictionaries, you can access the elements of a collection using identifiers called *keys*. Table 4-2 presents the different keys for graph collections.

TABLE 4-2 **Graph Collection Keys**

Collection Key	Description
GLOBAL_VARIABLES	All variables used in the application
LOCAL_VARIABLES	Variables local to this machine
MODEL_VARIABLES	Variables used in the model
TRAINABLE_VARIABLES	Variables capable of being trained by an optimizer
MOVING_AVERAGE_VARIABLES	Variables that maintain moving averages
SUMMARIES	Tensor summaries
QUEUE_RUNNERS	QueueRunners that provide input data
REGULARIZATION_LOSSES	Losses produced by regularization

Most of these collections store data related to variables, which I cover in Chapter 5. For now, it's simply important to know that graphs provide access to tensors, operators, and other types of data.

Creating GraphDefs

Many applications need to access graphs from other TensorFlow applications. The as_graph_def method makes this possible. This method returns a serialized form of a Graph called a GraphDef.

A GraphDef stores a graph's data in a special format called a *protocol buffer*, also known as a *protobuf*. This may be generated in text or binary form, and in text form, it looks like the JavaScript Object Notation (JSON).

In a GraphDef, every tensor and operation is represented by a node element. Each node has a name field, an op field, and one or more attr fields. The following text presents the general structure of a node element:

```
node {
  name: "..."
  op: "..."
  attr { ... }
  attr { ... }
  ...
}
```

The last element in a GraphDef is a versions element. This element identifies the version of the GraphDef structure.

The best way to understand GraphDefs is to look at an example. Suppose that an application contains the following code:

```
a = tf.constant(2.5)
b = tf.constant(4.2)
sum = a + b;
```

In text form, the content of the GraphDef is given as follows:

```
node {
  name: "Const"
  op: "Const"
  attr {
    key: "dtype"
    value { type: DT_FLOAT }
  }
  attr {
    key: "value"
    value {
```

```
      tensor {
        dtype: DT_FLOAT
        tensor_shape {}
        float_val: 2.5
      }
    }
  }
}
node {
  name: "Const_1"
  op: "Const"
  attr {
    key: "dtype"
    value { type: DT_FLOAT }
  }
  attr {
    key: "value"
    value {
      tensor {
        dtype: DT_FLOAT
        tensor_shape {}
        float_val: 4.2
      }
    }
  }
}
node {
  name: "add"
  op: "Add"
  input: "Const"
  input: "Const_1"
  attr {
    key: "T"
    value { type: DT_FLOAT }
  }
}
versions {
  producer: 22
}
```

This GraphDef has three nodes: two that represent tensors and one that represents the operation that adds the tensors. Real-world applications may have thousands of nodes. At the end of the list of nodes, the versions object identifies the version as 22.

The `write_graph` function in `tf.train` makes it possible to store a `GraphDef`'s data to a file. Its signature is given as follows:

```
write_graph(graph/graph_def, logdir, name, as_text=True)
```

The first argument can be set to a `Graph` or `GraphDef`. The last argument identifies if the content should be written in text or binary form. For example, the following code stores the current graph to a text file named `graph.dat`:

```
tf.train.write_graph(tf.get_default_graph(), os.getcwd(), 'graph.dat')
```

Similarly, an application can load a `GraphDef` from a file containing graph data by calling one of two routines:

>> `TextFormat.Merge(data, graphdef)`: Initializes a `GraphDef` from text elements

>> Creating `GraphDef`s: Converting a graph into a protocol buffer

The `TextFormat` class is provided in `google.protobuf`. For a complete discussion of accessing protocol buffers in Python, visit `https://developers.google.com/protocol-buffers/docs/pythontutorial`.

Creating and Running Sessions

As a Python developer, you're probably accustomed to having your programs processed line by line. But in a TensorFlow application, operations involving tensors aren't executed until they're stored in a graph and executed in a session. This section explains how you can code applications that create and execute sessions.

Creating sessions

As with graphs, only one session can be active at a time. But there's an important difference between sessions and graphs — every session must be explicitly created. You can create a `Session` by calling `tf.Session`, which accepts three optional arguments:

>> `target`: Name of the execution engine

>> `graph`: The `Graph` instance to be launched

>> `config`: A `ConfigProto` that configures the session's execution

A discussion of execution engines is in Chapter 11, which introduces the target parameter. Similarly, most of the settings in a ConfigProto relate to threads and devices, so Chapter 10 discusses the config parameter.

By default, a session accesses tensors and operations in the default graph. But if you set the graph parameter in tf.Session, the session will execute that graph instead.

Applications frequently call tf.Session inside a with statement. This statement ensures that code in the with block can access the new Session. The following code shows how this works:

```
with tf.Session() as sess:
    ...
```

Most of the example applications presented in this book create sessions with similar code.

Executing a session

The most important method of the Session class is run. This method accepts four arguments, and only the first is required:

>> fetches: Identifies one or more operations or tensors to be executed

>> feed_dict: Data to be fed into a tensor

>> options: Configuration options for the session's execution

>> run_metadata: Output data from the session

The fetches parameter accepts a wide range of data types. Most applications set this parameter equal to an operation, a tensor, or the name of an operation or tensor. You can also assign fetches to a list of tensors, operations, or names.

If you assign fetches to a tensor, run will return an ndarray with the same values and shape. The following code calls run with a two-element tensor:

```
tensr = tf.constant([2, 3])
with tf.Session() as sess:
    res = sess.run(tensr)
    print(res)                    # Prints [2, 3]
```

If you assign fetches to an Operation, run will return an ndarray containing the values of the tensor produced by the operation. The following code calls run with an operation that performs addition:

```
t1 = tf.constant(7)
t2 = tf.constant(2)
with tf.Session() as sess:
    res = sess.run(t1 + t2)
    print(res)                   # Prints 9
```

If you assign fetches to a collection of elements, run will return a similar collection containing the processed results. The following code calls run with a list containing two tensors:

```
t1 = tf.constant(9)
t2 = tf.constant(5)
with tf.Session() as sess:
    res1, res2 = sess.run([t1, t2])
    print(res1)                   # Prints 9
    print(res2)                   # Prints 5
```

The feed_dict parameter of run plays an important role in applications that process training data with batches. Chapter 5 discusses this parameter in detail.

Interactive sessions

Rather than send an entire script to an interpreter, many Python developers prefer to write code interactively. In this mode, the interpreter displays feedback as each line is processed.

To support interactive development, TensorFlow provides the Interactive Session class. An InteractiveSession serves the same role as a Session, but it makes itself the default session when it's constructed.

Instead of calling sess.run, you can evaluate tensors by calling their eval method. Similarly, you can execute operations by calling the run method of the Operation class.

An example clarifies how InteractiveSessions work. The following code is intended to be run in normal mode:

```
t1 = tf.constant(1.2)
t2 = tf.constant(3.5)
prod = tf.multiply(t1, t2)
with tf.Session() as sess:
    print("Product: ", sess.run(prod))
```

This code accomplishes the same result with an InteractiveSession:

```
t1 = tf.constant(1.2)
t2 = tf.constant(3.5)
prod = tf.multiply(t1, t2)
sess = tf.InteractiveSession()
print("Product: ", prod.eval())
```

The InteractiveSession class constructor accepts the same arguments as that of the Session class. Similarly, its run method accepts the same arguments as the run method of the Session class.

Writing Messages to the Log

All of the example code in Chapters 1 through 4 has relied on print to write data to standard output. But TensorFlow provides a logging mechanism with many more messaging capabilities than regular print. There are five points to know about TensorFlow logging:

» TensorFlow enables logging through the tf.logging package.

» TensorFlow logging is based on regular Python logging, and many tf. logging functions are identical to the methods of Python's Logger class.

» TensorFlow supports five logging levels. In order of severity, these are DEBUG, INFO, WARN, ERROR, and FATAL.

» To enable logging, an application needs to call tf.logging set_verbosity with the lowest level of severity that should be logged.

» By default, TensorFlow writes log messages to standard output. At the time of this writing, TensorFlow logging doesn't support writing messages to a log file.

For each logging level, tf.logging provides a similarly named function that writes a logging message at that level. As an example, the following code enables INFO messages (and messages of greater severity) and then writes an INFO message that displays the value of output:

```
tf.logging.set_verbosity(tf.logging.INFO)

with tf.Session() as sess:
    output = sess.run(...)
    tf.logging.info('Output: %f', output)
```

If output's value is 5.5, tf.logging.info will print the following message to standard output:

```
INFO:tensorflow:Output: 5.5
```

Table 4-3 lists set_verbosity, info, and other functions provided by tf.logging.

TABLE 4-3   ## Summary Data Functions

Function	Description
set_verbosity(level)	Enables logging for messages of the given severity level and greater severity
debug(msg, *args, **kwargs)	Logs a message at DEBUG severity
info(msg, *args, **kwargs)	Logs a message at INFO severity
warn(msg, *args, **kwargs)	Logs a message at WARN severity
error(msg, *args, **kwargs)	Logs a message at ERROR severity
fatal(msg, *args, **kwargs)	Logs a message at FATAL severity
flush()	Forces logging operations to complete
log(level, msg, *args, **kwargs)	Logs a message at the given severity level
log_if(level, msg, condition, *args)	Logs a message at the given severity level if the condition is true
log_first_n(level, msg, n, *args)	Logs a message at the given severity level at most *n* times
log_every_n(level, msg, n, *args)	Logs a message at the given severity level once every *n* times

The last three functions make it possible to control when messages are written to the log. The third parameter of `log_if` defines a condition that determines when the message should be logged. The following code logs the value of `output` if it's greater than 0:

```
tf.logging.log_if(tf.logging.INFO, 'Output: %f', (output > 0),
    output)
```

The third argument of `log_first_n` and `log_every_n` is an integer that determines how often should be performed. In `log_first_n`, the value sets the maximum number of times the function should write its message to the log. In `log_every_n`, the value tells the function to log its message once every *N* times it's called.

Visualizing Data with TensorBoard

Logging is fine for monitoring simple data, but in many cases, developers need to keep track of large, complex data sets. Practical applications may launch a session hundreds or thousands of times, and logging isn't sufficient to monitor how data changes with each execution.

The good news is that your TensorFlow installation contains TensorBoard. This powerful utility reads an application's data and displays it in a web page. Figure 4-2 gives an idea of what the TensorBoard page looks like in the Chrome browser.

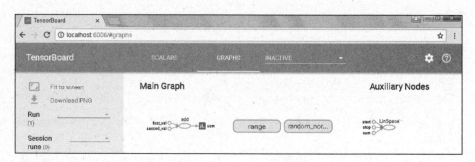

FIGURE 4-2:
TensorFlow can display many aspects of an application, including the structure of its graph.

The bad news is that TensorBoard requires specially formatted data called *summary data*, and generating this data isn't easy.

Running TensorBoard

When you install TensorFlow, the installer places the TensorBoard utility in the top-level scripts directory. If you can't execute the `tensorboard` command from a command line, add this directory to your system's PATH variable.

The `tensorboard` command accepts a handful of flags, including the following:

- » `--logdir DIR`: The directory containing the summary data
- » `--host HOST`: Identifies the host portion of the web page's URL
- » `--port PORT`: Identifies the port of the web page's URL

By default, TensorBoard's IP address is 127.0.0.1, which can be accessed as `localhost`. TensorBoard's default port is 6006. Therefore, TensorBoard's default URL is `http://localhost:6006`.

The `--logdir` flag is required, so you can't launch TensorBoard without data. You must set this flag to a directory that contains a special file called an *event file*. This file contains the summary data that TensorBoard needs to perform visualization. If the file is located in a directory named output, the following command tells TensorBoard to read the event file:

```
tensorboard --logdir=output
```

Generating summary data

At this point, you should understand how to create math operations and execute them in a session. This discussion introduces a new type of operation called a *summary operation*. This resembles other TensorFlow operations, but when a session executes a summary operation, the result is a protocol buffer that contains summary data. An application can write this buffer to a file whose content can be displayed with TensorBoard.

TensorBoard can illustrate many different types of data, and each type corresponds to a function of `tf.summary`. Table 4-4 lists six of the available functions.

Of these functions, the two most popular are `scalar` and `histogram`. `scalar` generates summary data for a single value that changes over multiple session executions. `histogram` generates data for a set of values that change over session executions. The `image` function generates data related to images and image analysis. Chapter 8 discusses images in detail.

TABLE 4-4

Summary Data Functions

Function	Description
scalar(name, tensor, collections=None)	Creates a summary operation that provides data about a scalar
histogram(name, values, collections=None)	Creates a summary operation that provides histogram data
audio(name, tensor, sample_rate, max_outputs=3, collections=None)	Creates a summary operation that provides data from an audio source
image(name, tensor, max_outputs=3, collections=None)	Creates a summary operation that provides data from an image
merge(inputs, collections=None, name=None)	Merges the specified summary operations into one summary operation
merge_all(key= tf.GraphKeys.SUMMARIES)	Merges summary operations into one summary operation

In my opinion, the best way to understand summary data is to look at example code. The following code performs three tasks:

» `tf.summary.scalar` generates operations that provide scalar data.

» `tf.summary.merge_all` combines them into one operation.

» `sess.run` executes the merged summary operation.

```
# Add two scalars
a = tf.constant(2.5)
b = tf.constant(4.5)
total = a + b;

# Create operations that generate summary data
tf.summary.scalar("a", a)
tf.summary.scalar("b", b)
tf.summary.scalar("total", total)

# Merge the operations into a single operation
merged_op = tf.summary.merge_all()

with tf.Session() as sess:
    _, summary = sess.run([sum, merged_op])
```

As shown, each entity of interest requires a separate operation to generate summary data. That is, the application needs to call `tf.summary.scalar` three times: once for each tensor to be analyzed. But you don't need to access the return values of each call to `tf.summary.scalar` because `tf.summary.merge_all` combines the data generation operations into one operation.

Creating custom summaries

Instead of calling the functions in Table 4-4, you can generate custom summary data by creating `Summary` objects. The `Summary` class is a Python wrapper for a protocol buffer containing summary data.

You can create a `Summary` instance by calling `tf.Summary` and setting its `value` parameter to a list of `Summary.Value` buffers. Each `Summary.Value` can have a `node_name`, a `tag`, and one of five data fields:

>> `simple_value` — a 32-bit floating-point value

>> `image` — an Image instance containing pixel data

>> `histo` — a HistogramProto containing data to be displayed in a histogram

>> `audio` — an Audio instance containing audio data

>> `tensor` — a TensorProto containing data related to tensors

The following code creates a custom summary and sets its `simple_value` field:

```
custom_summary = tf.Summary(value=[
    tf.Summary.Value(tag="num_tag", simple_value=5.0),
])
```

This code doesn't create an operation that generates summary data — it directly generates the summary data. In the preceding code, TensorBoard will display the content of `custom_summary` as though it had been generated with `tf.summary.scalar`.

Writing summary data

After you've generated summary data, the next step is to create a directory and write the summary data to the directory's event file. This process requires creating a `FileWriter` and calling its methods.

Creating a FileWriter

An application can create a FileWriter by calling its constructor:

```
tf.summary.FileWriter(logdir, graph=None, max_queue=10,
   flush_secs=120, filename_suffix=None)
```

The logdir parameter sets the name of the directory that should be created to contain the summary data. If you set the graph parameter, the graph's data will be added to the event file in the given directory. If you set filename_suffix, the suffix will be appended to the name of the generated event file.

A FileWriter updates the event file asynchronously, which means multiple write operations may be pending at once. The max_queue parameter identifies the maximum number of write operations that can be pending at a given time. The flush_secs parameter identifies how often the FileWriter should execute pending operations.

As an example, the following code creates a FileWriter and configures it to create a directory named log. The event file in this directory should contain summary data for the default graph.

```
fw = tf.summary.FileWriter("log", graph=tf.get_default_graph())
```

If this directory already exists, the constructor may create multiple event files. In many cases, it's a good idea to check if the directory exists and delete it, if necessary.

Printing data to the event file

The FileWriter constructor creates a directory with an event file. The File Writer's methods make it possible to write data to the event file. Table 4-5 lists these methods and provides a description of each.

TABLE 4-5

Methods of the FileWriter Class

Method	Description
add_summary(summary, global_step=None)	Adds summary data to the event file
add_event(event)	Adds event data to the event file
add_graph(graph, global_step=None, graph_def=None)	Adds summary data for the graph to the event file

Method	Description

`add_meta_graph(`
    `meta_graph_def,`
    `global_step=None)`
	Adds data from a `MetaGraphDef` to the event file

`add_run_metadata(`
    `run_metadata, tag,`
    `global_step=None)`
	Adds run metadata from a session to the event file

`add_session_log(`
    `session_log,`
    `global_step=None)`
	Adds data from a `SessionLog` to the event file

`flush()`	Executes pending write operations
`close()`	Flushes write operations and closes the event file
`reopen()`	Reopens the event file for writing summary data

`add_summary` prints summary data. That is, it writes summary data produced by a data generation operation to the event file. The following code demonstrates how this can be called:

```
# Merge operations into a single operation
merged_op = tf.summary.merge_all()

# Create the FileWriter
writer = tf.summary.FileWriter("summary")

with tf.Session() as sess:
    _, summary = sess.run([sum, merged_op])
    writer.add_summary(summary)
    writer.close()
```

`add_event` writes an `Event` to the event file. Like a `Summary` an `Event` is a Python wrapper for a protocol buffer. Each `Event` has a `wall_time` field that identifies the time and a `step` that identifies the global step. An `Event`'s data is specified by the `what` field, which can be set to one of the following values:

>> `file_version` —the version of the event file

>> `graph_def` — content of a `GraphDef` buffer

>> `summary` — an Summary containing summary data

>> `log_message` — LogMessage containing logged messages

>> `session_log` — SessionLog containing the session's state

>> `tagged_run_metadata` — TaggedRunMetadata containing metadata from the session

>> `meta_graph_def` — content of a `MetaGraphDef` buffer

As an example, the following code creates an `Event` whose `wall_time` is set to the current time and whose `what` field is associated with a `Summary`:

```
new_summary = tf.Summary(value=[
    tf.Summary.Value(tag="val", simple_value=9.0),
])
event = tf.Event(wall_time=time.time(), summary=new_summary)
file_writer.add_event(event)
```

Calling `add_graph` accomplishes the same result as setting the `graph` parameter in the `FileWriter`'s constructor. `add_meta_graph` prints the content of a `MetaGraphDef`, which I'll discuss in Chapter 5.

The `flush` method forces the `FileWriter` to execute any pending write operations to the event file. The `close` method also forces the `FileWriter` to execute pending write operations. After the operations have completed, the method closes the event file.

Putting Theory into Practice

The code in `ch4/two_graphs.py` demonstrates how an application can create multiple graphs and execute them in separate sessions. After executing each graph, the application calls `tf.train.write_graph` to write the graph's structure to a file. The application also creates a `FileWriter` and generates summary data that can be viewed with TensorBoard. Listing 4-1 presents the code:

LISTING 4-1: **Launching Multiple Graphs in Multiple Sessions**

```
# Enable logging
tf.logging.set_verbosity(tf.logging.INFO)

# Create tensors
t1 = tf.constant([1.2, 2.3, 3.4, 4.5])
t2 = tf.constant([5.6, 6.7, 7.8, 8.9])
t3 = tf.concat([t1, t2], 0)
t4 = tf.random_normal([8])
t5 = tf.tensordot(t3, t4, 1)
```

```
# Create operations to generate summary data
tf.summary.scalar("t1", t1[0])
tf.summary.scalar("t2", t2[0])
tf.summary.scalar("t3", t3[0])
tf.summary.scalar("t4", t4[0])
tf.summary.scalar("t5", t5)
merged_op = tf.summary.merge_all()

# Create FileWriter
file_writer = tf.summary.FileWriter("log", graph=tf.get_default_graph())

# Execute first graph
with tf.Session() as sess:

    # Execute the session
    dot_result, summary = sess.run([t5, merged_op])

    # Write the result to the log
    tf.logging.info('Result of dot product: %f', dot_result)

    # Print the summary data
    file_writer.add_summary(summary)
    file_writer.flush()

    # Obtain the GraphDef and write it to a file
    tf.train.write_graph(sess.graph, os.getcwd(), 'graph1.dat')

# Create second graph and make it default
graph = tf.Graph()
with graph.as_default():

    # Compute the average
    t6 = tf.random_uniform([8], 4.0, 8.0)
    t7 = tf.fill([8], 6.0)
    t8 = tf.reduce_mean(t6 + t7)

    # Execute first graph
    with tf.Session() as sess:

        # Execute the session
        sess.run(t8)

        # Obtain the GraphDef and write it to a file
        tf.train.write_graph(sess.graph, os.getcwd(), 'graph2.dat'
```

The first call to sess.run is particularly interesting. Its first argument is a list containing two elements. The first element, t5, is the result of an operation that combines t1, t2, t3, and t4. The second element, merged_op, combines five operations that generate summary data.

sess.run returns the value of t5 and the generated summary data. When these results are available, the application logs the value of t5 and prints the summary data to a file by calling the add_summary method of a FileWriter.

The first parameter in the FileWriter's constructor is log, so the FileWriter prints its data to an event file in the log directory. You can launch TensorBoard to visualize this data with the following command:

```
tensorboard --logdir=log
```

To view the generated data in TensorBoard, open a browser to http://local host:6006. If you click the HISTOGRAMS link at the top of the page, you can view tensors t1 through t4. Figure 4-3 shows what the histogram of t1 looks like.

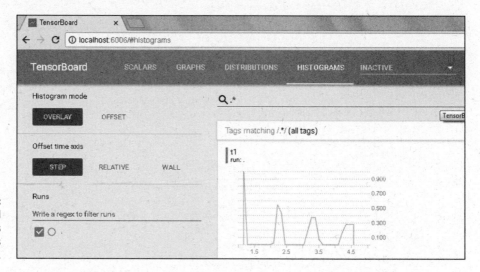

FIGURE 4-3:
A TensorBoard histogram plots the elements of a tensor.

Unlike t1 through t4, t5 only has one element. The application generates data for t5 by calling tf.summary.scalar, and you can view this data in TensorBoard by clicking the SCALARS link at the top of the page. The result isn't particularly interesting because the application only executed the session once. Chapter 5 explains how to execute sessions with multiple steps and view the resulting data in TensorBoard.

Chapter **5**

Training

Before the Internet, old-timers like me entertained ourselves by actually speaking to one another. One rip-roaring game was 20 Questions, in which one player thinks of an object and the other player asks questions to determine what the object is. The questioner is allowed to ask at most 20 yes/no questions, and a typical game goes something like this:

Q: Is it larger than a breadbox?

A: Yes.

Q: Can it move?

A: Yes.

Q: Is it an animal?

A: No.

Q: Does it move on wheels?

A: No.

Q: (Sigh) Is it an evil robot, Matt? Again?

A: THAT'S IT! You win!

In this chapter, I explain how the game 20 Questions is similar to the training methodology used in supervised machine learning.

Training in TensorFlow

In the game 20 Questions, the questioner starts with a guess and refines his understanding with each answer. This game resembles the training methodology used in supervised machine learning. An application starts with a general idea, or model, of the desired system. The application compares its model to experimental data, determines the difference between them, and repeatedly refines the model to reduce the difference.

The general training process is simple to understand, but implementing training with TensorFlow isn't easy. The process involves six steps:

1. **Construct a mathematical expression for the general model.**

2. **Declare variables to be updated as training is performed.**

3. **Obtain an expression for the loss, which is the difference between the model and observation.**

4. **Create an** `Optimizer` **with the loss from Step 3 and call its** `minimize` **method.**

5. **(Optional) Configure the second argument of the session's** `run` **method to feed batches of data to the session.**

6. **Execute the session by calling the session's** `run` **method.**

Judging from the questions on `StackOverflow.com`, many developers have difficulty grasping how these steps are performed. This chapter explains this training process and then presents example code that demonstrates how these steps can be implemented in a TensorFlow application.

Formulating the Model

Just as a game of 20 Questions starts with making a guess, machine learning starts with forming an initial mathematical model of the system. A number of factors determine the nature of this model, including the system's complexity, the structure of the input data, and the nature of the problem. Image data requires a different model than voice data. Classification problems require a different type of model than prediction problems.

This book focuses on two methods of mathematical modeling. The first involves approximating a set of data points with a shape. For example, if a system consists of two-dimensional points, you can predict future points by approximating the system with a two-dimensional line. Lines are determined by the equation y = mx + b, so this equation serves as the general model.

The second method involves creating artificial neural networks, or ANNs. Though inspired by biological phenomena, every ANN represents a mathematical relationship. Chapter 7 introduces this exciting topic and explains how you can construct ANNs in code.

Whether you model your system with a shape or a neural network, you need to refine the model until it resembles the observed data as closely as possible. This refinement entails updating the model's parameters, such as the *m* and *b* in y = mx + b. In a TensorFlow application, these trainable parameters are all instances of the `Variable` class.

TIP

When you're talking to customers, try not to use the term *guess*, as in "Golly, all of our guesses were way off base!" The preferred term is *initial estimate*, as in "Initial estimates proved inaccurate, but subsequent training runs will lead to better results."

Looking at Variables

At first glance, variables have a lot in common with tensors. Both store data in multidimensional arrays and both can be processed with TensorFlow operations.

But while a tensor can serve many purposes, most variables have only one purpose: to store data to be updated during training. A variable's value will change as training proceeds, and hopefully, each change will bring the model closer to the desired system.

Variables have three other important characteristics:

>> A variable maintains its value between successive executions of a session.

>> A variable must be specially initialized by an executing session.

>> A variable is an instance of the `Variable` class, not the `Tensor` class.

The last point is important. When working with variables, you need to call a new set of methods and functions. The following sections explain how to create and initialize variables.

Creating variables

An application can create variables by calling `tf.Variable`, whose first parameter sets the variable's initial value. For example, the following code creates a variable named `variableA` and sets its initial value equal to a tensor named `tensorA`:

```
tensorA = tf.constant([1.5, 2.5, 3.5])
variableA = tf.Variable(tensorA)
```

A variable's job is to hold data to be updated during training. Instead of initializing variables with constant values, many applications use random values. The following code creates a variable named `variableB` and sets its initial value to a tensor of normally distributed values:

```
variableB = tf.Variable(tf.random_normal([3]))
```

`tf.Variable` accepts a Boolean parameter called `trainable`. If you set this parameter to `True`, the variable can be updated by training. If you set it to `False`, the variable can't be updated by training.

Initializing variables

One important difference between variables and tensors is that you need to execute special operations to initialize variables. That is, before you can train a variable, you need to create an initialization operation and execute it in a session. If an application attempts to use an uninitialized variable, TensorFlow raises an error: Attempting to use uninitialized value. . ..

TensorFlow provides three functions that create operations that initialize variables. Table 5-1 lists them and provides a description of each.

TABLE 5-1 **Variable Initialization Functions**

Function	Description
`variable_initializer(var_list, name='init')`	Returns an operation that initializes the variables in the given list
`local_variables_initializer()`	Returns an operation that initializes all local variables
`global_variables_initializer()`	Returns an operation that initializes all global variables

Applications commonly call `global_variables_initializer` because it creates an operation that initializes every global variable in the session. The following code shows how you can call this function:

```
init = tf.global_variables_initializer()
...
with tf.Session() as sess:
    sess.run(init)
```

An application can check whether a variable has been initialized by calling `is_variable_initialized` with the variable's name.

Determining Loss

Training refines a model's variables to minimize the difference between your model and the observed data. Machine learning literature commonly refers to this difference as the *cost function*. TensorFlow's documentation refers to it as *loss*.

For example, if you model a set of points with a straight line, the expression for the model is y = mx + b. Of course, the points on the line won't exactly match the observed data, y_{obs}. If there are *N* points, you can represent the loss with the following expression:

$$loss = \frac{1}{N} \sum_{i=0}^{N-1} \left(y_{obs} - \left(mx + b \right) \right)^2$$

In a TensorFlow application, you can express the model and loss with the following code:

```
m = tf.Variable(tf.random_normal([]))
b = tf.Variable(tf.random_normal([]))
model = tf.add(tf.multiply(x, m), b)
loss = tf.reduce_mean(tf.pow(model - y, 2))
```

This method of computing loss is called *mean squared error,* and it's one of many methods available — maximum likelihood estimation and log likelihood estimation are also popular. Chapter 6 discusses statistical regression and the different ways you can compute loss.

If your model contains neural networks, you can't compute loss with a simple equation. Feed-forward networks require a special algorithm like backpropagation, and recurrent networks rely on backpropagation through time (BPTT). I discuss neural networks and backpropagation in Chapter 7. I introduce BPTT in Chapter 9.

REMEMBER

There's no right way to compute loss. The only requirement is that every decrease in loss must imply that the model is closer to the observed data. The process of improving the model by reducing loss is called *optimization*.

Minimizing Loss with Optimization

After you've formed an expression for the loss, the next step is to minimize the loss by updating the model's variables. This process is called *optimization*, and TensorFlow supports a variety of algorithms for this purpose. Choosing the right algorithm is critically important when coding machine learning applications.

Each optimization method is represented by a class in the `tf.train` package. Four popular optimization classes are the `GradientDescentOptimizer`, `Momentum Optimizer`, `AdagradOptimizer`, and `AdamOptimizer` classes. The following sections look at each of these classes, starting with the `Optimizer` class, which is the base class of TensorFlow's optimization classes.

The Optimizer class

You can't directly access the `Optimizer` class in code; applications need to instantiate one of its subclasses instead. But the `Optimizer` class is crucial because it defines the all-important `minimize` method:

```
minimize(loss, global_step=None, var_list=None, gate_gradients=1, aggregation_
    method=None, colocate_gradients_with_ops=False, name=None, grad_loss=None)
```

The only required argument is the first, which identifies the loss. By default, `minimize` can access every trainable variable in the graph. An application can select specific variables for optimization by setting the `var_list` argument.

`minimize` returns an operation that can be executed by a session's `run` method. Each execution performs two steps:

1. **Compute values that update the variables of interest.**

2. **Update the variables of interest with the values computed in Step 1.**

Just as you probably won't win 20 Questions with your first question, you probably won't optimize your model with a single call to `minimize`. Most applications perform optimization in a loop, and the following code gives an idea what an optimization loop looks like:

```
# Create the optimizer and obtain the operation
optimizer = tf.train.GradientDescentOptimizer(learn_rate)
optimizer_op = minimize(loss)

# Execute the minimization operation in a session
```

```
with tf.Session() as sess:
    for step in range(num_steps):
        sess.run(optimizer_op)
```

If the optimizer reaches a suitable minimum, it has *converged* to the minimum. If it fails to reach a minimum, the optimizer has *diverged*.

Each call to the session's `run` method minimizes the loss by updating variables. An application controls how updates are performed by creating a subclass of `Optimizer`. This discussion explores four popular `Optimizer` subclasses: `Gradient DescentOptimizer`, `MomentumOptimizer`, `AdagradOptimizer`, and `AdamOptimizer`.

TECHNICAL STUFF

The following discussion gets awfully nerdy, and if you're just getting started in machine learning, you don't really need to know the math. However, selecting the right optimizer can make a significant impact on the application's performance. Also, if you're interviewing for a lucrative TensorFlow job, you should be able to justify why you prefer the `AdamOptimizer` to the `GradientDescentOptimizer`.

The GradientDescentOptimizer

The `GradientDescentOptimizer` is the simplest and most common of the optimizers used in machine learning. If you look through online example code or textbooks on machine learning, you're likely to encounter this optimizer frequently.

Despite its popularity, few experts recommend the `GradientDescentOptimizer` over the alternatives. To see why, you need to understand the algorithm it uses to perform optimization. In this discussion, I present the theory of gradient descent and then explain how you can create and use `GradientDescentOptimizer`s in code.

The Gradient Descent algorithm

The `GradientDescentOptimizer` minimizes loss using the gradient descent algorithm, which relies on a crucial mathematical fact: A function decreases fastest at a point in the direction determined by its negative gradient at that point.

If you've taken calculus, you know that the derivative of a function at a point equals the function's slope at that point. That is, if f(x) is differentiable, its derivative with respect to x is denoted f'(x), and the slope at point *a* is denoted f'(a). Figure 5-1 shows what a function's derivative looks like.

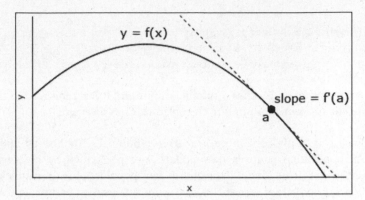

FIGURE 5-1:
The derivative at a point equals the slope of the curve at that point.

A function with multiple variables has multiple derivatives. As an example, f(x, y) has a derivative with respect to *x* and a derivative with respect to *y*. These are *partial derivatives*, and they're denoted with the following notation:

Partial derivative of f(x, y) with respect to x: $\frac{\partial f}{\partial x}$

Partial derivative of f(x, y) with respect to y: $\frac{\partial f}{\partial y}$

Figure 5-2 depicts the relationship $f(x, y) = 16 - 4x^2 - 2y^2$. At point (1, 2), the partial derivative with respect to *x* is −8, and the partial derivative with respect to *y* is −8.

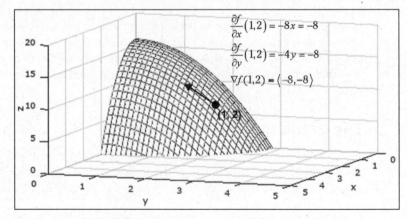

FIGURE 5-2:
The gradient points in the direction of steepest ascent.

Geometrically speaking, a *vector* is a quantity with a magnitude and a direction. A vector can be defined with components that identify its magnitudes in orthogonal directions. You can think of a vector as an arrow in space. If a vector points two units in the positive x-direction and three units in the negative y-direction, it can be represented as <2, -3>.

The gradient descent algorithm is concerned with a special type of vector called a *gradient*. A function's gradient is a vector whose components equal the function's partial derivatives. The gradient of *f* is denoted ∇*f*, and if the function has three variables, you can express its gradient as follows:

$$\nabla f(x,y,z) = \left[\frac{\partial f}{\partial x}, \frac{\partial f}{\partial y}, \frac{\partial f}{\partial z} \right]$$

If the function has two variables, its gradient vector will have two components. In Figure 5-2, the gradient at (1, 2) is the vector <-8, -8>. This vector is represented by the black arrow extending from the point (1, 2).

Suppose that the function in the figure represents a mountain in the Swiss Alps. If you're an Alpine climber, the gradient identifies the steepest direction of climbing. This designation isn't a coincidence. A function's gradient always points in the direction of steepest ascent. Similarly, the opposite vector identifies the steepest direction for descent.

After you understand the significance of the gradient, you're ready to tackle the gradient descent algorithm. This algorithm computes the gradient of the loss and updates the model's variables until the gradient of the loss falls to zero. To express this operation mathematically, I need to introduce some notation:

» The set of trainable variables is denoted θ. The values of the variables at Step *t* is denoted θ_t.

» The loss, which is a mathematical relationship containing the model's variables, is denoted $J(\theta)$. The gradient of the loss is $\nabla J(\theta)$.

» The learning rate, denoted η, is a value that affects how much θj changes from step to step.

With this notation, you can express each optimization step of the `Gradient DescentOptimizer` with the following equation:

$$\theta_t = \theta_{t-1} - \eta \nabla J(\theta)$$

This shows how the model's variables change with each training operation. As training continues, $\nabla J(\theta)$ should approach zero, which means that each new set of variables should be approximately equal to the previous set. At this point, optimization has completed because the optimizer has converged to a minimum.

The value of η is determined by the developer, and selecting this value is a crucial decision. If η is too large, the algorithm will progress quickly, but it may step around the minimum and never reach a final value.

If η is too small, the algorithm will move more precisely, but it will take a great deal of time. In addition, the optimizer may stop at a local minimum instead of a global minimum.

Creating a GradientDescentOptimizer

An application can perform optimization with the gradient descent algorithm by creating a GradientDescentOptimizer. The constructor is given as follows:

```
tf.train.GradientDescentOptimizer(learning_rate, use_
    locking=False, name='GradientDescent')
```

The learning_rate parameter sets η, the learning rate. The following code creates an optimizer and sets its learning rate to 0.1:

```
learn_rate = 0.1
optimizer = tf.train.GradientDescentOptimizer(learn_rate)
optimizer_op = optimizer.minimize(loss)
```

Many developers set η using trial and error, and initial estimates frequently range between 0.1 and 0.0001. A common method is to start with a large value of η and reduce the value until the optimizer converges successfully. Computer scientists have devised automatic methods for selecting η, but to the best of my knowledge, no method has gained widespread acceptance.

If you set the use_locking parameter to True, the GradientDescentOptimizer will acquire a lock that prevents other operations from modifying its variables. The variables can still be read normally.

Shortcomings

The gradient descent algorithm is the oldest and simplest algorithm for minimizing loss, but it has important disadvantages that every developer should be aware of.

The first disadvantage involves the difference between a local minimum and a global minimum. Optimization seeks the point of minimum loss across the entire range of the function. This value is the *global minimum* of the loss.

But a GradientDescentOptimizer may converge to a minimum that isn't global. This value is a *local minimum*, and Figure 5-3 illustrates the difference. In this figure, the function has two local minima surrounding the global minimum. If the optimizer reaches either of the local minima, it will halt optimization because the gradient of the loss, $\nabla J(\theta)$, equals 0.

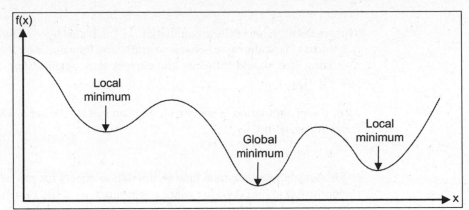

FIGURE 5-3:
A function may
have many local
minima, but only
one global
minimum.

You need to be aware of three other issues when using the gradient descent algorithm:

» It's generally slow to converge to a minimum value.

» It can only optimize differentiable functions.

» It may oscillate between values and never reach a minimum.

This last issue deserves explanation. If the learning rate is large, the algorithm may jump back and forth between a pair of points and never reach a minimum. This jumping is called *oscillation*, and it's a source of frequent frustration.

You can reduce the likelihood of oscillation by reducing the learning rate. Alternatively, you can create an optimizer whose learning rate changes from step to step. The following sections present three such optimizers: the `MomentumOptimizer`, the `AdagradOptimizer`, and the `AdamOptimizer`.

The MomentumOptimizer

The `MomentumOptimizer` has a lot in common with the `GradientDescent Optimizer`, but it usually converges faster with a reduced likelihood of oscillation. The `MomentumOptimizer` minimizes loss through the momentum algorithm, which uses preceding values of the loss gradient to update the current set of variables.

The momentum algorithm introduces a new quantity that TensorFlow calls the *accumulation*. This quantity, denoted v_t, is determined by the gradient of the current loss, the learning rate, and the preceding value of the accumulation:

$$v_t = \alpha v_{t-1} - \eta \nabla J(\theta)$$

The preceding value of the accumulation, v_{t-1}, is scaled by α, called the *momentum*. α is set to a constant value between 0 and 1, and its value indicates how much the preceding step should influence the current step. Applications commonly set α equal to 0.9.

After the accumulation is computed, you can update the set of variables with the following equation:

$$\theta_t = \theta_{t-1} + v_t$$

It's important to understand how accumulation affects the rate of convergence. If the optimizer moves quickly toward a minimum, αv_{t-1} will be significant, and the optimizer will approach the minimum even faster. If the optimizer is stuck between two values, αv_{t-1} will reduce the amount by which the variables are updated.

An application can create a `MomentumOptimizer` by calling its constructor:

```
MomentumOptimizer(learning_rate, momentum, use_locking=False, name='Momentum',
    use_nesterov=False)
```

The `use_locking` parameter has the same purpose as the `use_locking` parameter in the `GradientDescentOptimizer` constructor. That is, the optimizer will lock its variables' values if `use_locking` is set to `True`.

If `use_nesterov` is set to `True`, the optimizer adopts the Nesterov Accelerated Gradient descent algorithm, which is commonly shortened to NAG. The NAG algorithm modifies the momentum algorithm by updating variables *before* computing the loss. The following equations show how this algorithm works:

$$v_t = \alpha v_{t-1} - \nabla J\left(\theta - \alpha v_{t-1}\right)$$
$$\theta_t = \theta_{t-1} + v_j$$

The NAG algorithm generally converges faster than the gradient descent algorithm. The paper *On the Importance of Initialization and Momentum in Deep Learning* by Ilya Sutskever et al discusses the algorithm's performance in detail.

The AdagradOptimizer

The gradient descent algorithm and the momentum algorithm apply the same learning rate to each variable being trained. But different variables may converge to their minima at different rates. The adaptive gradient (Adagrad) algorithm takes this into account.

The Adagrad algorithm has two characteristics that have made it popular among academics and experts:

» The learning rate changes from variable to variable and from step to step. The learning rate at the tth step for the ith variable is denoted $\eta_{t,i}$.

» Adagrad methods compute *subgradients* instead of gradients. A subgradient is a generalization of a gradient that applies to nondifferentiable functions. This means AdaGrad methods can optimize both differentiable and nondifferentiable functions.

In 2011, John Duchi, Elad Hazan, and Yoram Singer described the first Adagrad algorithm in their paper *Adaptive Subgradient Methods for Online Learning and Stochastic Optimization*. The math is so ugly that I won't attempt to explain it. In case you're curious, here's the equation for the per-variable learning rate:

$$\eta_{t,i} = \frac{\eta}{\sqrt{G_{t,ii}}}$$

In this equation, $G_{t,ii}$ is the ith element of the diagonal of the matrix formed by taking the outer product of the subgradient of the loss with itself. After computing the learning rates, the optimizer updates the variables:

$$\theta_{t,i} = \theta_{t-1,i} - \eta_{t,i} g_t$$

Thankfully, TensorFlow developers don't have to worry about subgradients or outer products. This is because the TensorFlow API provides the `Adagrad Optimizer` class, whose constructor is given as follows.

```
AdagradOptimizer(learning_rate, initial_accumulator_value=0.1, use_locking=False,
    name='Adagrad')
```

One shortcoming of the Adagrad algorithm is that the learning rates always decrease in magnitude. As training continues, their values will eventually reach zero, bringing training to a halt.

The AdamOptimizer

The Adam (Adaptive Moment Estimation) algorithm closely resembles the Adagrad algorithm in many respects. It also resembles the Momentum algorithm because it takes two factors into account:

» The first moment vector: Scales the gradient by $1 - \beta_1$

» The second moment vector: Scales the *square* of the gradient by $1 - \beta_2$

These moment vectors are denoted m_t and v_t, respectively. The following equations show how their values change from step to step:

$$m_t = \beta_1 m_{t-1} + (1 - \beta_1) \nabla J(\theta)$$

$$v_t = \beta_2 v_{t-1} + (1 - \beta_2) \left[\nabla J(\theta) \right]^2$$

After computing these vectors, the optimizer updates the model's variables with the following equations:

$$\eta_t = \frac{\eta \sqrt{1 - \beta_2{}^t}}{1 - \beta_1{}^t}$$

$$\theta_t = \theta_{t-1} - \frac{\eta_t m_t}{\sqrt{v_t} + \varepsilon}$$

In the second equation, the purpose of ε is to prevent the denominator from reaching zero. For this reason, ε is usually set to a small value.

To employ the Adam algorithm, you need to create an instance of `AdamOptimizer`. The constructor is given as follows:

```
AdamOptimizer(learning_rate=0.001, beta1=0.9, beta2=0.999, epsilon=1e-08,
    use_locking=False, name='Adam')
```

TIP

When deciding on an optimizer, I always start with the `AdamOptimizer`, especially when working with images. The only exception is when I'm providing code to newcomers. In this case, I create a `GradientDescentOptimizer`, which doesn't scare anyone.

Feeding Data into a Session

Instead of processing all the test data with one call to a session's `run` method, applications frequently split the data into portions and call `run` once for each portion. There are at least three reasons to do so:

>> If the data is stored in a file or on a remote server, it may be more efficient to process one portion of data while another is loaded from the source.

>> Shuffling the portions of data increases the data's *stochasticity*. This process can improve convergence to a global minimum instead of a local minimum. I explain the rationale for data shuffling in the upcoming "Stochasticity" section.

>> Time constraints make it impractical to process all the data at once.

A portion of data processed in one session execution is called a *batch*. The process of transferring batches to a session is called *feeding data to the session*. To configure this in code, an application needs to perform three steps:

1. **Define placeholders to contain the data to be fed into the session.**

2. **Use the placeholders in the expressions for model and loss.**

3. **Set the second parameter of the session's `run` method to a dictionary that associates each placeholder with a source of data.**

Step 2 is trivial because you can process placeholders in the same way that you can process tensors. This discussion focuses on Steps 1 and 3. Later chapters present code that demonstrates how data can be fed into a session.

Creating placeholders

A *placeholder* is a constant `Tensor` that holds a batch of data to be fed into a session. You can create placeholders by calling the `tf.placeholder` function:

```
tf.placeholder(dtype, shape=None, name=None)
```

The first two arguments specify the type of the placeholder's elements and its size. The actual content of a placeholder is set by the running session, so there's no way to initialize a placeholder.

For example, the following code creates a placeholder that contains 32-bit floating-point values:

```
ph = tf.placeholder(tf.float32)
```

If a placeholder's shape isn't given, it can be set to a tensor of any shape. If the shape is given, assigning a tensor of a different shape will cause an error.

Defining the feed dictionary

Chapter 3 introduces the `Session` class and explains how you can execute a session by calling its `run` method. But the discussion doesn't mention `run`'s second argument, `feed_dict`, which makes it possible to feed data into the session. To feed data to a session, you need to assign `feed_dict` to a dictionary whose keys identify tensors in the session. Most applications set these keys to placeholders. Each value in `feed_dict` identifies a source of data to be passed to the tensor (usually a placeholder) identified by the key.

To demonstrate data feeding, the following code creates a placeholder, uses it in a model operation, and then feeds it into the session through the `feed_dict` parameter of the `run` method.

```
ph = tf.placeholder(tf.float32)
...
with tf.Session() as sess:
  sess.run(optimizer, feed_dict={ph: data_src})
```

When associating data with a placeholder, there's a catch: The data source can be a list of constants or a NumPy `ndarray`, but it can't be a tensor. The following code associates a placeholder with an `ndarray`:

```
ph = tf.placeholder(tf.float32)
vals = np.array([9., 8., 7.])
incr = tf.add(ph, 1.)
with tf.Session() as sess:
  res = sess.run(incr, feed_dict={ph: vals})
  print(res)
```

In this case, the printed result is `[10. 9. 8.]` because `feed_dict` passes the `vals` array to the session through the `ph` placeholder. If an application assigns `vals` to a tensor, TensorFlow will raise the following error: *The value of a feed cannot be a tf.Tensor object.*

Stochasticity

To keep optimizers from converging to a local minimum instead of a global minimum, many applications split their training data into small batches and feed them randomly to the session. This randomness, also called *stochasticity*, forces the optimizer to take larger jumps at first and smaller jumps as training progresses. This jumping increases the likelihood that the optimizer will find a global minimum.

If the gradient descent algorithm is employed to process stochastic data, it's referred to as the *stochastic gradient descent* algorithm. If you encounter the term SGD in machine learning literature, this algorithm is what it's referring to.

Monitoring Steps, Global Steps, and Epochs

In TensorFlow, each session execution that processes a single batch of data is called a *step*. Many TensorFlow functions and methods accept a parameter called `global_step`, which can be used to monitor the total number of steps executed by a session. In practice, `global_step` serves as the index of the batch being processed. You can access this index in code by calling `tf.train.global_step`.

You can also store the global step in a regular variable. This storage requires two operations:

1. Define a variable with an initial value of 0 and its `trainable` argument set to `False`.

2. Set the variable equal to the `global_step` parameter of the optimizer's `minimize` method.

If its `global_step` parameter is set to a variable, `minimize` will increment the variable each time a session processes a batch of data. The following code creates a variable named `gstep` and configures it to store the application's global step:

```
# Define the variable to hold the global step
gstep = tf.Variable(0, trainable=False)

# Configure the optimizer
learn_rate = 0.1
batch_size = 40
optimizer = tf.train.GradientDescentOptimizer(learn_rate).
            minimize(loss, global_step=gstep)

# Initialize variables
init = tf.global_variables_initializer()

# Launch session
with tf.Session() as sess:
    sess.run(init)

    for batch in range(batch_size):
        _, step, result = sess.run([optimizer, gstep, x_min])
        print("Step %d: Computed result = %f" % (step, result))
```

As you look at this code, a question may occur to you: Why keep track of the global step when you can access the loop index? To answer this question, suppose that you execute ten training batches and then restart your application. The loop variable will revert back to 0, but if you'd saved the global step to a file, you can restore it and use it as the current global step. I explain how to save variables to a file in the section "Saving variables," later in this chapter.

In the preceding example, the test executes each batch only once. In a real-world application, all the batches will be processed multiple times. A pass through every batch of a dataset is referred to as an *epoch*. For example, if a dataset is split into 50 batches, an epoch consists of 50 steps.

Many applications execute sessions in two loops: The outer loop iterates once for each epoch, and the inner loop executes once for each batch. The following code creates the two loops and calls `sess.run` with each iteration:

```
for epoch in range(num_epochs):
    for batch in range(num_batches):
        sess.run(...)
```

It's important to understand the difference between epochs and batches. Similar training loops are performed throughout this book's example code and examples on the Internet.

Saving and Restoring Variables

The `Saver` class makes it straightforward to load and store variables. By default, a `Saver` can access every variable in the session. But the first argument of the constructor can identify specific variables to be accessed. For example, the following code creates a `Saver` that can save/restore only two variables: `firstVar` and `secondVar`:

```
saver = tf.train.Saver([firstVar, secondVar])
```

After you create a `Saver`, you can store variables to a file by calling its `save` method. Then you can restore variables from a file by calling `restore`.

Saving variables

The `save` method stores variables and data related to the variables. By default, the method creates at least three binary files, each with the same name but a different suffix:

>> *filename*.data-*X*-of-*Y*: Stores variable values

>> *filename*.index: Holds the offset of each variable in the data file(s)

>> *filename*.meta: `MetaGraphDef` containing the structure of the graph that contains the variables

The data files contain variable values, and if the application has many variables, `save` will create multiple data files. If there's only one file, its name will be `filename.data-00000-of-00001`.

The index file contains a table that matches variable names to offsets in the index file. You can retrieve variables using the `restore` method, which I explain in the next section.

You can create these files by creating a `Saver` and calling its `save` method:

```
save(sess, save_path, global_step=None, latest_filename=None,
    meta_graph_suffix='meta', write_meta_graph=True, write_
    state=True)
```

These parameters are straightforward to understand. `sess` is the session containing the variables of interest and `save_path` identifies the path of the file to contain the saved data. The last element of `save_path` specifies the name of the files to be generated.

If `latest_filename` is set, `save` will create a text file that lists the paths of files involved in the save operation. If `global_step` is set, the value will be appended to each of the generated files.

For example, the following code creates a `Saver` and calls `save` to create the generated files (output.*) in the current directory:

```
saver = tf.train.Saver()
saver.save(sess, os.getcwd() + "/output")
```

If there aren't many variables to store, `save` will generate only three files: `output.data-00000-of-00001`, `output.index`, and `output.meta`.

Restoring variables

The `restore` method loads variables that have been stored previously. The process of restoring variables consists of two steps:

1. Call `import_meta_graph` to add the variables' nodes to the current graph.

2. Call `restore` to access the variable data.

The first step is simple. `tf.train.import_meta_graph` accepts the path of a `*.meta` file, reads graph data from the file, and adds the graph's nodes to the current graph. The function returns a `Saver` that lets you restore variables from the loaded graph.

For example, the following code imports graph data from `output.meta` and obtains a `Saver` that can be used to load variables:

```
saver = tf.train.import_meta_graph("output.meta")
```

After obtaining the `Saver`, an application can load variables by calling its `restore` method, whose signature is given as follows:

```
restore(sess, save_path)
```

As in the `save` method, `sess` identifies the session containing the variables, and `save_path` is the path to the file containing the variable data. This path must include the name of the three files without the suffix. As an example, the following code uses `saver` to load variables from `output` into the current graph:

```
saver.restore(sess, os.getcwd() + "/output")
```

Working with SavedModels

In addition to storing variables with a `Saver`, you can store your application's entire model by creating a `SavedModel`. As stated in the documentation, `SavedModel`s are "the universal serialization format for TensorFlow models" and serve as "the canonical way to export TensorFlow graphs."

To be precise, a `SavedModel` is a directory that contains a `*.pb` or `*.pbtxt` file. This file contains the application's model and stores graph definitions in `MetaGraphDef` protocol buffers. In addition to this file, a `SavedModel` may contain one or more of the following subdirectories:

>> **variables:** A directory containing the application's variables (files are similar to those produced by the Saver's save method, excluding the *.meta file)

>> **assets:** Auxiliary files that need to be loaded into the graph

>> **assets.extra:** User-provided files that don't need to be loaded into the graph

Saving and restoring a `SavedModel` isn't conceptually difficult, but the code gets a little complicated.

Saving a SavedModel

The process of saving an application's model to a `SavedModel` is similar to the process of storing variables. But instead of creating a `Saver`, you need to create a `tf.saved_model.builder.SavedModelBuilder`. The constructor accepts a single argument that identifies the top-level directory:

```
builder = tf.saved_model.builder.SavedModelBuilder("out")
```

After creating a `SavedModelBuilder`, you can add data to the model and save the model to the given directory. To add data to the model, you need to call one of two functions: `add_meta_graph` or `add_meta_graph_and_variables`. The signature of `add_meta_graph` is given as

```
add_meta_graph(tags, signature_def_map=None, assets_
    collection=None, legacy_init_op=None, clear_devices=False,
    main_op=None)
```

Metagraphs identify their capabilities and purposes with strings called *tags*. You can assign a metagraph's tags by setting the `tags` parameter. The `tf.saved_model.tag_constants` provides three common tags: `GPU`, `SERVING`, and `TRAINING`.

A graph's inputs and outputs form its *signature*. In code, a graph's signature is represented by a `SignatureDef`, and you can create this by calling the `build_signature_def` function of the `tf.saved_model.signature_def_utils` package:

```
build_signature_def(inputs=None, outputs=None, method_name=None)
```

To create the signature, you need to set `inputs` and `outputs` to dictionaries that associates names with `TensorInfo` protocol buffers. For the names, many applications use constants from `tf.saved_model.signature_constants`, which include `CLASSIFY_INPUTS`, `CLASSIFY_OUTPUT_CLASSES`, `PREDICT_INPUTS`, and `PREDICT_OUTPUTS`.

You can obtain a `TensorInfo` for a tensor by calling `tf.saved_model.utils.build_tensor_info` with the tensor. The following code returns a `TensorInfo` for a tensor named `input_vec`:

```
info = tf.saved_model.utils.build_tensor_info(input_vec)
```

The `method_name` parameter of `build_signature_def` is a string that serves as the signature's method name. You can set this to one of the strings in the `tf.saved_model.signature_constants` module, such as `CLASSIFY_METHOD_NAME`, `PREDICT_METHOD_NAME`, or `REGRESS_METHOD_NAME`.

The `add_meta_graph_and_variables` method is similar to `add_meta_graph`, but it has an extra parameter. The first parameter of `add_meta_graph_and_variables` is `sess`, which identifies the session that should provide the metagraph's variables.

After you've added metagraphs to a `SavedModel`, you can store the `SavedModel` by calling the `save` method. This accepts an `as_text` parameter that identifies whether the protocol buffer should be saved as a text file (`*.pbtxt`) or a binary file (`*.pb`). By default, `save` stores metagraph data in a binary file.

Loading a SavedModel

While it's complex to save metagraphs to a `SavedModel`, it's easy to load them. You need to know only one function:

```
tf.saved_model.loader.load(sess, tags, export_dir, **saver_kwargs)
```

This loads the `MetaGraphDef` protocol buffer from the directory given by `export_dir` with the tags given by `tags`. The `sess` parameter identifies the session that should contain the metagraph's variables, assets, and signatures.

Putting Theory into Practice

When I started learning TensorFlow, I found training difficult to understand. In addition to the theory, there are many new concepts to deal with, such as variables, optimizers, and placeholders.

To clarify how training works, I provide `ch5/simple_train.py` in the example code. The application is so simple that it doesn't even bother to formulate a model. Instead, it computes the loss with a simple quadratic equation: $x^2 - 4x + 5$. Figure 5-4 shows what this looks like.

As shown in Figure 5-4, the loss reaches a global minimum when `x_var` equals 2. Therefore, the optimizer's goal is to update `x_var` until it equals 2. The code in Listing 5-1 shows how you can accomplish this goal in TensorFlow.

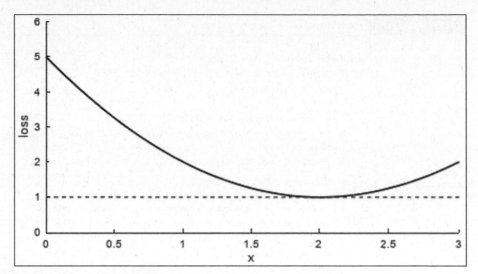

FIGURE 5-4:
The loss reaches
a minimum when
x equals 2.

| LISTING 5-1: | **Training in TensorFlow** |

```
# Define a trainable variable
x_var = tf.Variable(0., name='x_result')

# Define an untrainable variable to hold the global step
step_var = tf.Variable(0, trainable=False)

# Express loss in terms of the variable
loss = x_var * x_var - 4.0 * x_var + 5.0

# Find variable value that minimizes loss
learn_rate = 0.1
num_epochs = 40
optimizer = tf.train.GradientDescentOptimizer(learn_rate).minimize(loss, global_
    step=step_var)

# Initialize variables
init = tf.global_variables_initializer()

# Create the saver
saver = tf.train.Saver()

# Create summary data and FileWriter
summary_op = tf.summary.scalar('x', x_var)
file_writer = tf.summary.FileWriter('log', graph=tf.get_default_graph())
```

(continued)

LISTING 5-1: *(continued)*

```
# Launch session
with tf.Session() as sess:
    sess.run(init)

    for epoch in range(num_epochs):
        _, step, result, summary = sess.run([optimizer, step_var, x_var,
    summary_op])
        print('Step %d: Computed result = %f' % (step, result))

        # Print summary data
        file_writer.add_summary(summary, global_step=step)
        file_writer.flush()

    # Store variable data
    saver.save(sess, os.getcwd() + '/output')
    print('Final x_var: %f' % sess.run(x_var))
```

This code creates two variables: a trainable variable named x_var and an untrainable variable named step_var. loss is set to a quadratic equation whose independent variable is x_var.

The application calls tf.global_variables_initializer to obtain an operation for initializing its variables. The session must execute this operation before it can train the variables in the optimization process.

After creating the variables, the application creates a GradientDescentOptimizer and calls its minimize method to reduce the loss to a minimum. Then it assigns the global_step parameter of minimize to step_var. This assignment tells the session to increment step_var each time it performs a training operation.

After each training operation, print displays the global step and the current value of x_var. As training continues, x_var approaches 2, the point of minimum loss. Similarly, step_var approaches 40 because the training loop performs 40 iterations.

When optimization is complete, the application stores its variables to a file. The save method of the Saver instance stores variable data to three files in the current directory: output.data-00000-of-00001, output.index, and output.meta.

The code in ch5/restore_vars.py loads the value of x_var from the new data files. Listing 5-2 presents the code.

LISTING 5-2: **Loading Variables from a File**

```
# Create session
with tf.Session() as sess:

    # Load stored graph into current graph
    saver = tf.train.import_meta_graph('output.meta')

    # Restore variables into graph
    saver.restore(sess, os.getcwd() + '/output')

    # Display value of variable
    print('Variable value: ', sess.run('x_result:0'))
```

It's important to see that this code doesn't create a `Saver` by calling the class's constructor. Instead, it obtains a `Saver` by calling `import_meta_graph` with the name of the file containing graph data.

After obtaining the `Saver`, the application obtains the variable's value by calling the `Saver`'s `restore` method and the session's `run` method. Even though the variable's name was `x_var`, the application calls `run` with `x_output:0` because the variable's `name` parameter was set to `x_output`.

Visualizing the Training Process

The `ch5/simple_train.py` application prints the loss at each step using the following code:

```
print("Step %d: Computed result = %f" % (step, result))
```

TensorFlow provides a better way to monitor training. Chapter 4 covers the TensorBoard utility, which reads summary data generated by an application. The code in `ch5/simple_train.py` generates summary data for training by performing four steps:

1. Call `tf.summary.scalar` to create an operation that writes `x_var` to summary data.

2. Call `tf.summary.FileWriter` to create a `FileWriter`.

3. Execute the session with the operation from Step 1.

4. With each session execution, print the summary data by calling the `FileWriter`'s `add_summary` method.

For the last step, the following code prints the summary data:

```
file_writer.add_summary(summary, global_step=step)
```

The global_step parameter is important to understand. This parameter changes from step to step, and it tells TensorBoard to display a different value at each step. Figure 5-5 presents TensorBoard's output for the variable as training proceeds.

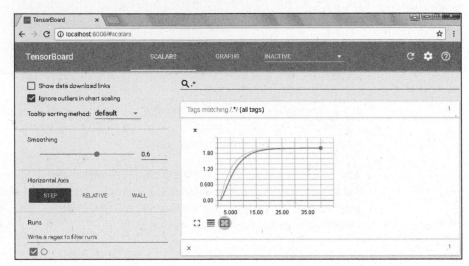

FIGURE 5-5: TensorBoard illustrates training by displaying variable values at each step.

In this example, the loss is so simple that the optimizer converges gently to the minimum when x equals 2. In real-world applications, the optimization process is never as smooth. Thankfully, TensorBoard can illustrate what's happening in the training process.

Session Hooks

After you understand how to save variables and generate summary data, you're ready to learn how to automate these operations with session hooks. Session hooks make it possible to monitor a session's state, access a session's data, and execute code at different points in the session's execution. To use session hooks, you need to perform two steps:

1. Create one or more SessionRunHook instances.

2. Create a MonitoredSession and configure it with the session hooks.

This discussion presents both steps. I also present code that demonstrates how these steps can be performed in practice.

Creating a session hook

To monitor a session's operation, you need to create a custom subclass of SessionRunHook or instantiate an existing subclass provided in the tf.train package. I refer to an instance of SessionRunHook or one of its subclasses as a *session hook*. To explain this topic, I present the methods of the SessionRunHook class and then introduce the subclasses provided by TensorFlow.

Life-cycle methods of SessionRunHook

When you associate a session hook with a session, the application calls the hook's methods at different stages in the session's life-cycle. To be specific, the application calls five methods of the SessionRunHook class:

» begin(): Called when the session is created

» after_create_session(session, coord): Called when the session's graph is finalized

» before_run(run_context): Called before the associated session starts executing

» after_run(run_context, run_values): Called after the associated session starts executing

» end(session): Called at the end of the session

It's important to see the difference between begin and after_create_session. An application calls begin immediately after the session has been created. At this point, you can access and modify the session's graph. But when the application calls after_create_session, the graph's structure is finalized and can't be changed.

The before_run and after_run methods both provide a run_context parameter. This is an instance of SessionRunContext, and it provides four members:

» session: The associated session

» original_args: A SessionRunArgs that contains the arguments of the session's run method

» stop_requested: A bool that identifies whether a stop is requested

» request_stop(): Tells the session to stop

If you want a session hook to read a value from the session's graph, you can code before_run to return a SessionRunArgs instance. You need to set the first argument of the SessionRunArgs constructor to the name of the variable or tensor to access.

If you added a return value to before_run, you can obtain the desired variable(s) or tensor(s) through the run_values argument of the after_run method. This SessionRunValues object has three fields:

>> results: The value(s) accessed by the return value of before_run

>> options: The RunOptions object used to configure the session's execution

>> run_metadata: The RunMetadata object containing information about the session's execution

This relationship between before_run and after_run can be confusing. To clarify how the two methods work together, the following code creates a subclass of SessionRunHook that prints information before and after the session runs.

```
class CustomHook(tf.train.SessionRunHook):
    def before_run(self, run_context):
        print("First argument: ", run_context.original_args.fetches);
        return tf.train.SessionRunArgs(loss)


    def after_run(self, run_context, run_values):
        print("Loss: ", run_values.results);
```

In this code, before_run returns a SessionRunArgs that identifies the name of the loss variable. When after_run is called, the results field of the run_values argument contains the current value of loss.

Subclasses of SessionRunHook

You can create your own subclasses of SessionRunHook and add code for different life-cycle methods. But in most cases, it's easier to instantiate an existing subclass. Table 5-2 presents the constructors of each session hook class in the tf.train package.

The first three session hook classes automate the processes of logging messages, saving variables, and generating summary data. You can specify how often the operation should be performed by setting a training step interval (every_n_iter or n_steps) or the time interval (every_n_secs or n_secs). Naturally, you can't set both types of intervals in the same method.

TABLE 5-2   **Session Hook Classes**

Class	Description
`LoggingTensorHook(tensors, every_n_iter=None, every_n_ secs=None, at_end=False, formatter=False)`	Logs values of a tensor after a given number of steps or after a given time
`CheckpointSaverHook(checkpoint_dir, save_secs=None, save_steps=None, saver=None, checkpoint_ baseline='model.ckpt', scaffold=None, listeners=None)`	Saves data to a checkpoint after a given number of steps or after a given time
`SummarySaverHook(save_steps=None, save_secs=None, output_dir=None, summary_writer=None, scaffold=None, summary_op=None)`	Generates summary data after a given number of steps or after a given time
`StepCounterHook(every_n_steps=100, every_n_secs=None, output_dir=None, summary_writer=None)`	Counts the number of steps per second
`StopAtStepHook(num_steps=None, last_step=None)`	Tells the session to stop after a number of steps have executed or a specific step has been reached
`NanTensorHook(loss_tensor, fail_on_nan_loss)`	Stops training if loss equals NaN
`GlobalStepWaiterHook(wait_until_step)`	Delays execution until the global step reaches a given value
`FinalOpsHook(final_ops, final_ops_feed_dict=None)`	Evaluates tensors at the end of a session
`FeedFnHook(feed_fn)`	Runs the given function and sets the session's feed dict

A `StepCounterHook` tells you about the session's performance by showing how many training steps are performed in the given time interval. To provide output, it generates summary data using a summary writer. In contrast, a `StopAt StepHook` tells the session to stop at a given global step value or after a specified number of training steps.

Creating a MonitoredSession

A `MonitoredSession` isn't a `Session`, but it contains a `Session` instance and provides methods for interacting with the session. For example, you can launch a `MonitoredSession`'s session by calling `run` and close the session by calling `close`.

To create a `MonitoredSession`, you need to call its constructor:

```
MonitoredSession(session_creator=None, hooks=None, stop_grace_period_secs=120)
```

The first parameter is a `SessionCreator` instance, which configures the underlying session. TensorFlow provides two subclasses of `SessionCreator`: `ChiefSessionCreator` and `WorkerSessionCreator`. The terms *chief* and *worker* refer to different types of processes in distributed applications.

You can associate session hooks with a `MonitoredSession` by setting the `hooks` parameter to a list of session hooks. The last parameter, `stop_grace_period_secs`, sets the number of seconds that a session thread can continue executing after an application calls `close`.

The `MonitoredSession` class also provides a method called `should_stop`. Applications frequently employ this method to determine whether the session should continue running. A session hook can stop a session through its `request_stop` method, which calls the monitored session's `should_stop` method. The following code demonstrates how `should_stop` can be used:

```
with tf.train.MonitoredSession(hooks=[custom_hook]) as sess:
    while not sess.should_stop():
        sess.run(...)
```

This `should_stop` method becomes particularly important for distributed TensorFlow applications. I discuss distributed applications and their sessions in Chapter 13.

Putting theory into practice

The code in the `ch5/monitor_train.py` module performs the same training operation as in the `ch5/simple_train.py` module. The difference is that monitor_train.py uses session hooks to save variables and generate summary data. Listing 5-3 presents the code.

LISTING 5-3: **Monitoring a Session with Session Hooks**

```
# Custom session hook
class CustomHook(tf.train.SessionRunHook):

    def begin(self):
        print('Beginning the session!')

    def before_run(self, run_context):
        return tf.train.SessionRunArgs(loss)
```

```python
    def after_run(self, run_context, run_values):
        if run_context.original_args != 'init':
            print('Loss: ', run_values.results)

    def end(self, session):
        print('The session is about to end!')

# Define a trainable variable
x_var = tf.Variable(0., name='x_result')

# Define an untrainable variable to hold the global step
step_var = tf.train.create_global_step()

# Express loss in terms of the variable
loss = x_var * x_var - 4.0 * x_var + 5.0

# Find variable value that minimizes loss
learn_rate = 0.1
num_epochs = 40
optimizer = tf.train.GradientDescentOptimizer(learn_rate).minimize(loss,
    global_step=step_var)

# Initialize variables
init = tf.global_variables_initializer()

# Create summary operation
summary_op = tf.summary.scalar('x', x_var)

# Create hooks
custom_hook = CustomHook()
checkpoint_hook = tf.train.CheckpointSaverHook(checkpoint_dir='ckpt_dir',
    checkpoint_basename='output', save_steps=10)
summary_hook = tf.train.SummarySaverHook(save_steps=10, output_dir='log',
    summary_op=summary_op)
hooks = [custom_hook, checkpoint_hook, summary_hook]

# Launch session
with tf.train.MonitoredSession(hooks=hooks) as sess:
    sess.run(init)

    for epoch in range(num_epochs):
        sess.run(optimizer)
```

This module creates three session hook instances:

>> CustomHook: Prints messages at different points in the session's execution

>> CheckpointSaverHook: Saves checkpoint data to a directory named ckpt_dir

>> SummarySaverHook: Saves summary data to a directory named log

After creating the session hooks, the module creates a MonitoredSession and configures it with the three hook instances. Then it initializes the session's variables and optimizes the model.

2
Implementing Machine Learning

Chapter 6

Analyzing Data with Statistical Regression

E verybody knows that machine learning is a fast-paced, exciting field for clever, future-minded people, and everybody knows that statistics is a boring, stodgy field for people who enjoy Muzak. So newcomers may find it odd to see a chapter on statistical analysis in a book on machine learning.

But machine learning and statistics have a lot in common. In fact, they have the same ultimate goal: to model real-world systems with mathematical relationships. Machine learning relies extensively on statistical methods, and this chapter presents three methods that play critical roles in TensorFlow development: linear regression, polynomial regression, and logistic regression. In addition, the example code in this chapter solidifies the manner in which TensorFlow applications perform training.

Analyzing Systems Using Regression

One of the most effective tools used by statisticians is regression. *Regression* analyzes a system by measuring the relationships between its variables. TensorFlow provides many capabilities for this analysis, and this chapter focuses on four types of regression:

>> **Linear regression:** Fitting a straight line to points in a dataset

>> **Polynomial regression**: Fitting a polynomial to points in a dataset

>> **Binary logistic regression:** Classifying points into one of two categories

>> **Multinomial logistic regression:** Classifying points into one of multiple categories

The following sections explore these simple operations.

Linear Regression: Fitting Lines to Data

Searching through your grandfather's attic, you find a mint condition first issue of *Commander Warpspeed's Journey into Space!* This rare comic book may be worth many thousands of dollars, so you decide to sell it. But how much should you ask for it?

An online search provides 40 selling prices that range from less than $5,000 to more than $10,000. Figure 6-1 illustrates these prices on a chart.

Computing the average selling price would be easy, but you want to know whether the price is rising or falling and by how much the price is rising or falling. To find a good selling price, you decide to approximate your data with a line that indicates the change in the book's price over time. This process is called *linear regression*, and the dashed gray line in Figure 6-1 identifies the general trend of the comic book's price.

The first step in TensorFlow training involves choosing an initial expression for the model (see Chapter 5). For linear regression, this decision is easy. The model is a line whose equation is $y = mx + b$, where m is the line's slope, and b is the y-intercept (the y-value when x equals 0). The goal of linear regression is to determine m and b so that the resulting line best approximates (or fits) the set of points.

The loss is also simple to compute. If the graph contains the point (x, y), the difference between the system and the model is $y - (mx + b)$.

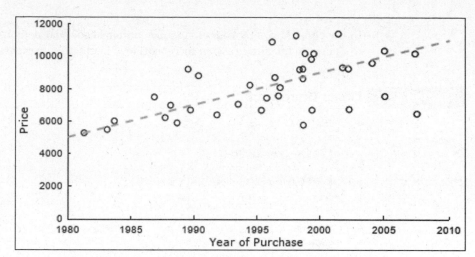

FIGURE 6-1:
The comic book's
value increases
over time.

In machine learning applications, values of the loss should always have the same sign. You can make sure all the loss values are positive by computing the square of the error at each point and take the average of the error values. If there are N points, you can compute the loss with the following equation:

$$loss = \frac{1}{N}\sum_{i=0}^{N-1}\left(y-\left(mx+b\right)\right)^2$$

This method of computing loss is called the *mean-squared error*, or MSE. In TensorFlow, you can compute it by calling the reduce_mean function. The following code shows how this function is used:

```
model = tf.add(tf.multiply(m, x), b)
loss = tf.reduce_mean(tf.pow(model - y, 2))
```

Having obtained an expression for the loss, the next step is to create an optimizer to minimize the loss. As the optimizer does its work, it will update the variables m and b, thereby obtaining a line that best approximates the change in the comic book's price over time.

To demonstrate this, the following code creates an optimizer, sets its learning rate to 0.1, and calls its minimize method:

```
optimizer = tf.train.GradientDescentOptimizer(0.1)
opt_op = optimizer.minimize(loss)
```

minimize returns an operation that you can use as the first argument of the session's run method (see Chapter 5). Note that you must call run repeatedly to ensure that the training converges to suitable values for *m* and *b*.

In the ch6 folder, `lin_regression.py` contains code that demonstrates how you can perform linear regression in TensorFlow. Listing 6-1 presents the code.

LISTING 6-1: **Linear Regression**

```
# Random input values
N = 40
x = tf.random_normal([N])
m_real = tf.truncated_normal([N], mean=2.0)
b_real = tf.truncated_normal([N], mean=3.0)
y = m_real * x + b_real

# Variables
m = tf.Variable(tf.random_normal([]))
b = tf.Variable(tf.random_normal([]))

# Compute model and loss
model = tf.add(tf.multiply(x, m), b)
loss = tf.reduce_mean(tf.pow(model - y, 2))

# Create optimizer
learn_rate = 0.1
num_epochs = 200
num_batches = N
optimizer = tf.train.GradientDescentOptimizer(learn_rate).minimize(loss)

# Initialize variables
init = tf.global_variables_initializer()

# Launch session
with tf.Session() as sess:
    sess.run(init)

    # Perform training
    for epoch in range(num_epochs):
        for batch in range(num_batches):
            sess.run(optimizer)

    # Display results
    print('m = ', sess.run(m))
    print('b = ', sess.run(b))
```

This module sets the number of batches equal to the number of input points. The training process executes 200 epochs, and each epoch performs 40 training steps.

Polynomial Regression: Fitting Polynomials to Data

You can easily extend the method of linear regression to polynomials. That is, the process of fitting a polynomial to a set of points uses essentially the same process as that used to fit a line.

To demonstrate, I explain how you can approximate data with a cubic polynomial. You can express every cubic polynomial with the following equation:

$$y = ax^3 + bx^2 + cx + d$$

Figure 6-2 illustrates how you can fit a cubic polynomial to a set of random points.

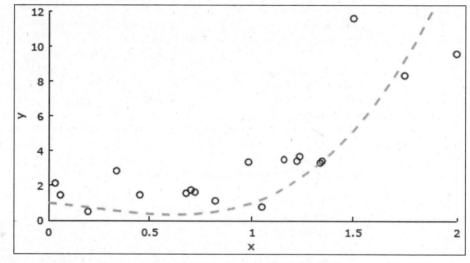

FIGURE 6-2:
Statistical
regression makes
it possible
to approximate
data with a
polynomial.

The code in ch6/poly_regression.py uses TensorFlow to fit a cubic polynomial to a set of random points. If you compare this code to the code in ch6/lin_regression.py, you'll see that the two modules closely resemble one another. The most important difference involves the expression for the model, which is computed as follows:

```
model = a * tf.pow(x, 3) + b * tf.pow(x, 2) + c * x + d
```

To obtain an expression for the loss, the module uses the same mean-squared error process that was used for linear regression. (See the section "Linear Regression: Fitting Lines to Data.") To minimize the loss, the module creates the same type of optimizer (GradientDescentOptimizer) used for linear regression. The code in Listing 6-2 shows how to do so.

LISTING 6-2: **Polynomial Regression**

```python
# Random input values
N = 40
x = tf.random_normal([N])
a_real = tf.truncated_normal([N], mean=3.)
b_real = tf.truncated_normal([N], mean=-2.)
c_real = tf.truncated_normal([N], mean=-1.)
d_real = tf.truncated_normal([N], mean=1.)
y = a_real * tf.pow(x, 3) + b_real * tf.pow(x, 2) + c_real * x + d_real

# Variables
a = tf.Variable(tf.random_normal([]))
b = tf.Variable(tf.random_normal([]))
c = tf.Variable(tf.random_normal([]))
d = tf.Variable(tf.random_normal([]))

# Compute model and loss
model = a * tf.pow(x, 3) + b * tf.pow(x, 2) + c * x + d
loss = tf.reduce_mean(tf.pow(model - y, 2))

# Create optimizer
learn_rate = 0.01
num_epochs = 400
num_batches = N
optimizer = tf.train.GradientDescentOptimizer(learn_rate).minimize(loss)

# Initialize variables
init = tf.global_variables_initializer()

# Launch session
with tf.Session() as sess:
    sess.run(init)

    # Perform training
    for epoch in range(num_epochs):
        for batch in range(num_batches):
            sess.run(optimizer)

    # Display results
    print('a = ', sess.run(a))
    print('b = ', sess.run(b))
    print('c = ', sess.run(c))
    print('d = ', sess.run(d))
```

You can apply the methodology used in poly_regression.py to polynomials of any degree. All you need to do is set the model to the general polynomial and create a variable for each of the polynomial's coefficients.

Binary Logistic Regression: Classifying Data into Two Categories

While linear and polynomial regression are concerned with identifying trends, logistic regression is concerned with placing data points into categories. If Points A and B belong to Category X and Points P and Q belong to Category Y, what category will Point J belong to?

The following sections look at systems with only two categories. Is the patient healthy or sick? Will the operation succeed or fail? This process of modeling systems with two categories is called *binary logistic regression*.

Setting up the problem

Binary logistic regression is concerned with testing the effect of one or more variables on a binary outcome. If patients take a new medication, will their symptoms disappear? If a candidate wears a red tie and blue pants on election day, will the public vote for that person?

To demonstrate the process of binary logistic regression, this discussion focuses on a question of obvious importance: How does the volume of my alarm clock affect my getting out of bed in the morning? I'm such a heavy sleeper that if the alarm doesn't sound, I'll lie in bed forever. But as the volume increases, the probability of me getting out of bed increases.

To examine the relationship between the alarm volume and my getting out of bed, I set my alarm to ring a different volume every morning for 40 days. Figure 6-3 illustrates the relationship between the alarm volume and my getting out of bed.

To model this mathematically, statisticians represent each category with a number. In this example, I associate Category 1 (Get Out of Bed) with 1 and Category 0 (Stay Asleep) with 0.

But I don't want the output to be limited to 0 and 1. I want a value between 0 and 1 that identifies the probability of me getting out of bed. This concept is important to understand: When you code applications that perform classification, the theory of probability takes center stage. This discussion doesn't provide a complete discussion of the subject, but I'll explain the math as it becomes necessary.

It should be clear that linear and polynomial regression won't help with this problem because their models produce values beyond 0 and 1. Also, straight lines and polynomials are too simplistic for practical classification.

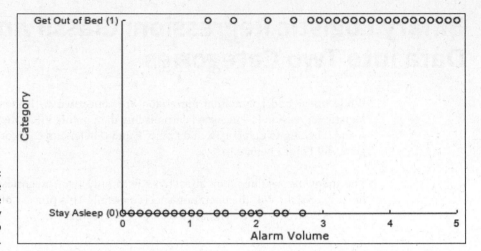

FIGURE 6-3:
As the volume
increases, the
chances of my
waking up
increase.

To classify data points, statisticians employ a different type of regression called *logistic regression.* Just as linear regression models systems with a line and polynomial regression uses a polynomial, logistic regression employs a type of curve called the logistic function.

Defining models with the logistic function

The logistic function plays a central role in applications that classify data points. Mathematicians express the logistic function with the following equation:

$$\sigma(x) = \frac{1}{1 + e^{-x}}$$

Figure 6-4 shows what the logistic function looks like for values of x between 8 and −8:

This function is shaped like an S, and because sigma (σ) is the Greek letter for S, this function is commonly referred to as the *sigmoid function*, or $\sigma(x)$. This function has three properties that make it suitable for classifying points into one of two categories:

» Its maximum value is 1, and the minimum value is 0.

» $\sigma(0) = 0.5$, which implies that a data point in the center is equally likely to belong to both categories.

» The function is symmetric around the *y*-axis — that is, $\sigma(-x) = 1 - \sigma(x)$.

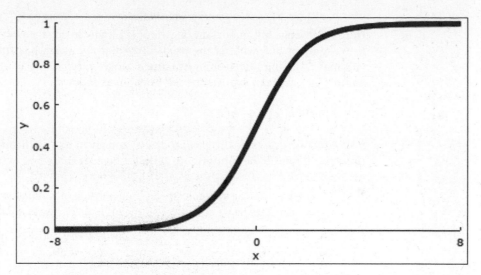

Having selected the logistic function, you can approximate the system with the model function $\sigma(mx+b)$. As with linear regression, the goal is to find values for m and b that bring the model as closely in line with real-world observation as possible.

The next step is to find an expression for the loss. One possible method is to use the mean-squared error (see the earlier sections on linear and polynomial regression). But there's a problem. The slope of the sigmoid function is nearly 0 at its extremes, which means gradient descent method will take a great deal of time to minimize the loss.

For this reason, applications that classify data points put aside mean-squared error and compute loss using a different method called maximum likelihood estimation.

Computing loss with maximum likelihood estimation

The goal of binary logistic regression is to obtain the sigmoid function that best approximates the available data. This function identifies the approximate probability of a point being classified in Category 1.

But what about the probability of a point being classified in Category 0? There are only two categories, so if we denote the probability of Category 1 as $\sigma(mx+b)$, the probability of Category 0 is $1 - \sigma(mx+b)$. For the sake of simplicity, I'll refer to the model function, $\sigma(mx+b)$, as h(x).

Here's a strange but important question: If I know in advance whether I'm going to wake up or not, what is the probability that my alarm has rung at a specific volume? Denoting my sleeping/waking state as y_i ($y_0 = 0$, $y_1 = 1$) and the alarm volume as x, you can express the relationship as follows:

$$L(y_i) = h(x)^{y_i} \left[1 - h(x) \right]^{(1-y_i)}$$

This equation expresses the *likelihood* of y_i, and given its significance in classification, you'll want to be comfortable with it. Consider these two extreme cases:

>> If h(x) represents the system perfectly, h(x) will equal 1 when y_i equals 1 and h(x) will equal 0 when y_i equals 0. This means L(y_i) will always equal 1.

>> If h(x) is always wrong, h(x) will always equal 0 when y_i equals 1 and h(x) will always equal 1 when y_i equals 0. This means L(y_i) will always equal 0.

In general, a likelihood function will produce a value somewhere between 0 and 1. The greater the likelihood, the more closely the model, h(x), resembles the system. The process of maximizing the likelihood is called *maximum likelihood estimation*. It should be clear that maximizing the likelihood minimizes the loss.

To simplify computation, statisticians take the logarithm of the likelihood. After this step, the maximum likelihood estimation method is referred to as the *log likelihood method*.

TensorFlow's optimizers work by minimizing loss. But when dealing with likelihood, the goal is to obtain greater values, not smaller values. To fix this issue, statisticians negate the expression for log likelihood. The resulting expression for the loss is given as follows:

$$loss = -y_i \log(h(x)) - (1 - y_i) \log(1 - h(x))$$

This and similar expressions are commonly used in binary logistic regression. The following section demonstrates how the logistic function and log likelihood can be used in practical code.

Putting theory into practice

The code in ch6/binary_logistic.py uses TensorFlow to perform binary logistic regression. Listing 6-3 presents the code.

LISTING 6-3: **Binary Logistic Regression**

```
# Input values
N = 40
x = tf.lin_space(0., 5., N)
y = tf.constant([0., 0., 0., 0., 0., 0., 0., 0., 0., 0.,
                 1., 0., 0., 1., 0., 0., 0., 1., 0., 0.,
                 1., 0., 1., 1., 1., 1., 1., 1., 1., 1.,
                 1., 1., 1., 1., 1., 1., 1., 1., 1., 1.])

# Variables
m = tf.Variable(0.)
b = tf.Variable(0.)

# Compute model and loss
model = tf.nn.sigmoid(tf.add(tf.multiply(x, m), b))
loss = -1. * tf.reduce_sum(y * tf.log(model) + (1. - y) * (1. - tf.log(model)))

# Create optimizer
learn_rate = 0.005
num_epochs = 350
optimizer = tf.train.GradientDescentOptimizer(learn_rate).minimize(loss)

# Initialize variables
init = tf.global_variables_initializer()

# Launch session
with tf.Session() as sess:
    sess.run(init)

    # Run optimizer
    for epoch in range(num_epochs):
        sess.run(optimizer)

    # Display results
    print('m =', sess.run(m))
    print('b =', sess.run(b))
```

This module accepts the data points in Figure 6-3 as input and computes values of m and b that best fit the data to the model function $\sigma(mx+b)$. Figure 6-5 depicts the computed model function superimposed over the training data.

On my system, the computed values are m = 4 and b = -13.5. mx + b equals 0 when x = 3.375, so the center of the sigmoid function is reached when the volume is set to 3.375.

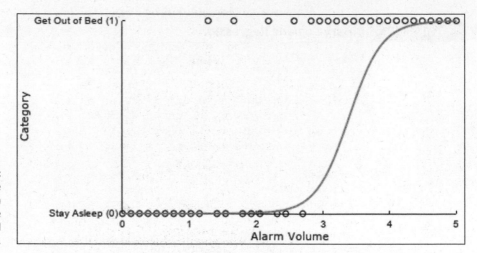

FIGURE 6-5:
After training, the
sigmoid function
approximates the
experimental
data.

Multinomial Logistic Regression: Classifying Data into Multiple Categories

Many machine learning applications need to classify points into more than two categories. This process is called multinomial logistic regression, and it resembles binary logistic regression in many respects. The primary difference is that it uses different functions to represent the model and loss.

To present this topic, I explain how you can use TensorFlow to recognize handwriting samples from the Modified National Institute of Science and Technology (MNIST) dataset. Each image contains a handwritten digit that belongs to one of ten categories.

The Modified National Institute of Science and Technology (MNIST) Dataset

To test machine learning applications, the National Institute of Standards and Technology (NIST) compiled a set of handwriting samples of numbers between 0 and 9. Yann LeCun created a subset of NIST's images called the Modified NIST (MNIST) database.

Unlike NIST's samples, MNIST's samples all have the same size and are all centered into 28-x-28 images. Each pixel is given as an unsigned byte between 0 (white) and 255 (black). Each image has a corresponding label that identifies the handwritten digit (0 through 9).

To run the multinomial logistic regression example, you need to download the MNIST dataset from `http://yann.lecun.com/exdb/mnist`. Four files are available:

» `train-images-idx1-ubyte.gz` — Training images

» `train-images-idx3-ubyte.gz` — Training labels

» `t10k-labels-idx1-ubyte.gz` — Test images

» `t10k-images-idx3-ubyte.gz` — Test labels

The training labels and test labels identify the digits written in the corresponding images. For example, the sixth label in the training dataset is 8. Figure 6-6 shows what the sixth image in the training dataset looks like.

FIGURE 6-6:
Each MNIST image contains a handwritten digit in a 28-x-28 pixel array.

If you decompress an MNIST file, you'll see that each file stores its data in a single data structure. Thankfully, you don't need to know anything about these structures because TensorFlow makes accessing MNIST data easy. The function to know is `read_data_sets`, which is provided by the `tensorflow.contrib.learn.datasets.mnist` package:

```
read_data_sets(train_dir, fake_data=False, one_hot=False, dtype=dtypes.float32,
    reshape=True, validation_size=5000, seed=None)
```

When this function executes, it searches for the four MNIST archives in the directory identified by the `train_dir` parameter. If any of the files can't be found, `read_data_sets` will download them, decompress them, and store them in the specified folder.

To understand the other arguments of `read_data_sets`, it's important to be familiar with the function's return value, which is an instance of the `Datasets` class. Each `Datasets` instance has three fields:

» `train` — a Dataset containing the MNIST training data

» `validation` — a Dataset containing validation data

» `test` — a Dataset containing data to be used for testing

Appropriately enough, each field of a `Datasets` instance is an instance of the `Dataset` class. Table 6-1 lists four members of this class and provides a description of each.

TABLE 6-1

Members of the Dataset Class

Function	Description
`images`	ndarray of images given as numpy arrays
`labels`	ndarray of category names for the images
`num_examples`	The number of examples in the dataset
`next_batch(batch_size, fake_data=False, shuffle=True)`	Returns the next batch of images

The first three fields are straightforward. The following code calls `read_data_sets`, and for each field, it prints the shape of the corresponding image array:

```
import tensorflow.contrib.learn as learn

dset = learn.datasets.mnist.read_data_sets('MNIST-data')
print("Training images: ", dset.train.images.shape)
print("Validation images: ", dset.validation.images.shape)
print("Test images: ", dset.test.images.shape)
```

On my system, the printed results are given as follows:

```
Training images:          (55000, 784)
Validation images:        (5000, 784)
Test images:              (10000, 784)
```

If you set one_hot to True in read_data_sets, the labels field of the resulting Dataset will contain one-hot vectors. A *one-hot vector* is a one-dimensional array in which one element's value is high, and the rest are low. By default, the high value is 1, and the low value is 0. If the one_hot parameter is set to True, each label will be provided as a one-hot vector with ten elements: a 1 in the position that identifies the digit and a 0 in every other position.

The next_batch method of the Dataset class provides MNIST data in batches. The first argument sets the size of each batch, the second argument identifies whether fake data should be generated, and the last argument indicates whether the MNIST data should be shuffled.

Defining the model with the softmax function

You can use the sigmoid function to classify points into two categories. (See the section "Defining models with the logistic function" for more information.) If a system (such as MNIST classification) has more than two categories, the sigmoid function won't be sufficient.

Instead, statisticians use an operation that can accept an array of values and return an array of values. This is the *softmax function*, which extends the sigmoid function to multiple variables. The jth term of the softmax function is denoted by $\sigma(x)_j$, and if the input array contains N terms, you can compute the softmax function of x_j with the following equation:

$$\sigma(x)_j = \frac{e^{x_j}}{\sum_{i=0}^{N-1} e^{x_i}}$$

When using this function, you need to be aware of two points:

» Each value in the output array lies between 0 and 1.

» The sum of the values in the output array will always equal 1.

In TensorFlow, you can perform the softmax operation by calling the softmax function in the tf.nn package:

```
softmax(input, dim=-1, name=None)
```

By default, every element of the input tensor is added together in the denominator of the softmax function. But if you set the dim parameter, only the values in the specified dimension will be included in the sum.

An example will clarify how this function works. If the input tensor is [3.2, -2.6, 1.7, 0.0, 4.9], calling `softmax` will return a 5-element tensor equal to [0.14835, 0.00045, 0.03310, 0.00605, 0.81205]. You can compute the first softmax value in the following way:

$$\sigma(x)_0 = \frac{e^{x_0}}{\sum_{i=0}^{4} e^{x_i}} = \frac{e^{3.2}}{\left(e^{3.2} + e^{-2.6} + e^{1.7} + e^0 + e^{4.9}\right)} = 0.14835$$

Each of the N values identifies the probability of the data point belonging to the corresponding category. The probability of the point belonging to Category 0 is 0.14835.

Computing loss with cross entropy

If h(x) is a model and y_i identifies a category, you can compute the likelihood of y_i for a given value of x in the following way:

$$L(y_i) = h(x)^{y_i} \left[1 - h(x)\right]^{(1-y_i)}$$

The concept of likelihood can be extended to systems with more than two outcomes. If a classifier has to choose between N categories, y_i can take any value between 0 and N-1. If the model is given as h(x), you can express the likelihood with the following equation:

$$L(y_0, y_1, \ldots y_{N-1}) = h(x)^{y_0} h(x)^{y_1} \cdots h(x)^{y_{N-1}} = \prod_{i=0}^{N-1} h(x)^{y_i}$$

Again, the likelihood will equal 1 if h(x) is always right, and it will equal 0 if h(x) is always wrong. To convert the likelihood into a suitable loss function, statisticians take the negative logarithm and arrive at the following expression:

$$loss = -\sum_{i=0}^{N-1} y_i \log(h(x))$$

In machine learning literature, this result is referred to as *cross entropy*. This term comes from information theory, and it refers to the usage of logarithms to determine how many bits should be used to represent messages. The following code defines a model by calling `tf.nn.softmax` and then computes the loss using cross entropy.

```
model = tf.nn.softmax(tf.matmul(x, m) + b)
loss = tf.reduce_mean(-tf.reduce_sum(y * tf.log(model)))
```

For improved performance, TensorFlow provides a function that combines the softmax function and cross entropy. This function is `tf.nn.softmax_cross_entropy_with_logits` and its signature is given as follows:

```
softmax_cross_entropy_with_logits(labels=None, logits=None, dim=-1, name=None)
```

You must identify each argument passed to this function by name. `logits` is set to the tensor that would be passed to softmax, and `labels` is set to a tensor containing the associated labels. `logits` and `labels` must have the same size.

TensorFlow also provides a function that combines the sigmoid function and cross entropy: `sigmoid_cross_entropy_with_logits`. Its signature is given as follows:

```
sigmoid_cross_entropy_with_logits(_sentinel=None, labels=None,
    logits=None, name=None)
```

`labels` and `logits` accept the same values as the corresponding arguments of `softmax_cross_entropy_with_logits`.

Putting theory into practice

The code in ch6/`multi_regression.py` demonstrates how you can use multinomial regression to load and classify images from the MNIST dataset. Listing 6-4 presents the code.

LISTING 6-4: **Multinomial Logistic Regression**

```
# Read MNIST data
dataset = learn.datasets.mnist.read_data_sets('MNIST-data', one_hot=True)

# Placeholders for MNIST images
image_holder = tf.placeholder(tf.float32, [None, 784])
label_holder = tf.placeholder(tf.float32, [None, 10])

# Variables
m = tf.Variable(tf.zeros([784, 10]))
b = tf.Variable(tf.zeros([10]))

# Compute loss
loss = tf.reduce_mean(
    tf.nn.softmax_cross_entropy_with_logits(
        logits=tf.matmul(image_holder, m) + b, labels=label_holder))
```

(continued)

LISTING 6-4: *(continued)*

```
# Create optimizer
learning_rate = 0.01
num_epochs = 25
batch_size = 100
num_batches = int(dataset.train.num_examples/batch_size)
optimizer = tf.train.GradientDescentOptimizer(learning_rate).minimize(loss)

# Initialize variables
init = tf.global_variables_initializer()

# Launch session
with tf.Session() as sess:
    sess.run(init)

    # Loop over epochs
    for epoch in range(num_epochs):

        # Loop over batches
        for batch in range(num_batches):
            image_batch, label_batch = dataset.train.next_batch(batch_size)
            _, lossVal = sess.run([optimizer, loss],
                feed_dict={image_holder: image_batch, label_holder: label_
batch})

    # Display the final loss
    print('Final loss: ', lossVal)
```

Instead of computing the model, this code computes the loss directly by calling
softmax_cross_entropy_with_logits. The last line of the code prints the final
value for the loss.

Chapter **7**

Introducing Neural Networks and Deep Learning

This chapter explains how neural networks operate and how to use them to analyze data in TensorFlow applications.

From Neurons to Perceptrons

For many, the topic of neural networks conjures visions of artificial brains, omniscient computers that predict the future, and other fixtures of science fiction. But practitioners of machine learning take a more down-to-earth view: Neural networks are useful computational tools, but they're not ideal for every application, and they're never completely reliable.

Biology inspired the development of neural networks, but their essential operation is statistical in nature. *Neural networks* analyze data to discover mathematical relationships between inputs and outputs. They should only be used as a last resort — if you already have clear rules that relate outputs to input data, you should use your rules instead.

It's important to see the difference between the operation of a neural network and statistical regression. When you use regression, you choose the precise shape of the model. But when you analyze data with a neural network, you choose a general shape for the model, and the network determines the details.

In my opinion, the best way to approach the topic of artificial neural networks is to see how they relate to biological neurons. This section explores the basic structure of neurons and then proceeds to perceptrons, which serve as mathematical abstractions of neurons.

Neurons

In the early 19th century, Santiago Ramón y Cajal took a close look at the cells that make up nerve tissue. Scientists refer to these nerve cells as *neurons*, and Figure 7-1 illustrates their basic structure.

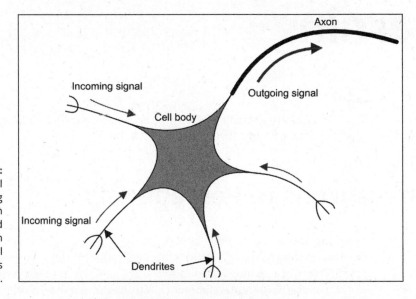

FIGURE 7-1: A nerve cell receives incoming signals through its dendrites and generates an outgoing signal that travels through the axon.

A neuron receives electrical stimulation through its *dendrites* and their branches. The chemicals in the cell body store electricity, and as incoming signals grow in strength, the neuron's voltage increases.

When the voltage in a neuron exceeds a certain value, called the *threshold,* the neuron transmits (or *fires*) an electrical signal. This signal travels through the axon and stimulates further neurons, as shown in Figure 7-1. In this manner, one neuron's firing may cause a series of other neurons to fire.

The study of neurons has progressed dramatically since the 19th century, and neurologists know that neurons do far more than just pass electricity from one cell to another. But for this chapter, you need to be familiar with only three points:

>> A neuron receives one or more incoming signals and produces one outgoing signal.

>> A neuron's output can serve as the input of another neuron.

>> Every neuron has a threshold, and the neuron won't produce output until its electricity exceeds the threshold.

If you understand these three points, you'll have no trouble grasping the abstract models of neurons.

Perceptrons

In 1962, Frank Rosenblatt devised a model for the neuron called the *perceptron.* Figure 7-2 shows how a perceptron can be represented graphically.

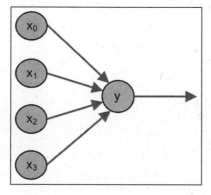

FIGURE 7-2:
Perceptrons resemble neurons in many respects.

Like a neuron, a perceptron receives multiple inputs and produces one output. But a perceptron's inputs are provided as numeric values instead of electrical pulses. In Figure 7-2, these values are denoted x_0 through x_3.

Similarly, the perceptron's threshold value is represented by a number. If the sum of the inputs exceeds the threshold, the perceptron's output will be 1. If the sum of the signals falls below the threshold, the output will be 0.

For example, suppose that x_0 is set to 0.5, x_1 is set to 1.5, x_2 is set to 2.5, and x_3 is set to -1.0. The sum of the signals is 3.5. If the perceptron's threshold value is 3.0, the perceptron will produce an output of 1. If the threshold value is 4.0, the perceptron will produce an output of 0.

Denoting the inputs as x_i and the output as y, a perceptron's output can be determined by the following relationship:

$$y = \begin{cases} 1 \text{ if } \sum_i x_i \geq \text{threshold} \\ 0 \text{ otherwise} \end{cases}$$

Like biological neurons, perceptrons can be connected together so that the output of one perceptron serves as the input of another. Figure 7-3 shows what this looks like. As shown, different perceptrons can have different numbers of inputs, but each always produces one output.

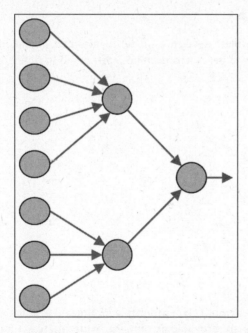

FIGURE 7-3:
Perceptrons can be combined together in a tree-like structure.

Historians and academics may find these simple perceptrons interesting, but in this primitive form, they can't be used for practical machine learning. This is because the perceptron's operation is static — its behavior can't be improved through training.

Improving the Model

After Rosenblatt published his initial vision of the perceptron, computer scientists updated his model in many ways. Three important changes are as follows:

>> Each incoming signal is assigned a weight that indicates its influence.

>> Instead of a threshold value, a constant called a bias is added to the incoming signals.

>> The sum of weighted inputs is passed to an activation function that determines the output.

These changes make neural networks suitable for machine learning. Modern developers refer to the elements of these networks as *nodes* instead of *perceptrons*.

Weights

In Figures 7-2 and 7-3, every input has equal influence in determining the output. But in a practical system, some inputs will have more influence than others on the decision-making process. In addition, some signals may have a negative influence on the outcome.

To reflect this unequal influence, computer scientists multiply each input by a value called a *weight*. Graphically, weights are represented by numbers associated with incoming connections. Figure 7-4 shows what a node looks like with weighted inputs.

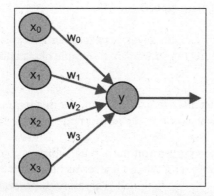

FIGURE 7-4:
Each input entering a node has an associated weight.

To determine the total effect of the inputs, a node multiplies each input by its weight and adds the products together. Then it compares the sum to its threshold. If the sum is greater than the threshold, the node produces an output value equal to 1. If not, the output value is 0.

Mathematically, weights are denoted as w_i, where i represents the weight of the ith input. Therefore, a node's operation can be expressed in the following relationship:

$$y = \begin{cases} 1 \text{ if } \sum_i w_i x_i \geq \text{threshold} \\ 0 \text{ otherwise} \end{cases}$$

For example, suppose that x_i = {3.5, -1.0, 2.5, -0.5} and w_i = {0.6, 1.2, 0.9, -0.2}. The sum of the weighted inputs can be computed as follows:

$$\sum_i w_i x_i = 3.5(0.6) - 1.0(1.2) + 2.5(0.9) - 0.5(-0.2) = 3.25$$

If the perceptron's threshold value is 4.0, the node will produce an output of 0 instead of 1.

Weights play a vital role in machine learning because they enable an application to update the neural network's behavior. As an application performs training, it updates the weights to improve the model.

Bias

A node fires when the weighted sum of its inputs exceeds a given threshold. Put another way, it produces positive output when the difference of the weighted sum and the threshold is greater than zero.

Rather than deal with the threshold, developers frequently replace it with a constant input called a *bias*. Figure 7-5 shows what a simple neural network looks like with an added bias.

The bias receives a weight just like every other input. For this reason, it makes sense to set the bias's value to 1, which is why the lowest node on the left is given as +1.

This book assumes that every perceptron has a bias, which is the same as saying that the threshold value equals zero. When I use terms like *inputs* or *input data*, you should assume that a bias value is included. Therefore, a perceptron produces a positive output when the weighted sum of its inputs is greater than zero.

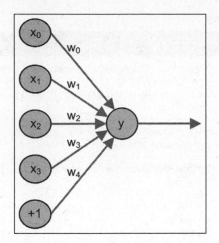

Activation functions

You can compute a node's output with the following relationship:

$$y = \begin{cases} 1 \text{ if } \sum_i w_i x_i \geq \text{ threshold} \\ \quad 0 \text{ otherwise} \end{cases}$$

The following equation expresses the same relationship using a more compact notation:

$$y = u\left(\sum_i w_i x_i\right)$$

Here, u(x) is called the *unit step function*. It returns 1 if its input is greater than 0 and returns 0 otherwise.

The unit step function is simple to understand, but it's not practical for machine learning. Computer scientists have devised many more suitable functions for producing a perceptron's output, and they're called *activation functions*.

A node's activation function accepts the weighted sum of the node's inputs and produces a single output value. In TensorFlow, an activation function accepts a tensor of values and returns a tensor containing output values. Table 7-1 lists seven of the activation functions supported by TensorFlow.

I like to divide these functions into two categories: rectifiers and classifiers. The distinction is simple: If a node's output identifies a category, set its activation function to a classifier. Otherwise, set the node's activation function to a rectifier.

TABLE 7-1   **Activation Functions**

Activation Function	Description
`tf.nn.relu(input, name=None)`	Returns the input value if positive, returns 0 otherwise
`tf.nn.relu6(input, name=None)`	Returns the input value if positive, up to a maximum of 6. Returns 0 otherwise
`tf.nn.crelu(input, name=None)`	Returns a concatenated tensor that separates the positive and negative portions of the input
`tf.nn.elu(input, name=None)`	Returns the input value if positive, returns the exponential of the input otherwise
`tf.nn.sigmoid(input, name=None)`	Returns $1/(1 + \exp(-x))$
`tf.nn.tanh(input, name=None)`	Returns $\tanh(x)$
`tf.nn.softsign(input, name=None)`	Returns $x/(\text{abs}(x) + 1)$

Rectifier functions

In an electrical circuit, a rectifier accepts an input signal and transmits an equal output signal if the input is positive. If the input signal is negative, the rectifier transmits an output of zero.

The rectified linear unit function, or ReLU, performs a similar operation. It returns the input if it's positive and returns 0 otherwise. Put another way, the ReLU function returns the maximum of the input and 0.

In TensorFlow, applications can perform ReLU operations by calling `tf.nn.relu`. Figure 7-6 illustrates the function's output over a range of input values.

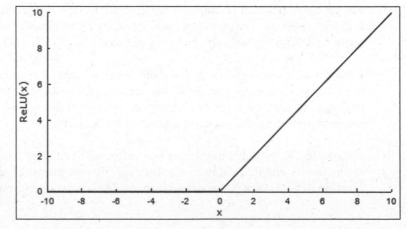

FIGURE 7-6: The rectified linear unit function (ReLU) only passes positive values.

`tf.nn.relu6` is similar to `tf.nn.relu`, but limits the maximum output to 6. This limitation reduces the likelihood of a node overreacting to large inputs. Figure 7-7 illustrates the behavior of `tf.nn.relu6`.

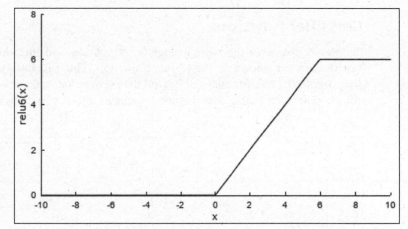

FIGURE 7-7:
The tf.nn.relu6
function clamps
the node's
maximum
output to 6.

`tf.nn.crelu` (Concatenated ReLU) produces an output tensor that is twice the size of the input tensor. The first half of the output contains a regular ReLU result (zero or positive input). The second half focuses on the negative part of the input (negative input or zero).

The ELU in `tf.nn.elu` stands for *Exponential Linear Unit.* This activation function returns the input value if it's greater than zero. If the input is zero or less, `tf.nn.elu` returns the exponential of the input minus one. Figure 7-8 shows what this looks like:

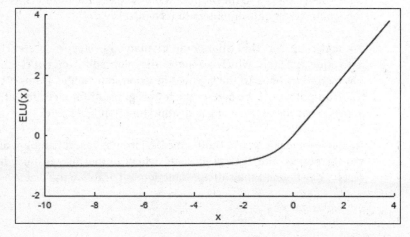

FIGURE 7-8:
The Exponential
Linear Unit (ELU)
function
proceeds
continuously
from positive to
negative values.

Unlike other rectifier functions, ELU is continuous at x = 0. According to Djork-Arné Clevert, Thomas Unterthiner, and Sepp Hochreiter at Johannes Kepler University, ELU provides faster learning than the regular ReLU function and better generalization.

Classifier functions

Chapter 6 discusses the topic of logistic regression and introduces the logistic function, better known as the sigmoid function. This function, which computes 1/(1 + exp(-x)), has a number of helpful properties that make it suitable for classifying points into categories. Figure 7-9 shows what tf.nn.sigmoid looks like.

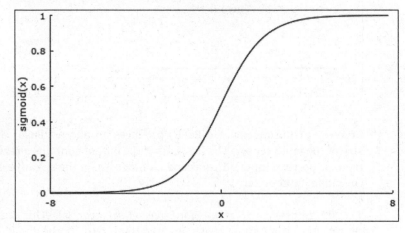

FIGURE 7-9: The sigmoid function is frequently employed to represent classification probability.

Though popular, the sigmoid function has one significant shortcoming: Its output ranges from 0 to 1. Because of this limited range, small changes in the input produce small changes in the output. In many cases, the differences in output may be too small for digital computers to recognize.

To make up for this shortcoming, many developers prefer the tf.nn.tanh activation function, which computes the hyperbolic tangent (tanh). This function has a similar shape to the sigmoid function, but ranges from -1 to 1. This means that computers will be better able to recognize differences in output. Figure 7-10 shows what the tf.nn.tanh activation function looks like.

In 2009, James Bergstra, Guillaume Desjardins, Pascal Lamblin, and Yoshua Bengio introduced the *softsign function*, which outperformed tanh in most of their tests. They defined the softsign function in the following way:

$$softsign(x) = \frac{x}{1+|x|}$$

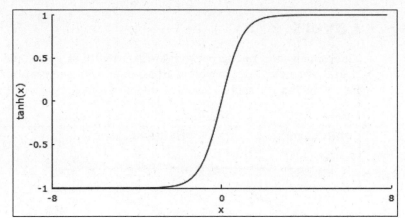

Figure 7-11 shows the softsign function for values of x between –8 and 8.

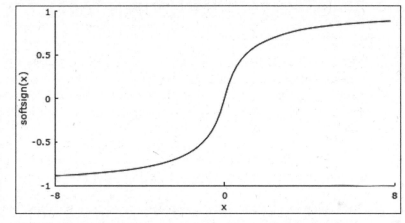

The gradient of the softsign function exceeds that of tanh throughout most of its domain. The larger gradient makes minor changes to the input easier to recognize.

Layers and Deep Learning

Individual nodes are too primitive to serve a useful purpose, but when you combine them into networks, you can create sophisticated tools for machine learning. This section explains how you can connect these nodes and explores the properties of the resulting neural networks.

Layers

The columns of a neural network are referred to as *layers*, and for this reason, neural networks are frequently called multilayer perceptrons (MLPs). Every neural net has at least two layers, and Figure 7-12 depicts an MLP with four.

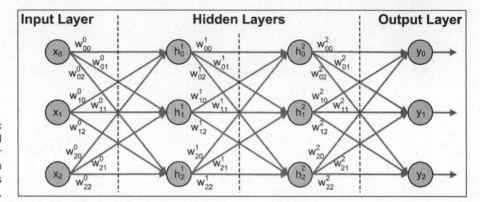

FIGURE 7-12: The neural network has four layers, and each layer has three nodes.

The layers of a neural network have specific names. The first layer, which provides input values, is called the *input layer*. The last layer, which provides output values, is called the *output layer*. The layers between the input layer and output layer are called *hidden layers*. Layers are numbered from left to right, starting with 0.

A layer is considered *dense* or *fully connected* if each of its nodes is connected to each node in the next layer. Every layer in Figure 7-12 is dense.

Each node in a hidden layer is denoted h_y^x, where x identifies the number of the layer and y identifies the index of the node in the layer. For example, h_1^2 identifies the second node in the third layer.

You can determine the output of each hidden node using the same methods discussed in the "Improving the Model" section. For example, if *func* is the activation function, the following equations compute the output of node h_0^1 and h_2^1:

$$h_0^1 = func\left(w_{00}^0 x_0 + w_{10}^0 x_1 + w_{20}^0 x_2 \right)$$
$$h_0^2 = func\left(w_{00}^1 h_0^1 + w_{10}^1 h_1^1 + w_{20}^1 h_2^1 \right)$$

Each weight in the network requires three values to uniquely identify it. Denoting a weight as w_{yz}^x, you can determine its position in the network as follows:

>> x identifies the layer containing the node producing the weighted signal.

>> y identifies the index of the node producing the signal to be weighted.

>> z identifies the index of the node receiving the signal.

For example, w_{01}^2 identifies a weight in the third layer (2). The weight applies to the signal leaving the first node (0) and entering the second node (1).

Deep learning

As you add more hidden layers to a network, it becomes capable of more sophisticated detection and classification. When an application uses a network with multiple hidden layers, it's making use of *deep learning*.

Deep learning has proven effective in many applications. Two famous examples include Google's AlphaGo program, which uses deep learning to beat professional Go players, and Google's 2012 demonstration of an application that recognized cat videos on YouTube.

Adding hidden layers to a network has two drawbacks. First, each hidden layer increases the amount of time needed to train the network. Second, each new hidden layer increases the chances of *overfitting*, which I discuss in the "Tuning the Neural Network" section.

Training with Backpropagation

As I discuss in Chapter 5, training updates your model so that it resembles the experimental data. The mathematical model represented by a neural network depends on the arrangement of the networks' nodes and their activation functions. To better understand this concept, consider the network in Figure 7-13.

Denoting the activation functions as f_0, f_1, and f_2, the neural network in Figure 7-13 represents the following mathematical relationship:

$$y(x_i) = f_2\left(w_{00}^1 f_0\left(w_{00}^0 x_0 + w_{10}^0 x_1 + w_{20}^0 x_2 + w_{30}^0 x_3\right) + w_{10}^1 f_1\left(w_{41}^0 x_4 + w_{51}^0 x_5 + w_{61}^0 x_6\right)\right)$$

The goal of training is to find the weights that bring y(x$_i$) as close as possible to the observed data. Put another way, the goal is to minimize the difference between y(x$_i$) and the observed data. As discussed in Chapters 5 and 6, this difference is called the loss, and one popular method of computing the loss is called the mean squared error (MSE).

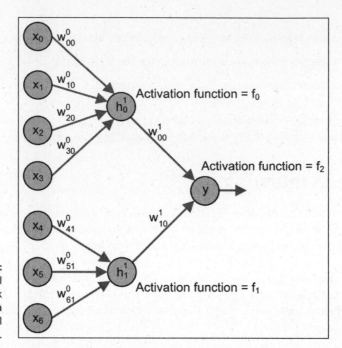

FIGURE 7-13:
Every neural network represents a mathematical relationship.

If you set $y(x_i)$ equal to a simple line or polynomial, you can easily compute the loss and pass its operation to an optimizer, such as the `GradientDescentOptimizer`. Chapter 5 covers the different optimization algorithms and their corresponding TensorFlow classes.

A neural network's model is more complicated, so the loss isn't as easy to compute. But in 1974, Paul Werbos was the first person to optimize the weights of a neural network using a method called *backpropagation*. Researchers have devised other algorithms for training neural networks since then, but because of its simplicity and speed, backpropagation remains the most popular method.

In essence, backpropagation extends the optimization algorithms from Chapter 5 to apply to neural networks. The general process involves six steps:

1. **Initialize the network's weights.**

2. **For the set of inputs x_i, compute $y(x_i)$.**

This computation is called *forward propagation*.

3. **For the set of inputs x$_i$, determine the loss.**

4. **For each weight, compute the partial derivative of the loss with respect to the weight.**

5. **Using the partial derivatives computed in Step 4, update each weight in the network.**

6. **Return to Step 2 and continue until the partial derivatives of the loss approach zero.**

To see how backpropagation computes partial derivatives, it helps to understand the chain rule of calculus. If p(x) = f(g(x)), you can express the derivative of p(x) in the following way:

$$p'(x) = f'(g(x))g'(x)$$

Backpropagation extends the chain rule to partial derivatives and derivatives involving sums of functions. In this manner, the algorithm determines the partial derivative of the loss with respect to each weight in the network.

Thankfully, you don't need to worry about partial derivatives or the chain rule because TensorFlow performs backpropagation automatically. But you do need to create the optimizer that backpropagation will employ to update the network's weights.

Implementing Deep Learning

After you have a solid grasp of nodes, weights, and the general structure of neural networks, you're ready to see how a practical application combines these elements in code. The `ch7/deep_learning.py` module demonstrates how you can use TensorFlow to implement deep learning.

Like the `ch6/multi_regression.py` module, `ch7/deep_learning.py` loads and classifies images from the MNIST dataset. But instead of using logistic regression, the module creates a neural network made up of fully connected layers. Listing 7-1 presents the code.

LISTING 7-1: **Classifying Images with Deep Learning**

```
# Read MNIST data
dataset = learn.datasets.mnist.read_data_sets('MNIST-data',
    one_hot=True)

# Placeholders for MNIST images
img_holder = tf.placeholder(tf.float32, [None, 784])
lbl_holder = tf.placeholder(tf.float32, [None, 10])

# Layer settings
hid_nodes = 200
out_nodes = 10

# Define weights
w0 = tf.Variable(tf.random_normal([784, hid_nodes]))
w1 = tf.Variable(tf.random_normal([hid_nodes, hid_nodes]))
w2 = tf.Variable(tf.random_normal([hid_nodes, hid_nodes]))
w3 = tf.Variable(tf.random_normal([hid_nodes, out_nodes]))

# Define biases
b0 = tf.Variable(tf.random_normal([hid_nodes]))
b1 = tf.Variable(tf.random_normal([hid_nodes]))
b2 = tf.Variable(tf.random_normal([hid_nodes]))
b3 = tf.Variable(tf.random_normal([out_nodes]))

# Create layers
layer_1 = tf.add(tf.matmul(img_holder, w0), b0)
layer_1 = tf.nn.relu(layer_1)
layer_2 = tf.add(tf.matmul(layer_1, w1), b1)
layer_2 = tf.nn.relu(layer_2)
layer_3 = tf.add(tf.matmul(layer_2, w2), b2)
layer_3 = tf.nn.relu(layer_3)
out_layer = tf.matmul(layer_3, w3) + b3

# Compute loss
loss = tf.reduce_mean(
    tf.nn.softmax_cross_entropy_with_logits(
        logits=out_layer, labels=lbl_holder))

# Create optimizer
learning_rate = 0.01
num_epochs = 15
batch_size = 100
num_batches = int(dataset.train.num_examples/batch_size)
```

```
optimizer = tf.train.AdamOptimizer(learning_rate).minimize(loss)
# Initialize variables
init = tf.global_variables_initializer()

# Launch session
with tf.Session() as sess:
    sess.run(init)

    # Loop over epochs
    for epoch in range(num_epochs):

        # Loop over batches
        for batch in range(num_batches):
            img_batch, lbl_batch = dataset.train.next_batch(batch_size)
            sess.run(optimizer, feed_dict={img_holder: img_batch,
                lbl_holder: lbl_batch})

    # Determine success rate
    prediction = tf.equal(tf.argmax(out_layer, 1), tf.argmax(lbl_holder, 1))
    success = tf.reduce_mean(tf.cast(prediction, tf.float32))
    print('Success rate: ', sess.run(success,
        feed_dict={img_holder: dataset.test.images,
            lbl_holder: dataset.test.labels}))
```

This application creates weights (w_i) and biases (b_i) by calling tf.Variable. Then it multiplies the input values by the weights and adds the biases. Each of the three hidden layers rectifies its output by calling tf.nn.relu.

The final layer (out_layer) performs similar multiplication and addition, but instead of calling tf.nn.relu, it passes its output to tf.nn.softmax_cross_entropy_with_logits. The module uses this output to select one of the ten output categories for MNIST images.

Tuning the Neural Network

The neural network in the preceding section is fine for demonstration, but it's not suitable for professional applications. To improve the accuracy and processing speed of their applications, professional developers use special routines that are collectively referred to as *tuning*. I like to call them the four "zations":

>> **Input standardization:** Preprocesses input data to statistically resemble training data

>> **Weight initialization:** Obtains suitable values for initial weights

>> **Batch normalization:** Processes data before the activation function to reduce the likelihood of saturation

>> **Regularization:** Reduces the likelihood of overfitting

Most developers agree that neural networks require some measure of tuning, but few agree on the best procedure. Rather than take sides, I focus on explaining how you can perform operations in TensorFlow applications.

Input standardization

A machine learning application should be able to analyze data it has never seen. But even if incoming data is completely new, it should have the same mean and standard deviation as the application's training data. This consistency ensures that the application won't be confused from one data set to the next.

For this reason, developers frequently transform input data to set the mean equal to 0 and the standard deviation equal to 1. This operation is called *standardization*, and TensorFlow's tf.nn package provides two functions that assist with standardization: moments and batch_normalization.

moments returns a tuple containing the mean and variance of the elements in a tensor's axis. Its signature is given as follows:

```
moments(x, axes, shift=None, name=None, keep_dims=False)
```

To set the mean and variance, assign x to the tensor to be analyzed and axes to an array of integers that identify the tensor's axes. If you set keep_dims to True, the returned mean and variance will have the same dimensionality as the input tensor.

batch_normalization accepts a tensor's mean and variance and standardizes the tensor's elements. Its signature is given as follows:

```
batch_normalization(x, mean, variance, offset, scale, variance_
    epsilon, name=None)
```

The `offset` parameter adds a constant to each value in the tensor, and `scale` multiplies each value by a constant. `variance_epsilon` identifies a value to be added to the denominator to ensure that TensorFlow doesn't divide by zero. Applications frequently set `offset` to 0.0, `scale` to 1.0, and `variance_epsilon` to 0.0001.

For example, the following code calls `moments` to obtain the mean and variance of a tensor. Then it calls `batch_normalization` to obtain a new tensor with standardized data:

```
input_data = tf.constant([1., 3., 5., 7., 9.])
stat_mean, stat_var = tf.nn.moments(input_data, 0)
standard_data = tf.nn.batch_normalization(input_data, stat_mean,
    stat_var, 0., 1., 0.0001, name=None)
```

This sets `standard_data` to [-1.4142, -0.7071, 0.0, 0.7071, 1.4142]. This tensor has a mean of 0 and a standard deviation of 1.

Weight initialization

When I started coding neural networks, I didn't give any thought to initializing weights — I just set them equal to small, random values. Researchers have analyzed this topic in detail and the following research papers present their results:

» 1998: "Efficient BackProp" by Yann Lecunn, Leon Bottou, Genevieve Orr, and Klaus-Robert Muller

» 2010: "Understanding the Difficulty of Training Deep Feedforward Neural Networks" by Xavier Glorot and Yoshua Bengio

» 2015: "Delving Deep into Rectifiers: Surpassing Human-Level Performance on ImageNet Classification" by Kaiming He, Xiangyu Zhang, Shaoqing Ren, and Jian Sun

Each of these papers presents a different methodology for initializing the weights of a neural network. TensorFlow supports these methodologies by providing functions of the `tf.contrib.keras.initializers` package. Each function is named after the chief researcher of the corresponding method, and Table 7-2 lists five of the available functions.

In Table 7-2's descriptions, `insize` and `outsize` refer to the sizes of the neural network's layers. That is, `insize` is the number of nodes in the layer providing the weights, and `outsize` is the number of nodes in the layer receiving the weights.

TABLE 7-2   ## Weight Initialization Functions

Function	Description
`lecun_uniform(seed=None)`	Returns uniformly distributed values between -sqrt(3/insize) and sqrt(3/insize)
`glorot_uniform(seed=None)`	Returns uniformly distributed values between -sqrt(6/(insize+outsize)) and sqrt(6/(insize+outsize))
`glorot_normal(seed=None)`	Returns normally distributed values with a standard deviation of sqrt(2/(insize+outsize))
`he_uniform(seed=None)`	Returns uniformly distributed values between -sqrt(6/insize) and sqrt(6/insize)
`he_normal(seed=None)`	Returns normally distributed values with a standard deviation of sqrt(2/insize)

Each of these functions accepts a `seed` that initializes the random number generator. Each function returns an `Initializer` whose `__call__` method accepts the shape of the random weights and returns the weights in an ndarray.

For example, the following code initializes an array of four normally distributed weights using `lecun_uniform`:

```
import time
init = tf.contrib.keras.initializers.lecun_uniform(time.time())
weights = init([4])
with tf.Session() as sess:
    result = sess.run(weights)
    print(result)              # Prints the ndarray containing weight values
```

In addition to the functions listed in Table 7-2, TensorFlow provides the `xavier_initializer` function in the `tf.contrib.layers` package:

```
xavier_initializer(uniform=True, seed=None, dtype=tf.float32)
```

When `uniform` is set to `True`, this function generates weights using the same method as the `glorot_uniform` function. When `uniform` is set to `False`, it generates weights using the same method as `glorot_normal`.

Batch normalization

In 2015, Sergey Ioffe and Christian Szegedy wrote an influential research paper that addresses the problem of *saturation*, which occurs when a node's activation function reaches an extreme value. Saturation is a major issue for functions like the sigmoid and tanh, whose slopes approach zero at their extremes. If the node's optimizer uses some form of gradient descent, the small slope will lead to slow training.

Another problem is that a small change to a saturated node's input will produce a small change to the output. The output change may be so small that the application can't perceive it.

To reduce the likelihood of saturation, Ioffe and Szegedy recommend fixing the mean and variance of each layer's input. This process is similar to the input standardization process, but it affects every layer of the network, not just the first.

Unfortunately, normalizing a layer's input limits the layer's flexibility. To remedy this issue, Ioffe and Szegedy recommend computing the mean and variance of each batch and normalizing the values of each batch independently. This process is called *batch normalization* (BN).

Batch normalization behaves differently depending on whether it's used during training or testing. During training, BN computes the mean and variance for each batch and uses the results to compute a scaling factor (gamma) and a shifting factor (beta). The following equations illustrate how BN computes and uses these values:

Batch mean: $\mu_B = \dfrac{1}{N} \sum_{0}^{N-1} x_i$

Batch variance: $\sigma_B^2 = \dfrac{1}{N} \sum_{0}^{N-1} (x_i - \mu_B)^2$

Normalization: $\widehat{x_i} = \dfrac{x_i - \mu_B}{\sqrt{\sigma_B^2 + \varepsilon}}$

Scaling and shifting: $y_i = \gamma \widehat{x_i} + \beta$

BN uses the mean and variance of individual batches to estimate the mean and variance of the entire population. TensorFlow computes the population's mean using a moving average and computes the population's variance using a moving variance. During testing, BN scales and shifts input values using the population mean and variance instead of the batch mean and variance.

To implement batch normalization in code, TensorFlow provides `tf.contrib.layers.batch_norm`. Table 7-3 lists its parameters and presents a description of each.

TABLE 7-3   **Parameters of tf.contrib.layers.batch_norm**

Parameter	Default	Description
`inputs`	--	Tensor of input values to be normalized
`decay`	`0.999`	Multiplication constant used to compute the moving mean and variance
`center`	`True`	Whether beta should be added to the normalized tensor
`scale`	`False`	Whether the normalized tensor should be scaled by gamma
`epsilon`	`0.001`	Factor to prevent division by zero
`activation_fn`	`None`	Activation function
`param_initializers`	`None`	Initializers for beta, gamma, the moving mean, and the moving variance
`param_regularizers`	`None`	Regularizers for beta and gamma
`updates_collections`	`tf.GraphKeys.UPDATE_OPS`	One or more collections to hold the normalization operations
`is_training`	`True`	Whether the normalization should update the moving mean and moving variance
`reuse`	`None`	Whether variables can be reused
`variables_collections`	`None`	Collections to store the normalization variables
`outputs_collections`	`None`	Collections to store the normalization outputs
`trainable`	`True`	Whether to add normalization variables to the graph's trainable collection
`batch_weights`	`None`	Weights to scale the batch mean and variance
`fused`	`False`	Whether to use fused normalization (faster)
`data_format`	`DATA_FORMAT_NHWC`	Format of the input data
`zero_debias_moving_mean`	`False`	Factor for updating the moving mean
`scope`	`None`	Scope to contain normalized variables
`renorm`	`False`	Whether to use extra variables during normalization
`renorm_clipping`	`None`	Dictionary that provides values for renormalization
`renorm_decay`	`0.99`	Factor to update moving mean/variance during renormalization

TensorFlow uses the `decay` parameter to compute the population's mean and variance. The following equations show how the computation is performed:

$$\mu_P = \mu_P decay + \mu_B (1 - decay)$$
$$\sigma_P^2 = \sigma_P^2 decay + \sigma_B^2 (1 - decay)$$

The `center` and `scale` parameters determine whether the values of the inputs parameter should be shifted and scaled. The function will shift the input values if `center` is `True` and will scale the input values if `scale` is `True`.

It's important to see the difference between `is_training` and `trainable`. Setting `is_training` to `True` tells the function that the normalization is being performed during a training run, which means it should update the population's mean and variance. Setting `trainable` to `True` tells the function to store its normalization variables in the graph collection represented by the `TRAINABLE_VARIABLES` key.

The last three parameters of `batch_norm` relate to *renormalization*. This process improves normalization when an application's batches are small or dependent on one another.

Regularization

One of the most difficult tasks in machine learning involves finding the right structure for a neural network. If you add too few nodes, your network will be too simple to classify data accurately. This is called *underfitting*.

If you add too many nodes, your network will tailor itself specifically for your training set and will be unsuitable for analyzing general data. This problem is called *overfitting*, and it's a serious issue in machine learning.

The process of updating a neural network (or other machine learning algorithm) to analyze general data is called *regularization*. Researchers have devised many methods for regularizing networks, and this section focuses on two:

>> **Dropout:** Randomly removes nodes from the network

>> **L1/L2 regularization:** Reduces weights by increasing the loss

For both methods, I explain how the regularization works and how you can perform it using TensorFlow.

Dropout

The dropout process randomly removes one or more nodes from a network. For each node removed, dropout removes the node's incoming and outgoing connections and their weights.

In TensorFlow, you can configure dropout for a neural network by adding a dropout layer. Adding this layer involves calling the `tf.nn.dropout` function:

```
dropout(x, keep_prob, noise_shape=None, seed=None, name=None)
```

In this function, `x` is the tensor containing values from the preceding layer, and `keep_prob` is a scalar with the same type as `x`. The function returns a tensor with the same size as `x`.

`dropout` sets each of its output values to 0 or `1/keep_prob` times the corresponding input value. More precisely, `dropout` sets an output value to 0 with a probability of `1-keep_prob` and sets the output value to `1/keep_prob` times the input value with a probability of `keep_prob`.

L1/L2 regularization

L1 and L2 regularization prevent overfitting by reducing the network's weights. Both methods increase the loss by a value that depends on two factors: the network's weights and a constant denoted λ.

L1 regularization increases the loss by λ multiplied by the absolute value of the weight to be updated. Therefore, when the algorithm updates the weight w_0 through backpropagation, it adds a value to the loss equal to $\lambda|w_0|$.

L2 regularization increases the loss by $\lambda/2$ multiplied by the square of the weight to be updated. Therefore, when the algorithm updates w_0, it adds $\lambda|w_0|^2/2$ to the loss.

In both cases, the loss increases when the weights increase and decreases when the weights decrease. Therefore, the regularization process tends to reduce nonessential weights to zero, thereby simplifying the model and (hopefully) avoiding overfitting.

To perform L1/L2 regularization in TensorFlow, you can call `tf.contrib.layers.l1_regularizer` or `tf.contrib.layers.l2_regularizer`:

» `l1_regularizer(lambda, scope=None)`: Returns a function that performs L1 regularization

» `l2_regularizer(lambda, scope=None)`: Returns a function that performs L2 regularization

These functions return special functions called *regularizers*. After you've obtained a regularizer, you can regularize a set of weights by calling `tf.contrib.layers.apply_regularization`:

```
apply_regularization(regularizer, weights_list=None)
```

Many TensorFlow functions accept regularizers as arguments. One important function is `tf.contrib.layers.fully_connected`, which I discuss in the "Improving the Deep Learning Process" section.

Managing Variables with Scope

When building applications with neural networks, keeping track of weights is a major priority. Hidden layers accept weighted inputs and produce weighted outputs. Without proper management, it's easy for the names of one layer's weights to clash with the names of another layer's weights.

Variable scope

In deep learning applications, layers frequently assign the same names to their weights. To keep the variables separate, TensorFlow makes it possible to define a variable's *scope*. An application can define a scope by calling `tf.variable_scope`:

```
tf.variable_scope(name_or_scope, default_name=None, values=None,
    initializer=None, regularizer=None, caching_device=None, partitioner=None,
    custom_getter=None, reuse=None, dtype=None, use_resource=None)
```

Applications commonly call this function as part of a `with` statement, as in the following code:

```
with tf.variable_scope("MyScope")
  ...
```

If an application creates variables using `tf.get_variable` inside a `with` block, TensorFlow will prepend the scope's name to the variable's name. That is, if the application creates a new variable named `MyVar`, the variable's full name will be `MyScope/MyVar`.

Chapter 5 explains how to create variables with `tf.Variable`, but if an application wants to create a variable inside a scope, the function to call is `tf.get_variable`:

```
get_variable(name, shape=None, dtype=None, initializer=None, regularizer=None,
    trainable=True, collections=None, caching_device=None, partitioner=None,
    validate_shape=True, use_resource=None, custom_getter=None)
```

If the `name` parameter identifies a variable in the current scope and the scope's `reuse` parameter is set to `True`, `get_variable` will return the existing variable. The following code shows how `tf.get_variable` can be used:

```
with tf.variable_scope("MyScope"):
    var = tf.get_variable("var", [1])

with tf.variable_scope("MyScope", reuse=True):
    same = tf.get_variable("var")  # Same as var
```

If the `name` parameter of `variable_scope` doesn't correspond to an existing variable in the scope, the function will create a new variable. The `initializer` parameter determines the variable's initial value. If this parameter isn't set, the initial value is determined by the `initializer` parameter of the surrounding scope. If the `initializer` parameter of the surrounding scope isn't set, TensorFlow will initialize the variable using Glorot initialization.

Retrieving variables from collections

As discussed in Chapter 4, a graph stores operations and tensors in a set of collections. An application can retrieve variables from a collection by calling `tf.get_collection`:

```
tf.get_collection(key, scope=None)
```

The `key` parameter identifies one of the graph's collections. One important key is `tf.GraphKeys.TRAINABLE_VARIABLES`, which identifies the collection containing the graph's trainable variables.

The `scope` parameter identifies the scope from which the variables should be retrieved. For example, the following code accesses a list containing all the trainable variables in the `hidden_layer_1` scope:

```
tf.get_collection(tf.GraphKeys.TRAINABLE_VARIABLES, 'hidden_layer_1')
```

Scopes for names and arguments

Just as `tf.variable_scope` creates a scope for variables, `tf.name_scope` creates a scope for tensors and operations. This function is simple to use, and the following code shows how it works:

```
with tf.name_scope('block1'):
    t = tf.constant([1., 2.], name='tens')
```

This example creates the tensor `t` inside a name scope whose identifier is `block1`. As a result, TensorFlow sets `t`'s full identifier to `block1/tens`.

The `tf.contrib.framework` package provides a useful function called `arg_scope`:

```
arg_scope(list_ops_or_scope, **kwargs)
```

This function creates a scope that inserts arguments into the scope's listed operations. That is, for each operation identified in the first argument, `arg_scope` inserts the arguments provided in the second argument.

An example clarifies how argument scoping works. As a result of the following code, every call to `foo` inside the scope will have `var` set to `39`:

```
from tensorflow.contrib.framework import arg_scope
with arg_scope([foo], var=39):
    ...
```

To make an operation accessible in an argument scope, you must decorate the operation's definition with `@add_arg_scope`. If a function requires many parameters and must be called multiple times, you can significantly reduce the amount of required code by setting arguments in an argument scope.

Improving the Deep Learning Process

In the "Implementing Deep Learning" section, I present an application that classifies MNIST images using an untuned neural network. This section presents an application that performs the same operation, but uses tuning mechanisms (normalization and regularization) to improve the network's accuracy and performance. But before I discuss the code, I'd like to introduce an improved method of creating fully connected layers.

Creating tuned layers

In Listing 7-1, earlier in this chapter, the application creates fully connected layers with low-level arithmetic operations, such as `tf.add` and `tf.matmul`. But TensorFlow provides a more sophisticated way to create fully connected layers through the `tf.contrib.layers.fully_connected` function.

This function accepts many parameters that tune the layer's behavior, such as weight initialization, normalization, and regularization. Table 7-4 lists the function's parameters and provides a description of each.

TABLE 7-4   **Parameters of tf.contrib.layers.fully_connected**

Parameter	Default	Description
inputs	--	Tensor of input values
num_outputs	--	Number of output values produced by the layer
activation_fn	tf.nn.relu	Function that produces the layer's output values
normalizer_fn	None	Function to process output values
normalizer_params	None	Parameters to be passed to the normalization function
weights_initializer	initializers.xavier_initializer()	Function that initializes the layer's weights
weights_regularizer	None	Function that regularizes the weights
biases_initializer	tf.zeros_initializer	Function that initializes the layer's biases
biases_regularizer	None	Function that regularizes the biases
reuse	None	Bool that specifies whether the layer and its weights should be reused
variables_collections	None	List of variable collections or dictionary containing a list of collections for each variable
outputs_collections	None	Collection to contain the outputs
trainable	True	Bool that specifies whether the layer's variables should be added to the graph's trainable variables
scope	None	Scope of the layer's variables

Applications need to set `inputs` to a tensor with at least two dimensions. If `fully_connected` is adding an input layer, applications should set `inputs` to a placeholder that provides the session with data. For successive layers, applications should set `inputs` to the return value of the function that created the preceding layer.

`fully_connected` returns a tensor containing the layer's output values. `num_outputs` parameter determines the size of this output tensor. It's important to see that `num_outputs` controls the number of nodes in the fully connected layer.

The `activation_fn` parameter specifies the activation function that will compute the outputs of the layer's nodes. By default, `fully_connected` sets this parameter to the `tf.nn.relu` rectification function, which is suitable for hidden layers. If a layer is intended to provide output, you'll probably need to associate a different function with `activation_fn`.

The `normalizer_fn`, `normalizer_params`, `biases_initializer`, and `biases_regularizer` parameters determine the tuning process used for the layer. `normalizer_fn` specifies a function to normalize the layer's values. This function will receive any arguments provided in the `normalizer_params` parameter.

If `normalizer_fn` is set, `fully_connected` ignores `biases_initializer` and `biases_regularizer`. Otherwise, the function calls `biases_initializer` to set the layer's bias values and regularizes the biases with the `biases_regularizer` function.

By default, the fully connected layer initializes its weights using the Glorot method. You can customize how weights are initialized by assigning `weights_initializer` to a function that returns an `Initializer`, such as `lecun_uniform`. You can also specify a function to regularize the layer's weights by setting `weights_regularizer`.

The `scope` parameter defines a variable scope for the fully connected layer. Weights and biases created by the layer will be stored within this scope. The `reuse` parameter identifies whether the layer and its variables can be reused.

Putting theory into practice

The code in the `ch7/tuned_learning.py` module performs the same MNIST classification as the `ch7/deep_learning.py` module presented earlier in this chapter. The difference is that it tunes the neural network to improve accuracy and performance. It also creates fully connected layers by calling `tf.contrib.layers.fully_connected` instead of `tf.add` and `tf.matmul`. Listing 7-2 presents the code.

LISTING 7-2: **Deep Learning with Tuning**

```python
# Read MNIST data
dataset = learn.datasets.mnist.read_data_sets('MNIST-data',
    one_hot=True)

# Placeholders for MNIST images
img_holder = tf.placeholder(tf.float32, [None, 784])
lbl_holder = tf.placeholder(tf.float32, [None, 10])
train = tf.placeholder(tf.bool)

# Layer settings
hid_nodes = 200
out_nodes = 10
keep_prob = 0.5

# Create layers
with tf.contrib.framework.arg_scope(
    [fully_connected],
    normalizer_fn=tf.contrib.layers.batch_norm,
    normalizer_params={'is_training': train}):
        layer1 = fully_connected(img_holder, hid_nodes, scope='layer1')
        layer1_drop = tf.layers.dropout(layer1, keep_prob, training=train)
        layer2 = fully_connected(layer1_drop, hid_nodes, scope='layer2')
        layer2_drop = tf.layers.dropout(layer2, keep_prob, training=train)
        layer3 = fully_connected(layer2_drop, hid_nodes, scope='layer3')
        layer3_drop = tf.layers.dropout(layer3, keep_prob, training=train)
        out_layer = fully_connected(layer3_drop, out_nodes,
            activation_fn=None, scope='layer4')

# Compute loss
loss = tf.reduce_mean(
    tf.nn.softmax_cross_entropy_with_logits(
        logits=out_layer, labels=lbl_holder))

# Create optimizer
learning_rate = 0.01
num_epochs = 15
batch_size = 100
num_batches = int(dataset.train.num_examples/batch_size)
optimizer = tf.train.AdamOptimizer(learning_rate).minimize(loss)

# Initialize variables
init = tf.global_variables_initializer()

# Launch session
with tf.Session() as sess:
    sess.run(init)
```

```
# Loop over epochs
for epoch in range(num_epochs):

    # Loop over batches
    for batch in range(num_batches):
        img_batch, lbl_batch = dataset.train.next_batch(batch_size)
        sess.run(optimizer, feed_dict={img_holder: img_batch,
            lbl_holder: lbl_batch, train: True})

# Determine success rate
prediction = tf.equal(tf.argmax(out_layer, 1), tf.argmax(lbl_holder, 1))
success = tf.reduce_mean(tf.cast(prediction, tf.float32))
print('Success rate: ', sess.run(success,
    feed_dict={img_holder: dataset.test.images,
        lbl_holder: dataset.test.labels, train: False}))
```

This module employs three methods to tune its multi-layer neural network:

>> It sends the output of each fully-connected layer to a dropout layer. The module sets keep_prob to 0.5, so the dropout layer sets half of its inputs to 0.

>> The module calls tf.contrib.layers.batch_norm to perform batch normalization on the hidden layers.

>> By default, tf.contrib.layers.fully_connected initializes the network's weights using the Glorot method.

Each hidden layer has 200 nodes, and the output layer has 10 nodes. Before creating the layers, the module defines an argument scope by calling tf.contrib.framework.arg_scope. arg_scope accepts a list containing a function (fully_connected) and the arguments to insert inside the function.

Each call to fully_connected sets the scope argument to a different value. Creating this scope changes the names of the layer's variables. An application can retrieve these variables by calling tf.get_collection.

The first three fully_connected calls don't set activation_fn, so the layers' nodes compute their output using the default ReLU activation function. The last fully_connected call sets activation_fn to None, so each node of the output layer returns the weighted sum of its inputs. The tf.nn.softmax_cross_entropy_with_logits function accepts these weighted sums and selects one of the ten categories.

Chapter **8**

Classifying Images with Convolutional Neural Networks (CNNs)

This chapter explains how you can code image recognition applications using TensorFlow and convolutional neural networks (CNNs). These applications are similar to the vanilla neural networks from Chapter 7, but they include layers specifically intended for image classification.

Filtering Images

If you've used image editing applications like Adobe Photoshop, you're probably familiar with filtering tools, which add effects, such as blurring, sharpening, or embossing, to images. Mathematically, these tools perform their operations using a process called *convolution*. This process plays a critical role in image recognition, and while it's not important to grasp all the gory details, it's good to understand the general process.

Convolution

Image convolution replaces each pixel of an image with the result of a two-dimensional dot product. This dot product accepts two matrices and returns the sum of the products of their corresponding elements.

For example, suppose that A and B are two 3-x-3 matrices whose elements are given as follows:

$$A = \begin{vmatrix} 1 & 2 & 3 \\ 4 & 5 & 6 \\ 7 & 8 & 9 \end{vmatrix} \quad B = \begin{vmatrix} -10 & -9 & -8 \\ -7 & -6 & -5 \\ -4 & -3 & -2 \end{vmatrix}$$

You can compute the two-dimensional dot product of A and B by multiplying corresponding pairs of values and adding the results together:

$$1(-10)+2(-9)+3(-8)+4(-7)+5(-6)+$$
$$6(-5)+7(-4)+8(-3)+9(-2)=-210$$

The first matrix involved in image convolution is the MxN rectangle surrounding one of the image's pixels. The second MxN matrix involved in the dot product is commonly called a *kernel*, but TensorFlow refers to it as a *filter*. The filter's elements determine what effect the filter will have on the image.

For example, if you denote an image as a matrix M, the pixel in the ith row and jth column is $m_{i,j}$. If you denote the filter as a matrix K, the element in the ith row and jth column is $k_{i,j}$. With this notation, the convolution process obtains the new value of $m_{i,j}$ with the following dot product:

$$m_{i,j}(filtered) = \begin{vmatrix} m_{i-1,j-1} & m_{i-1,j} & m_{i-1,j+1} \\ m_{i,j-1} & m_{i,j} & m_{i,j+1} \\ m_{i+1,j-1} & m_{i+1,j} & m_{i+1,j+1} \end{vmatrix} \bullet \begin{vmatrix} k_{0,0} & k_{0,1} & k_{0,2} \\ k_{1,0} & k_{1,1} & k_{1,2} \\ k_{2,0} & k_{2,1} & k_{2,2} \end{vmatrix}$$

$$= m_{i-1,j-1}k_{0,0} + m_{i-1,j}k_{0,1} + m_{i-1,j+1}k_{0,2} + m_{i,j-1}k_{1,0} + m_{i,j}k_{1,1} +$$
$$m_{i,j+1}k_{1,2} + m_{i+1,j-1}k_{2,0} + m_{i+1,j}k_{2,1} + m_{i+1,j+1}k_{2,2}$$

When filtering an image, this dot product must be computed for each pixel in the original image. This operation presents an important concern: How do you find the pixels surrounding $m_{i,j}$ if the pixel lies on the image's border?

TECHNICAL STUFF

Instead of computing a dot product for each pixel, many engineers perform convolution by converting the image and filter to the frequency domain. This process, called *fast convolution*, involves computing the Fast Fourier Transform (FFT) for each row and column of the image and filter.

This book, like other fine works of machine learning literature, employs the term convolution to refer to the process of computing a matrix of 2-D dot products. But the technical term for this is *cross-correlation*. Convolution reverses one of the operands before computing the dot products and the algorithm presented here doesn't reverse either operand.

Averaging Filter

A good way to understand image filtering is to walk through an example. This section focuses on the grainy image depicted in Figure 8-1.

FIGURE 8-1:
The image's mottled appearance is the result of noise.

Mathematically, an image's noise can be thought of as unwanted variation between adjacent pixels. You can reduce this variation by replacing each pixel with the average of itself and the pixels immediately surrounding it. You can accomplish this by convolving the image with a filter like the following:

$$kernel = \begin{vmatrix} \frac{1}{9} & \frac{1}{9} & \frac{1}{9} \\ \frac{1}{9} & \frac{1}{9} & \frac{1}{9} \\ \frac{1}{9} & \frac{1}{9} & \frac{1}{9} \end{vmatrix}$$

Denoting the pixel in the ith row and jth column as m_{ij}, you can compute the filtered value of m_{ij} in the following way:

$$m_{i,j}(filtered) = \frac{1}{9}m_{i-1,j-1} + \frac{1}{9}m_{i-1,j} + \frac{1}{9}m_{i-1,j+1} + \frac{1}{9}m_{i,j-1} + \frac{1}{9}m_{i,j} +$$

$$\frac{1}{9}m_{i,j+1} + \frac{1}{9}m_{i+1,j-1} + \frac{1}{9}m_{i+1,j} + \frac{1}{9}m_{i+1,j+1}$$

This type of filter is called a *box filter* or an *averaging filter*. After convolution, the filtered pixels form the image illustrated in Figure 8-2:

FIGURE 8-2:
Convolution with the box filter reduces the amount of noise in the image.

The box filter removed a lot of the image's noise, but it also removed detail that isn't noise. To improve on the box filter, engineers have devised a more effective noise-reduction filter called the *Gaussian filter.* The filter's elements are determined by values of the Gaussian curve.

Filters and features

Image filtering can do more than just add effects. One critical application involves finding an image inside a larger image. Consider the 7-x-7 filter presented in Figure 8-3.

kernel =	1.0	0.8	0.8	0.8	0.8	0.8	1.0
	0.8	0.8	0.0	0.8	0.0	0.8	0.8
	0.8	0.8	0.8	0.8	0.8	0.8	0.8
	0.8	0.8	0.8	0.8	0.8	0.8	0.8
	0.8	0.0	0.8	0.8	0.8	0.0	0.8
	0.8	0.8	0.0	0.0	0.0	0.8	0.8
	1.0	0.8	0.8	0.8	0.8	0.8	1.0

FIGURE 8-3:
The filter's elements correspond to the pixels of the smiley face.

If you look closely at the filter matrix, you'll see that its elements identify the pixel values of the grayscale image on the right. In other words, the filter defines its own small image — a smiley face. The dot product of an image with itself produces a large value, so if an image contains a 7-x-7 smiley face, the convolution of the image with this filter will produce a large value at the point where the smiley face is located.

This property of convolution makes it possible to locate images inside a larger image. For example, an image of an airplane should have a cockpit, two wings, and a fuselage. If you use one filter for the cockpit, one for the wings, and one for the fuselage, a high convolution value for each filter indicates the presence of an aircraft.

These subimages of interest are called *features,* and an application can check whether a feature is present in an image by convolving the image with an appropriate filter. A high convolution result indicates that the feature is present in the image.

Feature detection analogy

When it comes to image filtering, you can easily get wrapped up in the math and forget what's going on. So here's a strange analogy: Imagine that you have a magnifying glass and a high resolution image of a large crowd of people. As you move the glass over the image, you get a better look at each person in the crowd.

Suppose that you engrave your face on the glass. Afterward, you magically enchant the glass to display a number that identifies how closely the engraving matches the image underneath the glass. The largest number will appear when the glass is directly over your face.

Now suppose that you have other magnifying glasses, each with an engraved image of a member of your family. If you examine the numbers displayed by the different magnifying glasses, you'll be able to locate each of your family members and thereby locate your family in the crowd.

In this analogy, each magnifying glass is a filter, and each engraved image is a feature. The process of moving the glass over the image and reading the number corresponds to convolution.

Setting convolution parameters

When you categorize images using convolution, you don't set the filters' elements directly. Instead, you provide input images and their corresponding categories. The application's job is to determine which filters best support correct categorization. In this manner, filters resemble the weights of the neural networks discussed in Chapter 7.

Even though you can't set the filters' elements, you can set many of the filters' properties, such as their number and size. You can also configure three other aspects of convolution:

>> `stride`: Shifting the filter from one 2-D dot product to the next

>> `dilation`: Expanding the filter's size by inserting zero-valued elements

>> `padding`: Accounting for pixels near the edge of the image

These parameters play an important role in determining how an application performs convolution. The following sections explore each of them in detail.

Stride

After each two-dimensional dot product, the convolution process moves the filter one pixel to the right. When all the dot products have been computed for a row of pixels, convolution moves the filter one pixel down and continues computing two-dimensional dot products.

This behavior is the default, but developers can customize how the convolution is performed by setting the *stride*. Stride determines how much the filter shifts after each dot product. To set the stride, you need to provide two values: the horizontal pixel shift and the vertical pixel shift. The default stride is always (1, 1).

For example, if you set the stride to (2, 3), the filter will shift two pixels to the right after each dot product. After completing all the dot products for one row, the filter will shift three pixels down and start computing further dot products. This increased stride reduces the amount of computation needed for the convolution, but also reduces the amount of detail. In this book, stride will always be set to (1, 1).

Dilation

The term *dilation* usually refers to stretching or expanding part of the body, such as the pupil of the eye. In image processing, dilation refers to stretching the elements of a filter. As with stride, you can specify dilation by providing two values: one that sets horizontal stretching and one that sets vertical stretching. The default value is (1, 1), which indicates that no stretching should be performed.

As dilation increases, the effective size of the filter increases but the number of nonzero elements doesn't change. Instead, dilation inserts zeros between the filter's elements.

For example, if you set the dilation to (2, 1), the convolution will insert a zero between each horizontal pair of elements in the filter. These zero elements won't contribute any values to the two-dimensional dot products.

By changing the dilation, applications can efficiently detect features of varying sizes. For a thorough discussion of the topic, I recommend the 2015 paper *Multi-Scale Context Aggregation by Dilated Convolutions* by Fisher Yu and Vladlen Koltun (ICLR 2016).

Padding

If a filter's size is NxN, convolution computes an NxN two-dimensional dot product for each pixel in the input image. If a pixel lies on the edge of the image or near the edge, it isn't clear how the NxN dot product should be computed.

In TensorFlow, developers can configure the processing of border pixels in one of two ways. The first method involves ignoring pixels that lie on or near the image's edge. The advantage of ignoring these pixels is that every pixel in the resulting image will be accurate. The disadvantage is that the output image will be smaller than the input image.

The second method involves expanding the image and inserting zeros beyond its original borders. If a pixel lies on the edge of the image, the dot product will take these zeros into account. As a result, the output image will be the same size as the input image, but the output pixels on/near the edges won't be completely accurate because they were computed with zeros.

Convolutional Neural Networks (CNNs)

A traditional neural network receives a series of input values, multiplies each input value by a weight, and passes the processed data through a series of layers. This approach is fine for general-purpose data analysis, but it's not sufficient for processing images and similar 2-D/3-D data. Image classification requires convolution, and for this reason, neural networks intended for image classification are called convolutional neural networks, or CNNs.

CNNs resemble regular neural networks in a number of ways, but they have two distinguishing characteristics:

>> A CNN contains convolution layers that use rectangular filters to perform convolution.

>> A CNN uses pooling layers to reduce the dimensionality of output images.

After the convolution layers and pooling layers have done their jobs, CNNs use fully connected layers to provide output. Figure 8-4 illustrates the structure of a minimal CNN:

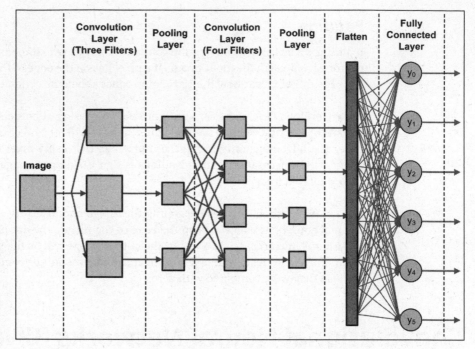

FIGURE 8-4:
Convolutional neural networks contain convolution layers, pooling layers, and at least one fully connected layer.

This network has two convolution layers that produce one output image for each filter. The pooling layers reduce the size of the images produced by convolution. This section explains what these layers accomplish and how they work together.

Creating convolution layers

In a TensorFlow application, an image is a tensor that contains a matrix for each of an image's channels. By channels, I mean the components that make up the image's pixels. For example, a grayscale image has one channel, so its tensor consists of one matrix. An RGB image has three channels, so its tensor will have three channels.

A convolution layer accepts a batch of images, performs convolution with a set of filters, and returns an output tensor containing the convolution results. The size of each output image depends on the size of the input images and the use of padding in the convolution.

You can create a convolution layer by calling tf.layers.conv2d. Table 8-1 lists the parameters of this function and presents the default value of each.

TABLE 8-1   ## Arguments of tf.layers.conv2d

Argument	Default	Description
inputs	--	Tensor containing input image
filters	--	Number of filters to be used
kernel_size	--	Size of the kernel (one value for an NxN square, two values for an MxN rectangle)
strides	(1, 1)	Amount the filter should shift between 2-D dot products
padding	'valid'	Method of processing pixels near the image's edge
data_format	'channels_last'	Order of the elements in the input tensor
dilation_rate	(1, 1)	Extent by which the filter should be horizontally/vertically stretched
activation	None	Activation function
use_bias	True	Bool that identifies whether the layer uses a bias
kernel_ initializer	None	Initializer for the filter's values (weights)
bias_ initializer	tf.zeros. initializer()	Initializer for the layer's biases
kernel_ regularizer	None	Regularizer for the filter's values (weights)
bias_ regularizer	None	Regularizer for the layer's biases
activity_ regularizer	None	Regularizer for the layer's output
trainable	True	Bool that identifies whether to add the filter's elements to the graph's trainable variables
name	None	Name of the layer
reuse	False	Bool that identifies whether to reuse the weights of a similarly-named scope

An application must set inputs to a tensor whose shape depends on the data_format parameter. If you set data_format to channels_last (the default value), the inputs tensor should have a shape equal to [batch_size, height, width, channels]. If you set data_format to channels_first, the inputs tensor should have a shape equal to [batch_size, channels, height, width].

The `filters` parameter identifies the number of filters used by the convolution layer. The `kernel_size` parameter identifies the size of each filter. If you set this parameter to a single value, N, the size of each filter will be NxN. If you set it to two values, such as [M, N], the size of each filter will be MxN.

The earlier "Setting convolution parameters" section talks about the stride and dilation characteristics of image filters. In `tf.layers.conv2d`, you can set these properties with the `strides` and `dilation_rate` parameters.

The `padding` parameter tells the layer how to process the image's boundary pixels. If you set `padding` to `valid`, the layer will ignore boundary pixels and return an output image smaller than the input image. If you set `padding` to `same`, the layer will pad the input image with zeros and produce an output image with the same size as the input image.

`tf.layers.conv2d` returns a tensor whose shape depends on the shape of the input image, the number of filters, and the `padding` parameter. For example, if the input's shape is [N, height, width, num_channels] and the `padding` is set to `same`, the output's shape will be [N, height, width, num_filters].

The number of channels does not affect the shape of the output. While performing convolution, `tf.layers.conv2d` combines the channels together, so a grayscale input image and an RGB input image will produce output images of the same size. If you'd like to perform channel-specific filtering, the function to use is `tf.nn.depthwise_conv2d`.

If an application sets `padding` to `valid`, each output image will be smaller than the input image. The reduction in size depends on the dimensions of the convolution filters. For example, if `padding` is `valid`, the filter size equals [X, Y], and the input's shape is [N, height, width, num_channels], the shape of each output image will be [N, height − (Y − 1), width − (X − 1), num_filters].

Creating pooling layers

A convolution layer produces an output image for each filter, so a CNN with many filters will produce many images. These images require a great deal of memory, so developers reduce the size of the images by following convolution layers with *pooling layers*.

A pooling layer subdivides an image's pixels into rectangular blocks and replaces each block with a single pixel. Figure 8-5 shows how this process works. The pooling operation divides a 9-x-8 matrix into 3-x-2 blocks and replaces each block with a single value.

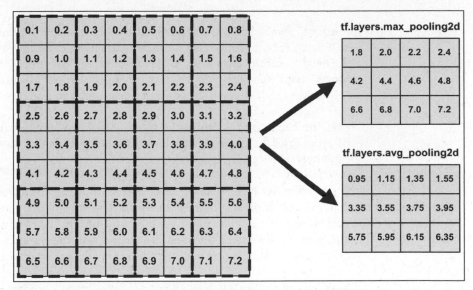

FIGURE 8-5:
A pooling layer accepts an input image, splits it into blocks, operates on each block, and returns a condensed image.

Figure 8-5 depicts two methods of pooling. The first finds the largest value in the input block and stores that value in the output image. You can create a pooling layer that performs this operation by calling tf.layers.max_pooling2d.

The second pooling method computes the average value of the pixels in the input block and stores that value in the output image. You can create a pooling layer that uses this method by calling tf.layers.avg_pooling2d.

Of the pooling functions provided by the tf.layers package, max_pooling2d is the most popular. This popularity makes sense because a high maximum value clearly indicates the presence of a filter's feature in the image. Table 8-2 lists the parameters of tf.layers.max_pooling2d and provides a description of each.

TABLE 8-2   **Parameters of tf.layers.max_pooling2d**

Parameter	Default	Description
inputs	——	Input 4-D tensor
pool_size	——	The size of the block used for pooling
strides	——	The shift from one pooling operation to the next
padding	'valid'	The padding algorithm: valid or same
data_format	'channels_last'	Specifies the shape of the input image
name	None	Provides a name for the layer

As with `tf.layers.conv2d`, the shape of the input tensor depends on `data_format`. If `data_format` is `channels_last`, the input tensor's shape should be [batch_size, height, width, channels]. If `data_format` is `channels_first`, the input tensor's shape should be [batch_size, channels, height, width]. Regardless of `data_format`, each element in the input tensor must be a `tf.float32`.

To set the height and width of the block used for pooling, you need to assign `pool_size` to a list or tuple of two integers. For the pooling illustrated in Figure 8-5, the application set `pool_size` to [2, 2].

`strides` identifies how much the block shifts (in pixels) from one pooling operation to the next. If the horizontal shift equals the vertical shift, you can set `strides` to one integer. If not, you can set `strides` to a tuple or list of two integers, where the first sets the vertical shift and the second sets the horizontal shift. For the pooling illustrated in Figure 8-5, the application set `strides` to 2.

If a pooling operation involves a point near the image's border, the computation will depend on the `padding` parameter. If you set `padding` to `valid`, the pooling won't take border pixels into account. If you set `padding` to `same`, the function will pad the image with zeros before pooling its values.

Putting Theory into Practice

Once you understand convolution, convolution layers, and pooling layers, you're ready to examine some code. This section presents an application that classifies images. But instead of classifying images of the MNIST dataset, this application classifies images from a dataset called CIFAR-10.

Processing CIFAR images

To test practical image recognition applications, the Canadian Institute for Advanced Research (CIFAR) provides the CIFAR-10 and CIFAR-100 datasets. Like the MNIST dataset, these datasets contain images and their classification labels. Unlike the MNIST images, the CIFAR images are in color and have a size equal to 32-x-32 pixels. This discussion explains how to obtain the CIFAR-10 dataset and access its content in a TensorFlow application.

The CIFAR-10 dataset

The main site for the CIFAR-10 and CIFAR-100 datasets is `www.cs.toronto.edu/~kriz/cifar.html`. The site provides three links for downloading the

CIFAR-10 dataset: one for the Python version, one for the Matlab version, and a binary version. This section focuses on the Python version, and I recommend that you download it to your development system.

Before proceeding, I recommend that you download and decompress the archive to the ch8 directory. Inside the decompressed directory, you'll find a folder named cifar-10-batches-py. This folder contains five files containing training images (data_batch_1 through data_batch_5) and a file containing test images (test_batch).

Accessing CIFAR-10 images and labels

CIFAR serializes the data in the CIFAR-10 files using a process called *pickling*. To read the data in Python, an application needs to import pickle and invoke its load method with the CIFAR file. As an example, the following code accesses the data in data_batch_2:

```
import pickle
with open('cifar-10-batches-py/data_batch_2', 'rb') as imgfile:
    dict = pickle.load(imgfile)
    imgfile.close()
```

The result is a dictionary with four keys:

» b'batch_label': Description of the batch (b' training batch 2 of 5')

» b'labels': A list of the 10,000 labels of the batch's images

» b'data': An ndarray containing the batch's image data

» b'filenames': A list of the 10,000 PNGs that contain image data (b'stealth_fighter_s_001650.png')

Each image label is provided as an integer between 0 and 9. These values correspond to the ten categories that identify the content of the corresponding image. These categories are airplane (0), automobile (1), bird (2), cat (3), deer (4), dog (5), frog (6), horse (7), ship (8), and truck (9). As an example, Figure 8-6 shows what a Category 7 image looks like.

The ndarray provided by the data key contains 8-bit unsigned integers in a 10,000-x-3,072 element matrix. This matrix contains 10,000 rows, and each row contains a 32-by-32 image with red, green, and blue components (32 x 32 x 3 = 3,072).

Classifying CIFAR images in code

The code in ch8/cifar_cnn.py demonstrates how you can use TensorFlow to load CIFAR-10 images and classify them with a convolutional neural network. Listing 8-1 presents the module's code.

LISTING 8-1: **Classifying CIFAR-10 Images**

```
# Set parameters
image_size = 32
num_channels = 3
num_categories = 10
num_filters = 32
filter_size = 5
num_epochs = 200
batch_size = 10
num_batches = int(50000/batch_size)
keep_prob = 0.6

# Read CIFAR training data
train_data = None
train_labels = None
for file_index in range(5):
    train_file = open('cifar-10-batches-py/data_batch_' + str(file_index+1),
    'rb')
    train_dict = pickle.load(train_file, encoding='latin1')
    train_file.close()

    if train_data is None:
        train_data = np.array(train_dict['data'], float)/255.0
        train_labels = train_dict['labels']
```

```
        else:
            train_data = np.concatenate((train_data, train_dict['data']), 0)
            train_labels = np.concatenate((train_labels, train_dict['labels']), 0)


    # Preprocess training data and labels
    train_data = train_data.reshape([-1, num_channels, image_size, image_size])
    train_data = train_data.transpose([0, 2, 3, 1])
    train_labels = np.eye(num_categories)[train_labels]


    # Read CIFAR test data
    test_file = open('cifar-10-batches-py/test_batch', 'rb')
    test_dict = pickle.load(test_file, encoding='latin1')
    test_file.close()
    test_data = test_dict['data']
    test_labels = test_dict['labels']


    # Preprocess test data and labels
    test_data = test_data.reshape([-1, num_channels, image_size, image_size])
    test_data = test_data.transpose([0, 2, 3, 1])
    test_labels = np.eye(num_categories)[test_labels]


    # Placeholders for CIFAR images
    img_holder = tf.placeholder(tf.float32, [None, image_size, image_size, num_
        channels])
    lbl_holder = tf.placeholder(tf.float32, [None, num_categories])
    train = tf.placeholder(tf.bool)


    # Create convolution/pooling layers
    conv1 = tf.layers.conv2d(img_holder, num_filters, filter_size, padding='same',
        activation=tf.nn.relu)
    drop1 = tf.layers.dropout(conv1, keep_prob, training=train)
    pool1 = tf.layers.max_pooling2d(drop1, 2, 2)
    conv2 = tf.layers.conv2d(pool1, num_filters, filter_size, padding='same',
        activation=tf.nn.relu)
    drop2 = tf.layers.dropout(conv2, keep_prob, training=train)
    pool2 = tf.layers.max_pooling2d(drop2, 2, 2)
    conv3 = tf.layers.conv2d(pool2, num_filters, filter_size, padding='same',
        activation=tf.nn.relu)
    pool3 = tf.layers.max_pooling2d(conv3, 2, 2)
    conv4 = tf.layers.conv2d(pool3, num_filters, filter_size, padding='same',
        activation=tf.nn.relu)
    drop3 = tf.layers.dropout(conv4, keep_prob, training=train)
```

(continued)

LISTING 8-1: *(continued)*

```python
# Flatten input data
flatten = tf.reshape(drop3, [-1, 512])

# Create connected layers
with tf.contrib.framework.arg_scope(
    [tf.contrib.layers.fully_connected],
    normalizer_fn=tf.contrib.layers.batch_norm,
    normalizer_params={'is_training': train}):
        fc1 = tf.contrib.layers.fully_connected(flatten, 512)
        fc2 = tf.contrib.layers.fully_connected(fc1, num_categories,
    activation_fn=None)

# Compute loss
loss = tf.reduce_mean(
    tf.nn.softmax_cross_entropy_with_logits(
        logits=fc2, labels=lbl_holder))

# Create optimizer
learning_rate = 0.0005
optimizer = tf.train.AdamOptimizer(learning_rate).minimize(loss)
# Initialize variables
init = tf.global_variables_initializer()

# Launch session
with tf.Session() as sess:
    sess.run(init)

    # Loop over epochs
    for epoch in range(num_epochs):

        # Loop over batches
        for batch in range(num_batches):
            batch_start = random.randint(0, batch_size*
    (num_batches-1)-1)
            batch_end = batch_start + batch_size
            img_batch = train_data[batch_start:batch_end, :]
            lbl_batch = train_labels[batch_start:batch_end, :]
            sess.run(optimizer, feed_dict={img_holder: img_batch,
                lbl_holder: lbl_batch, train: True})

        # Determine success rate
    prediction = tf.equal(tf.argmax(fc2, 1), tf.argmax(lbl_holder, 1))
    accuracy = tf.reduce_mean(tf.cast(prediction, tf.float32))
    print('Accuracy: ', sess.run(accuracy, feed_dict={img_holder: test_data,
        lbl_holder: test_labels, train: False}))
```

The application assumes that the user has downloaded the CIFAR-10 dataset for Python. It also assumes that the user has decompressed the archive into a directory named cifar-10-batches-py in the ch8 folder.

The module starts by loading the CIFAR-10 training images and labels. Then it performs four operations:

>> Concatenates the training images into one (50,000 x 3,072) ndarray. Concatenates the training labels into one (50,000 x 1) ndarray.

>> Converts the elements of the image ndarray to floating-point values.

>> Reshapes the image ndarray to [50,000, 32, 32, 3]. The last element identifies the number of channels per pixel (R, G, and B).

>> Converts the label ndarray to a one-shot ndarray (50,000 x 10).

This is a book on TensorFlow, so it may seem odd that the application preprocesses data using NumPy instead of TensorFlow. But there's an important reason: Sessions can't feed tensors into placeholders during training. Another reason is that TensorFlow stores tensor operations in the graph but does not store NumPy operations.

To process the image data, the application creates four convolution layers and three pooling layers. Each convolution layer uses 32 filters of size 5 x 5, and each uses a ReLU to serve as its activation function. The pooling layers set their block sizes to 2 x 2 and their strides to 2.

To understand the code, it's crucial to understand how the input tensor's size changes from layer to layer. Each batch contains ten images, so the initial size of each input tensor is [10, 32, 32, 3].

>> The first convolution layer has 32 filters, so the shape of the output tensor is [10, 32, 32, 32].

>> The first pooling layer shrinks each image dimension by one-half, so the output tensor's shape is [10, 16, 16, 32].

>> The second convolution layer has 32 filters, so the shape of the output tensor is [10, 16, 16, 32].

>> The second pooling layer shrinks each image dimension by one-half, so the output tensor's shape is [10, 8, 8, 32].

>> The third convolution layer has 32 filters, so the shape of the output tensor is [10, 8, 8, 32].

>> The third pooling layer shrinks each image dimension by one-half, so the output tensor's shape is [10, 4, 4, 32].

>> The fourth convolution layer has 32 filters, so the shape of the output tensor is [10, 4, 4, 32].

When the convolution is finished, the module flattens the image data and passes it to two fully connected layers. The first fully connected layer has 512 nodes and uses a ReLU to serve as its activation function. The second fully connected layer has ten nodes.

Performing Image Operations

TensorFlow provides many functions that perform general-purpose image processing. To present these functions, I divide them into five categories:

>> Image conversion

>> Color processing

>> Rotating and mirroring

>> Resizing and cropping

>> Convolution

The following sections introduce these functions and demonstrate their usage. The example application shows how to generate summary data for an image and visualize it with TensorBoard.

Converting images

The `tf.image` package provides functions that convert images between different file formats, color profiles, and data types. Table 8-3 lists these functions and provides a description of each.

TABLE 8-3   ## Image Conversion Functions

Function	Description
`decode_bmp(contents,` `. channels=None, name=None)`	Convert BMP-formatted image data into a tensor
`decode_gif(contents,` `. name=None)`	Convert GIF-formatted image data into a tensor

`decode_png(contents,`
`. channels=None, dtype=None,`
`. name=None)`
	Convert PNG-formatted image data into a tensor

`decode_jpeg(contents,`
`. channels=None, ratio=None,`
`. fancy_upscaling=None,`
`. try_recover_truncated=None,`
`. acceptable_fraction=None,`
`. dct_method=None,`
`. name=None)`
	Convert JPEG-formatted image data to a tensor

`decode_image(contents,` `. channels=None, name=None)`	Detects format of image data and converts data to a tensor

`encode_png(image,`
`. compression=None,`
`. name=None)`
	Converts a tensor containing image data to PNG encoding

`encode_jpeg(image,`
`. format=None,`
`. quality=None,`
`. progressive=None,`
`. optimize_size=None,`
`. chroma_downsampling=None,`
`  density_unit=None,`
`. x_density=None,`
`. y_density=None,`
`. xmp_metadata=None,`
`. name=None)`
	Converts a tensor containing image data to PNG encoding

`rgb_to_grayscale(images,` `  name=None)`	Convert one or more images from RGB to grayscale
`rgb_to_hsv(images,` `  name=None)`	Convert one or more images from RGB to HSV
`grayscale_to_rgb(images,` `  name=None)`	Convert one or more images from grayscale to RGB
`hsv_to_rgb(images,` `  name=None)`	Convert one or more images from HSV to RGB

`convert_image_dtype(image,`
`  dtype, saturate=False,`
`  name=None)`
	Change the data type of the image tensor's elements

The shape of an image's tensor depends on the nature of the image. For simple 2-D images, such as in a JPEG, the tensor's shape is [height, width, num_channels]. For a sequence of frames, such as the images in a GIF animation, the shape is [num_frames, height, width, num_channels].

In Table 8-3, the decode_* functions convert a zero-dimensional string tensor into a suitable image tensor. For example, if an application loads data from smiley.jpg into a tensor named smiley_tensor, decode_jpeg will return a decompressed tensor whose shape is [height, width, num_channels].

A TensorFlow application can read BMP, GIF, PNG, and JPEG images, but it can only write data to PNGs and JPEGs. These write operations are made possible by encode_png and encode_jpeg.

Keep in mind that TensorFlow's decode/encode functions don't accept files, but instead read and write zero-dimensional string tensors. TensorFlow provides a number of method to create string tensors from files, and one method involves three steps:

1. Call tf.string_input_producer with an array of file names.

2. Create a WholeFileReader by calling tf.WholeFileReader.

3. Call the reader's read method with the queue from Step 1.

To demonstrate how this process works, the following code reads data from smiley.png and writes it to smiley.jpg:

```
queue = tf.train.string_input_producer(['smiley.png'])
reader = tf.WholeFileReader()
_, png_data = reader.read(queue)
img_tensor = tf.image.decode_png(png_data)
jpeg_data = tf.image.encode_jpeg(img_tensor)
with tf.Session() as sess:
    tf.train.start_queue_runners()
    jpeg_file = open('smiley.jpeg', 'wb+')
    jpeg_file.write(jpeg_data.eval())
    jpeg_file.close()
```

The last function in Table 8-3, convert_image_dtype, converts the pixels of an image from one data type to another. This is particularly important because different image-processing operations require different data types. For example, convolution requires tensors containing floating-point elements while PNG encoding requires unsigned integers. The following code converts the elements of img to single-precision floating-point values:

```
img = tf.image.convert_image_dtype(img, tf.float32)
```

convert_image_dtype assumes that all integer values are non-negative and that all floating-point values lie between 0.0 and 1.0. The function performs scaling in addition to conversion, so it multiplies tf.float32 values by 256 when converting to tf.uint8 and it divides tf.uint8 values by 256 when converting to tf.float32.

Color processing

The second category of functions in tf.image change the color content of an image. Table 8-4 lists nine of these functions.

TABLE 8-4   Color-Processing Functions

Function	Description
adjust_brightness(image, delta)	Adds the given delta to the image's pixel values
adjust_contrast(images, contrast_factor)	Adjust contrast by the given factor
adjust_gamma(image, gamma=1, gain=1)	Perform gamma correction
adjust_hue(image, delta, name=None)	Change the image's hue content by the given delta
adjust_saturation(image, saturation_factor, name=None)	Update the image's saturation by a given value
random_brightness(image, max_delta, seed=None)	Adds a random value to the image's pixel values
random_contrast(image, lower, upper, seed=None)	Adjust contrast by a random value
random_hue(image, max_delta, seed=None)	Change the image's hue content by a random amount
random_saturation(image, lower, upper, seed=None)	Update the image's saturation by a random value

These functions are easy to understand. The adjust_*xyz* functions update an image's property by a specific amount. The random_*xyz* functions update an image's property by a random amount.

adjust_contrast and random_contrast change the deviation of the image's pixels from the mean. To be specific, if a pixel's component equals *x* and the average value is x_{avg}, calling adjust_contrast with a factor of *k* updates *x* in the following way:

$$x = k\left(x - x_{avg}\right) + x_{avg}$$

The random_*xyz* functions accept one or two bounds for the random value. For example, the following code changes the contrast of img by a random factor that lies between 0.1 and 0.2:

```
tf.image.random_contrast(img, 0.1, 0.2)
```

adjust_hue and random_hue operate on RGB images. Both functions convert the image's pixels to floating-point values and then convert the image to HSV. Then they add an offset to the hue channel and convert the image back to RGB and the pixels' original data type.

Rotating and mirroring

The tf.image package also provides functions that rotate and mirror (flip) the pixels of an image. Table 8-5 lists six of these functions and provides a description of each.

TABLE 8-5 **Rotation and Mirroring Functions**

Function	Description
rot90(image, k=1, name=None)	Rotates an image counterclockwise by a multiple of 90 degrees
flip_left_right(image)	Mirrors an image horizontally
random_flip_left_right(image, seed=None)	Mirrors an image horizontally half the time
flip_up_down(image)	Mirrors an image vertically
random_flip_up_down(image, seed=None)	Mirrors an image vertically half the time
transpose_image(image)	Mirrors an image along its main diagonal

rot90 rotates an image in a counterclockwise orientation by a multiple of 90 degrees. The precise angle of rotation equals $90(k \mod 4)$, where k is the second argument of rot90.

It's important to see the difference between transpose_image and the functions that flip the image vertically and horizontally. transpose_image flips an image along the diagonal running from the upper-left to the lower-right.

The following code shows how an application can decode PNG data and then rotate, flip, and transpose the image.

```
img_tensor = tf.image.decode_png(smiley)

# Rotate CCW by 270 degrees
rot_tensor = tf.image.rot90(img_tensor, 3)
rot_png = tf.image.encode_png(rot_tensor)

# Flip horizontal
flip_tensor = tf.image.flip_left_right(img_tensor)
flip_png = tf.image.encode_png(flip_tensor)

# Transpose
transpose_tensor = tf.image.transpose_image(img_tensor)
transpose_png = tf.image.encode_png(transpose_tensor)
```

Figure 8-7 illustrates the results of the operations performed in the example code.

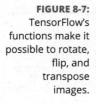

FIGURE 8-7: TensorFlow's functions make it possible to rotate, flip, and transpose images.

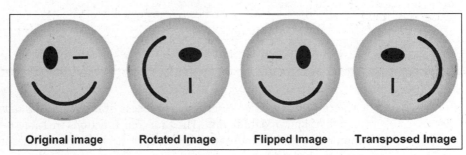

Original image **Rotated Image** **Flipped Image** **Transposed Image**

The random_flip_left_right and random_flip_up_down functions are helpful when you want to train an application to recognize images that may have been flipped. These functions flip their images half the time and leave their images unchanged half the time.

Resizing and cropping

Applications frequently need to enlarge, shrink, or crop the content of an image. Table 8-6 lists the functions of tf.image that perform these operations.

TABLE 8-6 **Resizing and Cropping Functions**

Function	Description
resize_nearest_neighbor(images, size, align_corners=False, name=None)	Resize using nearest-neighbor interpolation
resize_bilinear(images, size align_corners=False, name=None)	Resize using bilinear interpolation
resize_bicubic(images, size align_corners=None, name=None)	Resize using bicubic interpolation
resize_area(images, size, align_corners=False, name=None)	Resize using area interpolation
resize_images(images, size, method=ResizeMethod.BILINEAR, align_corners=False)	Resize using the specified interpolation method
central_crop(image, fraction)	Crop a central portion of the input image
resize_image_with_crop_or_pad(image, target_height, target_width)	Crop or pad the image until its size equals the given width and height
crop_and_resize(image, boxes, box_ind, crop_size, method=None, extrapolation_value=None, name=None)	Crop a portion of the image and resize the image to the given dimensions

The term *interpolation* refers to the process of inserting new data points within a range of known data points. The first four functions in Table 8-6 use interpolation to resize their input image or images. Each of them resizes its image(s) using a different interpolation method.

The resize_nearest_neighbor function resizes its images using *nearest-neighbor interpolation*. This function computes the color of an internal point by determining which pixel is closest to it and assigning the pixel's color. If you call this function to enlarge an image, the result will contain only the colors in the original. If you enlarge an image *n*-fold, its colors will be repeated *n* times.

The `resize_bilinear` function resizes images using *bilinear interpolation*. This determines the color of an internal point by finding the linear combination of the pixels surrounding it. This provides excellent results without significant processing, and for this reason, it's the default interpolation method employed by TensorFlow and many graphics cards.

To understand bilinear interpolation, it helps to look at one-dimensional interpolation, or linear interpolation. Suppose that P is a point on a line between Pixels A and B. The distance from P to the center of A is denoted t, and the distance from P to the center of B is given by 1 - t. Linear interpolation sets the color of P with the following equation:

$$P_{color} = tA_{color} + (1-t)B_{color}$$

When t equals 1, the color at P equals the color at A. When t equals 0, the color at P equals the color at B. If t = 0.5, the resulting color will equal the average of the colors of A and B. Interpolated values form straight lines, and Figure 8-8 depicts the lines used to interpolate between four points.

FIGURE 8-8:
Linear interpolation finds internal points by computing the linear combination of existing points.

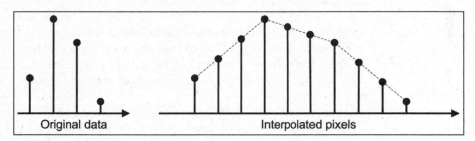

Bilinear interpolation is similar to linear interpolation, but computes the value of two-dimensional points located between four pixels. For example, suppose that P is surrounded by four pixels: A, B, C, and D. Locating P requires two interpolation parameters, t_1 and t_2. Figure 8-9 depicts a point P, its four surrounding pixels, and the two interpolation parameters.

Bilinear interpolation determines the color of an internal point by scaling the colors of surrounding pixels by the interpolation parameters. The following equation shows how bilinear interpolation computes the color at point P, which is surrounded by A, B, C, and D:

$$P_{color} = t_1 t_2 A_{color} + (1-t_1)t_2 B_{color} + t_1(1-t_2)C_{color} + (1-t_1)(1-t_2)D_{color}$$

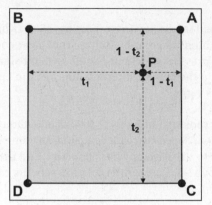

resize_bicubic resizes images using bicubic interpolation. Bicubic interpolation is similar to bilinear interpolation, but instead of finding the linear combination of four surrounding pixels, it determines the color of an internal point by evaluating a cubic polynomial involving 16 surrounding points. Bicubic interpolation produces smoother images than bilinear interpolation, but requires significantly more processing.

central_crop determines the dimensions of the cropped image by scaling the dimensions of the original image. For example, if you set the fraction parameter to 0.25, the cropped width will equal one-quarter of the original width, and the cropped height will equal one-quarter of the original height.

resize_image_with_crop_or_pad resizes its image without using interpolation. If the specified dimensions are smaller than the image, the function will crop the image from its center so that the final image has the specified dimensions. If the specified dimensions are larger than the image, the function will pad the image with zeros.

crop_and_resize can perform multiple crop operations. Each row of boxes identifies a portion of the image to be cropped, and each element of box_ind sets the index of the cropped image in the output. The function uses bilinear interpolation to resize each cropped image to crop_size.

Convolution

In addition to creating convolution layers, TensorFlow applications can perform simple convolution by calling tf.nn.conv2d:

```
tf.nn.conv2d(input, filter, strides, padding, use_cudnn_on_
    gpu=None, data_format='NHWC', name=None)
```

The format of input depends on the data_format parameter. That is, if an application sets data_format to NHWC, the shape of the input tensor should be [batch, height, width, channels]. If data_format is set to NCHW, the tensor's shape should be [batch, channels, height, width].

To perform convolution, you should assign filter to a tensor with the same shape as input. As it performs 2-D dot products, the function shifts the filter by intervals given in the strides tensor. You must set strides equal to a 1-D tensor with four elements. To shift the dot products by 1 in each direction, set strides to [1, 1, 1, 1].

If a 2-D dot product involves a pixel on or near the image's border, the computation will depend on the padding parameter. If you set padding to VALID, the convolution won't compute dot products involving border pixels. If you set padding to SAME, the function will pad the image with zeros before performing convolution.

TIP

The functions tf.layers.conv2d and tf.nn.conv2d have similar names but serve markedly different purposes. tf.layers.conv2d creates a convolution layer in a CNN, while tf.nn.conv2d performs a single convolution operation. Be sure not to confuse the two.

TECHNICAL
STUFF

In addition to conv2d, the tf.nn package provides a function called conv2d_transpose. This function performs regular convolution, but returns the transpose of the resulting image.

Putting Theory into Practice

The code in the ch8/img_proc.py module demonstrates how an application can remove noise from an image by performing convolution with a 3-x-3 filter whose elements equal 1/9. In addition to convolution, this module performs four operations:

» Changes the image's contrast by calling tf.image.adjust_contrast

» Mirrors the image horizontally by calling tf.image.flip_left_right

» Converts the data to PNG format and writes the data to a PNG file

» Generates summary data for viewing the image in TensorBoard

The ch8/img_proc.py module reads data from input_aircraft.png and writes its result to output_aircraft.png. Figure 8-10 depicts the input image and the output image.

Listing 8-2 presents the code that implements the module's operations using
TensorFlow.

LISTING 8-2:   **General-Purpose Image Processing**

```
# Load and pre-process PNG data
queue = tf.train.string_input_producer(['input_aircraft.png'])
reader = tf.WholeFileReader()
_, png_data = reader.read(queue)
orig_tensor = tf.image.decode_png(png_data)
img_tensor = tf.reshape(orig_tensor, [-1, 1, 232, 706])
img_tensor = tf.transpose(img_tensor, [0, 2, 3, 1])
img_tensor = tf.image.convert_image_dtype(img_tensor, tf.float32)

# Remove noise using a box filter
conv_filter = np.zeros([3, 3, 1, 1])
conv_filter[0, 0, :, :] = 0.1111
conv_filter[0, 1, :, :] = 0.1111
conv_filter[0, 2, :, :] = 0.1111
conv_filter[1, 0, :, :] = 0.1111
conv_filter[1, 1, :, :] = 0.1111
conv_filter[1, 2, :, :] = 0.1111
conv_filter[2, 0, :, :] = 0.1111
conv_filter[2, 1, :, :] = 0.1111
conv_filter[2, 2, :, :] = 0.1111
```

```
img_tensor = tf.nn.conv2d(img_tensor, conv_filter, [1, 1, 1, 1], 'SAME')

# Increase contrast
img_tensor = tf.reshape(img_tensor, [232, 706, 1])
img_tensor = tf.image.adjust_contrast(img_tensor, 0.8)

# Flip horizontal
img_tensor = tf.image.flip_left_right(img_tensor)

# Create summary data and FileWriter
img_tensor = tf.reshape(img_tensor, [1, 232, 706, 1])
img_tensor = tf.image.convert_image_dtype(img_tensor, tf.uint8)
summary_op = tf.summary.image('Output', img_tensor)
file_writer = tf.summary.FileWriter('log')

# Store result to PNG
img_tensor = tf.reshape(img_tensor, [232, 706, 1])
img_tensor = tf.image.encode_png(img_tensor)
with tf.Session() as sess:
    coord = tf.train.Coordinator()
    threads = tf.train.start_queue_runners(coord=coord)

    # Execute session
    output_data, summary = sess.run([img_tensor, summary_op])

    # Write output PNG data to file
    output_file = open('output_aircraft.png', 'wb+')
    output_file.write(output_data)
    output_file.close()

    # Print summary data
    file_writer.add_summary(summary)
    file_writer.flush()

    # Wait for threads to terminate
    coord.request_stop()
    coord.join(threads)
```

As you look at this code, it's important to keep track of the image's shape and data type. After the application decodes the input image, the tensor's shape is [232, 706, 1], and its elements are 8-bit unsigned integers. But before the convolution can be performed, the application converts the tensor's shape to [1, 232, 706, 1] and its elements to 32-bit floating-point values.

Before it can update the image's contrast, the application converts the image tensor's shape back to [232, 706, 1]. Later on, the module converts the image's shape to [1, 232, 706, 1] and its type to `tf.uint8` so that the module can generate summary data. Lastly, the application converts the tensor's shape to [232, 706, 1] so that it can encode the data to PNG format.

The process of generating summary data for an image is similar to that of generating data for a tensor. The only difference is that the application needs to call `tf.summary.image` instead of `tf.summary.scalar` or `tf.summary.histogram`. The function's signature is given as follows:

```
tf.summary.image(name, tensor, max_outputs=3, collections=None,
    family=None)
```

The `name` parameter provides the label that TensorFlow will associate with the image. The function accepts the image data through the `tensor` parameter, and the tensor's shape must be [batch_size, height, width, num_channels].

As an example, the `ch8/img_proc.py` module creates an operation that generates summary data for `img_tensor` with the following code:

```
summary_op = tf.summary.image('Output', img_tensor)
```

After creating this operation, the application executes it in a session and uses a `FileWriter` to print the protocol buffer to an event file. When launched, TensorBoard will read this event file and display the graphical content of `img_tensor`.

Chapter **9**

Analyzing Sequential Data with Recurrent Neural Networks (RNNs)

S uppose that you want a neural network to predict the next word in the phrase "My hovercraft is full of. . .." As any Monty Python fan (or a casual web search) will tell you, the obvious answer is "eels." But how can you train a neural network to arrive at the answer?

You can feed the network every sentence ever written on the Internet, but there's still a problem. To make the prediction, the neural network needs to recognize that the words form an *ordered sequence*. That is, the network needs to understand that the phrase "My hovercraft is full of" is a different phrase than "full is My of hovercraft."

None of the neural networks discussed in Chapters 1 through 8 of this book are capable of recognizing sequences. As a consequence, they can't use past analysis to solve future problems. For example, a CNN can classify an image, but it can't classify later images based on previous classifications. To make up for these shortcomings, machine learning researchers invented recurrent neural networks, or RNNs.

Recurrent Neural Networks (RNNs)

Most neural networks, such as convolutional neural networks, transfer data in one direction: from the input layer to the output layer. For this reason, they're called *feed-forward* networks. In contrast with feed-forward networks, recurrent neutral networks, or RNNs, make use of *feedback*. That is, they send data from a later node to an earlier node in the network.

Figure 9-1 depicts a simple RNN. The overall structure resembles that of a regular network, but the result of the output node is delayed and fed back into the output node. This feedback is the primary characteristic that distinguishes RNNs from other neural networks.

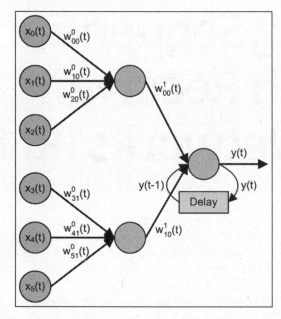

FIGURE 9-1:
A recursive neural network feeds past data back into one or more nodes.

Another important characteristic of RNNs is that they execute in *stages*. For example, if an RNN needs to parse words in audio or text, it will execute one stage for each word. With each stage, the RNN receives new data to process. It's important to see the difference between training steps and stages: One training step may require multiple processing stages.

In Figure 9-1, the network's stage is identified by t. This doesn't measure clock time, as in 1.37 seconds, but measures discrete time, which starts at 0 and increments by 1 with each new stage. Therefore, the initial input values are denoted $x_i(0)$, the next set of inputs are denoted $x_i(1)$, and so on.

An RNN makes use of previous processing stages by accessing delayed values. In Figure 9-1, delayed values are provided by the Delay element. If the current stage is 4, the value leaving the Delay element will be y(3). If the current stage is 5, the value leaving the element will be y(4).

Just as the network's values change from stage to stage, their associated weights also change. For example, if the RNN in Figure 9-1 has N stages, the application needs to compute a different set of weights for y(0) through y(N-1). If an RNN has many delayed values, computing the weight of each value can dramatically increase the time needed for training.

RNNs and recursive functions

To better understand how RNNs work, it helps to see how they relate to recursive functions. For example, the following function computes the factorial of N using recursion:

```
def factorial(N):
    if n == 1:
        return 1
    else:
        return N * factorial(N-1)
```

This function calls itself repeatedly and provides a new input value with each call. Recursive functions can be rewritten using loops, as demonstrated in the following function:

```
def factorial(N):
    x = 1
    for i in range(2, N+1):
        x *= i
    return x
```

A lengthy recursive function requires a significant amount of memory because of all the data that needs to be pushed onto the stack. To prevent overflow, Python sets the default maximum recursion limit to 1000.

Similarly, the processing requirements for an RNN increase with each new stage. Just as Python sets a maximum recursion limit, every RNN has a fixed number of stages it can process.

The process of converting a recursive function to a loop-based function is called *unrolling.* To better visualize an RNN, you can unroll it by inserting nodes for each stage to be processed. For example, suppose that the RNN in Figure 9-1 has three stages. Figure 9-2 shows what the RNN looks like after unrolling (weights removed for clarity).

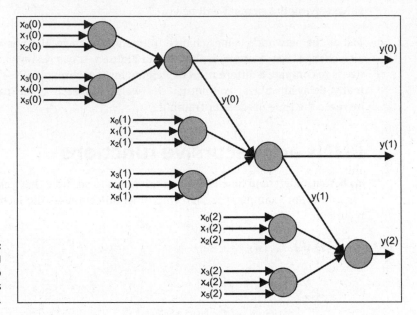

As shown in Figure 9-2, y(2) depends on current inputs (the weighted sums of $x_i(2)$) and the outputs of preceding stages. Developers refer to the combined results of past stages as the node's *state*.

Put simply, the difference between an RNN and a regular neural network is that one or more nodes of an RNN have state. If a node has state, it can apply the results of preceding stages to the current stage. This ability to use past results explains why RNNs are so popular when it comes to processing language and other sequential data.

Training RNNs

As illustrated in Figure 9-2, earlier in this chapter, unrolling an RNN results in a feed-forward network that receives its inputs at different stages ($x_i(0)$, $x_i(1)$, and so on). This behavior implies that RNNs can be trained like regular feed-forward networks. A popular training method is called backpropagation through time (BPTT), which applies the method of backpropagation to RNNs. Chapter 7 discusses the basic theory of backpropagation.

As you design RNNs with more processing stages, the number of nodes grows dramatically. As a result, RNNs suffer from two issues that plague all complex neural networks: vanishing gradients and exploding gradients. Chapter 7 explains these issues and the way they degrade the performance of neural networks.

To make up for the shortcomings of BPTT, researchers have devised alternative training methods. Truncated backpropagation through time (TBPTT) uses a limited number of stages for training. Real-time recurrent learning (RTRL) doesn't unroll RNNs, but trains with the partial derivatives of the network's outputs and states with respect to its weights.

Instead of focusing on new training methods, some researchers have invented entirely new variants of RNNs. These variants provide all the benefits of RNNs, but aren't as susceptible to vanishing gradients and exploding gradients. The most popular variants are long short-term memory (LSTM) cells and gated recurrent units (GRUs). This chapter discusses both of these variants and demonstrates how they can be used.

Creating RNN Cells

Just as vanilla neural networks are made up of nodes, RNNs are made up of *cells*. In most RNN literature, a cell is a part of an RNN that receives input and produces a single output value.

The cells of a TensorFlow RNN aren't quite as straightforward. According to the documentation, the cell of a TensorFlow RNN "is anything that has a state and performs some operation that takes a matrix of inputs. This operation results in an output matrix. . .." In other words, an RNN cell has a state, operates on an input matrix, and produces an output matrix.

In a TensorFlow application, the process of building an RNN starts with creating a cell. To be specific, the process consists of three steps:

1. **Create an instance of an RNN cell class with the number of units per cell.**

   Each cell class is a subclass of `tf.nn.rnn_cell.RNNCell`.

2. **Call a function, such as `tf.nn.static_rnn`, that creates an RNN based on the cell.**

   This function accepts a list of input tensors and returns the RNN's output and state.

3. **Use the output from Step 2 to compute the loss.**

   Minimize the loss by launching an optimizer in a session.

The RNNCell class plays a central role in this discussion. It can't be instantiated in code, but it's important because it serves as the base class of TensorFlow's RNN cell classes, which include BasicRNNCell, BasicLSTMCell, LSTMCell, and GRUCell. Figure 9-3 presents seven TensorFlow classes that inherit from RNNCell.

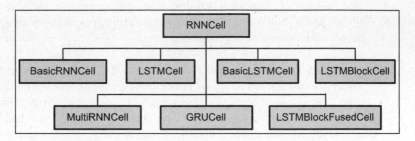

FIGURE 9-3:
Each subclass of RNNCell represents a different kind of RNN cell.

The RNNCell class defines properties and methods that can be accessed through its instances. Table 9-1 lists seven properties of an RNNCell.

TABLE 9-1

Properties of the RNNCell Class

Property	Description
state_size	The shape(s) of the cell's state(s)
output_size	The shape of the cell's output
graph	Graph of operations contained in the cell
losses	Losses to be applied to the cell's processing
update	Tensors used to update the cell's weights
variables	List of the cell's variables
weights	List of the cell's weights
scope_name	Name of the scope containing the variables

The state of an RNNCell can be represented by one or more tensors. Therefore, an application can assign state_size to an integer, a TensorShape, a tuple of integers, or a tuple of TensorShapes. Applications must assign output_size to an integer or a TensorShape.

The rest of the properties in Table 9-1 are straightforward. The losses property identifies a tensor or list/tuple of tensors that identify losses that the cell should apply during its processing. The last three properties in the table provide access to the cell's variables and variable scope.

In addition to properties, the `RNNCell` class defines a set of methods, and most of them customize the cell's behavior. Table 9-2 lists four particularly helpful methods and provides a description of each.

TABLE 9-2   ## Methods of the RNNCell Class

Method	Description
`add_loss(losses, inputs=None)`	Add loss tensors
`add_update(updates, inputs=None)`	Add updates to the cell's weights
`add_variable(name, shape, dtype=None, initializer=None, regularizer=None, trainable=true)`	Adds a new variable to the layer
`zero_state(batch_size, dtype)`	Returns a zero-filled tensor for initializing the cell's state

Of the listed methods, `zero_state` is particularly popular. It creates a zero-filled tensor or list of zero-filled tensors suitable for initializing an RNN's state. The shape of the return value depends on the method's `batch_size` parameter and the cell's `state_size` property.

Creating a basic RNN

The simplest subclass of `RNNCell` is `BasicRNNCell`. Its constructor is given as follows:

```
BasicRNNCell(num_units, activation=tf.nn.tanh, reuse=None)
```

The `num_units` parameter sets the number of hidden units in the cell. This parameter determines the RNN's learning capacity. That is, as the number of units increases, the size of the cell's state memory increases. Unfortunately, so does the training time. Also, if you set `num_units` too high, you run the risk of overfitting.

The second parameter of the constructor sets the cell's activation function. By default, RNN cells rely on the inverse tangent (tanh) to produce their output.

The last parameter, `reuse`, specifies whether applications can access identically named variables created by the cell.

After creating an instance of the cell, an application can construct an RNN by calling one of a handful of functions in the tf.nn package. The simplest of these functions is static_rnn:

```
static_rnn(cell, inputs, initial_state=None, dtype=None,
    sequence_length=None, scope=None)
```

Applications must assign inputs to a list of input matrices. For each input matrix in the list, the function creates a cell to receive and process the matrix. The number of rows in the input matrix equals the application's batch size. In this discussion, I refer to this number as batch_size.

By default, static_rnn assumes that the RNN's sequence length equals the number of columns in the input matrix. An application can customize this length by setting sequence_length to a one-dimensional tensor of batch_size values. Each value of sequence_length sets the length of the sequence for the corresponding row of the input matrix.

As its name implies, the initial_state parameter initializes the RNN's state. Applications must provide a state value for each row of the input matrix, so if the cell's state_size is an integer, an application must set initial_state to a matrix of shape [batch_size, state_size]. If state_size is a tuple, an application must set initial_state to a tuple of tensors of shapes [batch_size, element_size], where element_size is size of the corresponding element in state_size.

If an application sets the initial_state parameter, static_rnn will use the state's elements to determine the data type of the RNN's elements. If an application doesn't set initial_state, it must specify the data type with the dtype parameter. TensorFlow doesn't set a default data type for an RNN's content.

static_rnn returns a tuple containing two elements: the RNN's output and final state. The output contains batch_size elements, and the shape of the final state is determined by the cell's state_size.

The relationship between the number of units, state, inputs, and outputs can be confusing, so it helps to look at a basic example. The following code creates a BasicRNNCell with five units:

```
new_cell = tf.nn.rnn_cell.BasicRNNCell(5)
```

Because the RNN cell has five units, each row in the cell's output matrix will have a length of five.

For this example, each input matrix has two rows, and each row has four elements. If the application needs to provide three input matrices, it can set the RNN's input with this code:

```
inputs = [tf.constant([[1.,2.,3.,4.], [1.,2.,3.,4.]]),
    tf.constant([[1.,2.,3.,4.], [1.,2.,3.,4.]]),
    tf.constant([[1.,2.,3.,4.], [1.,2.,3.,4.]])]
```

After creating new_cell, an application can create a new RNN and pass it the list of input matrices with the following code. The dtype parameter specifies that the RNN's state and output should be composed of floating-point values:

```
output, state = tf.nn.static_rnn(new_cell, inputs, dtype=tf.float32)
```

Because inputs contains three input matrices, the structure of the new RNN contains three cells. Each cell produces an output matrix with the same number of rows as the input matrix. Figure 9-4 gives an idea of what a simple RNN looks like.

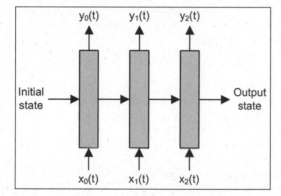

FIGURE 9-4: TensorFlow creates one RNN cell for each input matrix. Each cell produces one output matrix.

In Figure 9-4, $x_i(t)$ identifies the input matrices provided in the inputs parameter, and $y_i(t)$ identifies the output matrices returned by static_rnn. The initial state enters the first cell, which passes its state to the second cell, which passes its state to the third cell, which returns its state in static_rnn.

The precise values of output and state aren't important, but it's helpful to look at their shapes. Every RNN produces a list of output matrices, and the size of the list is determined by the size of the list of input matrices. Therefore, output is a list of three matrices. Because each input batch contained two rows, each output matrix has two rows. Each row has five values because the cell has five units.

The shape of the cell's state is determined by the batch size and the number of units in the cell. In this example cell, the state's shape is [2, 5] because the batch size is two and the cell contains five units.

Predicting text with RNNs

Because I'm a living national treasure, I extracted a portion of H.P. Lovecraft's short story *Herbert West–Reanimator* into the ch9/lovecraft.txt file. The ch9/rnn_lovecraft.py module reads this text and uses an RNN to predict how H.P. Lovecraft would add words to phrases. I'm sure we can all agree that this application is vitally important to humanity's cultural development, and Listing 9-1 presents the code.

LISTING 9-1: **Predicting Text with an RNN**

```
# Split text into words
python3 = sys.version_info[0] == 3
with open('lovecraft.txt', 'r') as f:
    input_str = f.read().lower()
    if python3:
        trans = input_str.maketrans('', '', string.punctuation)
        input_str = input_str.translate(trans)
    else:
        input_str = input_str.decode('utf-8').translate(None, string.
    punctuation)
    words = input_str.split()
    num_words = len(words)

# Convert words to values
word_freq = collections.Counter(words).most_common()
vocab_size = len(word_freq)
lookup = dict()
for word, _ in word_freq:
    lookup[word] = len(lookup)
input_vals = np.asarray([[lookup[str(word)]] for word in words])
input_vals = input_vals.reshape(-1,)

# Set values
input_size = 6
batch_size = 10
num_hidden = 600

# Placeholders
input_holder = tf.placeholder(tf.float32, [batch_size, input_size])
label_holder = tf.placeholder(tf.float32, [batch_size, vocab_size])
```

```
# Reshape input and feed to RNN
cell = tf.nn.rnn_cell.BasicRNNCell(num_hidden)
outputs, _ = tf.nn.static_rnn(cell, [input_holder], dtype=tf.float32)

# Compute loss
weights = tf.Variable(tf.random_normal([num_hidden, vocab_size]))
biases = tf.Variable(tf.random_normal([vocab_size]))
model = tf.matmul(outputs[-1], weights) + biases
loss = tf.reduce_mean(tf.nn.softmax_cross_entropy_with_logits(logits=model,
    labels=label_holder))

# Create optimizer and check result
optimizer = tf.train.AdagradOptimizer(0.1).minimize(loss)
check = tf.equal(tf.argmax(model, 1), tf.argmax(label_holder, 1))
correct = tf.reduce_sum(tf.cast(check, tf.float32))

# Execute the graph
start_time = time.time()
with tf.Session() as sess:
    sess.run(tf.global_variables_initializer())
    input_block = np.empty([batch_size, input_size])
    label_block = np.empty([batch_size, vocab_size])

    step = 0
    num_correct = 0.
    accuracy = 0.
    while accuracy < 95.:
        for i in range(batch_size):
            offset = np.random.randint(num_words-(input_size+1))
            input_block[i, :] = input_vals[offset:offset+input_size]
            label_block[i, :] = np.eye(vocab_size)[input_vals[offset+input_
    size]]
        _, corr = sess.run([optimizer, correct],
            feed_dict={input_holder: input_block, label_holder: label_block})
        num_correct += corr
        accuracy = 100*num_correct/(1000*batch_size)
        if step % 1000 == 0:
            print('Step', step, '- Accuracy =', accuracy)
            num_correct = 0
        step += 1

# Display timing result
duration = time.time() - start_time
print('Time to reach 95% accuracy: {:.2f} seconds'.format(duration))
```

To start, the module reads the content of lovecraft.txt into a string, splits the string into words, and associates each word with a number. A word's number is determined by its frequency. That is, the module associates the most common word with 0, the second most common word with 1, and so on.

After obtaining the array of numbers corresponding to the words, the module creates an RNN cell with 600 hidden layers. It uses the RNN cell to call tf.nn.static_rnn, which provides the RNN's output values. To determine loss, the module multiplies the RNN's outputs by a matrix of weights and adds biases to the products. Then it creates an AdagradOptimizer to minimize the loss.

For each training run, the application constructs a batch containing ten (batch_size) sequences of six (input_size) values each. As a result, the RNN can only recognize dependencies between at most six consecutive words. For each six-value sequence, the desired label is the seventh value, which represents the desired word to be predicted.

The application doesn't perform a fixed number of training runs. Instead, it continues training until the prediction accuracy exceeds 95 percent. For every thousand training runs, the application prints the prediction accuracy.

Creating multilayered cells

An application can improve an RNN's analyzing power by stacking cells together in sequence. This stacking process connects the output of one cell to the input of another. A TensorFlow application can stack RNN cells by creating an instance of the tf.contrib.rnn.MultiRNNCell class, whose constructor is given as follows:

```
MultiRNNCell(cells, state_is_tuple=True)
```

To create an MultiRNNCell, an application needs to set the first parameter to a list of RNNCell instances. The returned cell will contain the listed instances in sequence.

The second parameter sets the form of the cell's state. If you set state_is_tuple to True, the cell will provide its state as a tuple that contains an element for each of the combined cells. If you set this parameter to False, the cell concatenates the states of the individual cells.

As an example, the following code creates two BasicRNNCells and then creates a MultiRNNCell that stacks the cells together:

```
brc1 = tf.nn.rnn_cell.BasicRNNCell(3)
brc2 = tf.nn.rnn_cell.BasicRNNCell(3)
multi_cell = tf.nn.rnn_cell.MultiRNNCell([brc1, brc2])
```

As a result of this code, `multi_cell` stacks `brc1` and `brc2` together, connecting the output of `brc1` to the input of `brc2`.

Creating dynamic RNNs

The `static_rnn` function assumes that you know the length of your input data in advance. It requires that the input data be provided in a list of matrices, where each matrix has size [`batch_size, input_size`]. When an application calls `static_rnn`, TensorFlow creates the entire RNN structure in the current graph.

The `dynamic_rnn` function gives you more flexibility when providing input data. It tells TensorFlow to form the graph structure dynamically instead of building it in advance. The signature of `dynamic_rnn` is given as follows:

```
dynamic_rnn(cell, inputs, sequence_length=None, initial_state=None, dtype=None,
    parallel_iterations=None, swap_memory=False, time_major=False, scope=None)
```

Most of these parameters are identical to those of `static_rnn`. The primary difference is that applications can set `inputs` to a different shape. This shape depends on batch size, the maximum sequence length, and the function's `time_major` parameter. The default value of `time_major` is `False`, which means applications must assign inputs to a tensor of size [`batch_size, max_sequence, ...`] or a nested tuple. If an application sets `time_major` to `True`, it must assign inputs to a tensor of size [`max_sequence, batch_size, ...`] or a nested tuple.

TensorFlow can execute operations without temporal dependency in parallel. The `parallel_iterations` parameter controls how many such operations should be executed at once, and the default value is 32.

If an application sets `swap_memory` to `True`, TensorFlow will swap tensors between the GPU and CPU during the training process, incurring a small performance penalty. Chapter 11 explains how to execute TensorFlow operations on a GPU.

Like `static_rnn`, `dynamic_rnn` returns the output and state of the constructed RNN. The following code demonstrates how `dynamic_rnn` can be used:

```
example_cell = tf.nn.rnn_cell.BasicRNNCell(4)
output, state = tf.nn.dynamic_rnn(example_cell,
         example_input, dtype=tf.float32)
```

In my experiments, `dynamic_rnn` provides slightly better performance than `static_rnn`.

Long Short-Term Memory (LSTM) Cells

As RNNs process more stages, their unrolled networks get larger, and they become more susceptible to vanishing gradients. Because RNNs have a fixed number of stages, they can't analyze sequences with long-term dependencies. That is, if an RNN can process a maximum of N stages, it won't recognize any dependency between Element 0 and Element N+1.

To make up for these shortcomings, Sepp Hochreiter and Jürgen Schmidhuber proposed a modification to the RNN's structure in their 1997 paper *Long Short-Term Memory*. In essence, they proposed to reduce the size of an RNN's state by restricting when the RNN accepts data. To be specific, an LSTM uses three types of restrictions:

>> Restrict when the RNN accepts input data

>> Restrict the elements stored in the RNN's state

>> Restrict when the RNN produces output data

Hochreiter and Schmidhuber called their new type of cell a *long short-term memory (LSTM) cell*, often shortened to *LSTM*. Because of its restrictions, an LSTM processes and stores only the data it needs to make predictions.

One major advantage of LSTMs is size. To process a sequence of data, an LSTM requires fewer nodes than a comparable RNN. Also, because an LSTM can block the storage of irrelevant data, its state can examine sequences with long-term dependencies.

To implement these restrictions, Hochreiter and Schmidhuber added three gates to the RNN cell structure: the input gate, forget gate, and the output gate. Figure 9-5 gives an idea of how these gates control the connectivity of an LSTM cell.

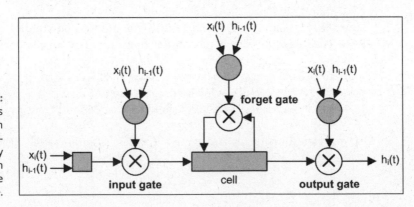

FIGURE 9-5: An LSTM reduces the size of an RNN by preventing unnecessary data from cluttering the RNN's state.

A BRIEF LITERARY DIGRESSION

In the 1887 novel, *A Study in Scarlet*, Dr. John Watson meets Sherlock Holmes for the first time. Despite Holmes's deductive capabilities, Watson is stunned to learn that the detective knows nothing about philosophy, literature, or astronomy. Holmes responds in the following way:

"I consider that a man's brain originally is like a little empty attic, and you have to stock it with such furniture as you choose. A fool takes in all the lumber of every sort that he comes across, so that the knowledge which might be useful to him gets crowded out, or at best is jumbled up with a lot of other things so that he has a difficulty in laying his hands upon it. Now the skillful workman is very careful indeed as to what he takes into his brain-attic. He will have nothing but the tools which may help him in doing his work. . .."

Each gate maintains its own weights and biases to determine when it should open and close. To be precise, the three gates operate by multiplying signals by the result of a sigmoid function (σ). For the input and output gates, the function determines how much of the signal should be allowed to pass. For the forget gate, the function determines whether the data should be stored in the cell's state (1) or discarded (0).

Denoting the state of the input gate as i_t, the state of the forget gate as f_t, and the state of the output gate as o_t, the following equations show how these gates work:

$$i_t = \sigma\left[w_i\left(x_i, h_{i-1}\right) + b_i\right]$$
$$f_t = \sigma\left[w_f\left(x_i, h_{i-1}\right) + b_f\right]$$
$$o_t = \sigma\left[w_o\left(x_i, h_{i-1}\right) + b_o\right]$$

Keep in mind that, inside of the gates, the underlying cell behaves like an RNN cell. That is, it relies on the tanh function (by default) to serve as its activation function.

Holmes' viewpoint closely resembles that of the inventors of the LSTM. While a regular RNN stores all the data it receives, an LSTM stores only the data it needs and discards everything else. This improved efficiency explains why applications based on LSTMs have better performance and flexibility than applications based on RNNs.

Creating LSTMs in code

In TensorFlow, the process of creating an LSTM is similar to that of creating a regular RNN: Create an instance of a cell class and form an RNN based on the cell. The second step requires the same static_rnn and dynamic_rnn functions discussed in the earlier section "Creating RNN cells."

The tf.nn.rnn_cell package provides a handful of classes that represent LSTM cells, and the fundamental classes are BasicLSTMCell, and LSTMCell. The first is simpler to use, but the second provides more customization options.

Setting the State

In a regular RNN, you can set the initial state with a matrix of size [batch_size, state_size]. But to initialize the state of an LSTM network, you need to provide a tuple containing two state matrices: one that identifies the cell state and one that identifies the hidden state.

To simplify initialization, the tf.nn.rnn_cell module provides a class named LSTMStateTuple, and its constructor accepts the two state matrices. Denoting the batch size as batch_sz and the state size as state_sz, the following code creates an LSTMStateTuple suitable for initializing the state of an LSTM network:

```
cstate = tf.placeholder(tf.float32, [batch_sz, state_sz])
hstate = tf.placeholder(tf.float32, [batch_sz, state_sz])
init = tf.nn.rnn_cell.LSTMStateTuple(cstate, hstate)
```

After creating the LSTMStateTuple, the application can assign it to the initial_state parameter in functions like static_rnn and dynamic_rnn.

The BasicLSTMCell class

From a developer's perspective, the BasicLSTMCell class is nearly identical to BasicRNNCell. Like the BasicRNNCell constructor, the BasicLSTMCell constructor accepts the number of units that should be generated per cell. The full constructor is given as follows:

```
BasicLSTMCell(num_units, forget_bias=1.0, state_is_tuple=True,
    activation=tf.nn.tanh, reuse=None)
```

The forget_bias parameter adds an initial bias to the input of the forget gate. This added bias prevents the cell from forgetting information at the start of training.

After you create a `BasicLSTMCell`, you can create an RNN based on LSTM cells by calling `static_rnn` or `dynamic_rnn`. As an example, the following code creates an LSTM network from a cell with seven units:

```
lstm_cell = BasicLSTMCell(7)
output, state = tf.nn.dynamic_rnn(lstm_cell,
        lstm_input, dtype=tf.float32)
```

By default, the LSTM's state contains two matrices in a tuple. Therefore, the state returned by `static_rnn` and `dynamic_rnn` is a tuple containing two matrices.

The LSTMCell class

LSTMs discard irrelevant data, so they have no way of measuring the time interval between input events. To add this capability, Felix Gers and Jürgen Schmidhuber proposed an improvement to the LSTM's structure in their 2000 paper, *Recurrent Nets that Time and Count*.

This modification involves adding special *peephole connections* between the cell's state and its gates. These connections enable the gates to take state data into account when controlling the flow of information.

You can enable peephole connections by creating `LSTMCells` instead of `Basic LSTMCells`. The `LSTMCell` constructor is given as

```
LSTMCell(num_units, use_peepholes=False, cell_clip=None, initializer=None,
    num_proj=None, proj_clip=None, num_unit_shards=None, num_proj_shards=None,
    forget_bias=1.0, state_is_tuple=True, activation=None, reuse=None)
```

The `cell_clip` parameter makes it possible to prevent exploding gradients from occurring. If you assign this parameter to a floating-point value, the function will limit the output of the cell's activation function to that value.

To reduce the dimensionality of input data, you can multiply input tensors by a matrix called the *projection matrix*. The `num_proj` parameter identifies the desired dimensionality of the projection's output. If you set `num_proj` to a value greater than 0, you can set `proj_clip` to a floating-point value that limits the projection's result to the range [`-proj_clip`, `proj_clip`].

Predicting text with LSTMs

The code in the ch9/lstm_lovecraft.py module performs the same text prediction as the code in the ch9/rnn_lovecraft.py module. The only difference is that it creates an RNN based on a BasicLSTMCell instead of a BasicRNNCell. It creates the RNN with the following code:

```
cell = tf.nn.rnn_cell.BasicLSTMCell(num_hidden)
outputs, _ = tf.nn.static_rnn(cell, [input_holder], dtype=tf.
    float32)
```

The rest of the code in ch9/lstm_lovecraft.py is identical to that in ch9/rnn_lovecraft.py. The application reads text from lovecraft.txt and feeds batches of six-element sequences into the RNN. It multiplies the RNN's outputs by a matrix of weights, adds biases to the products, and minimizes the loss with an AdagradOptimizer.

As expected, my experiments support the conclusion that LSTMs process sequences more efficiently than vanilla RNNs. On my system, RNNs require an average of 35.54 seconds to reach 95 percent accuracy and LSTMs require an average of 33.48 seconds.

Gated Recurrent Units (GRUs)

In 2014, Kyunghyun Cho, Bart van Merrienboer, Dzmitry Bahdanau, and Yoshua Bengio wrote a paper entitled *On the Properties of Neural Machine Translation: Encoder-Decoder Approaches*. In this paper, they proposed a new variant of RNN for examining variable-length sequences called a Gated Recursive Convolutional Network. Today, developers refer to their network structure as a Gated Recurrent Unit, or GRU.

Like LSTMs, GRUs use gates to control the flow of data to and from a cell. But the two cells have three important differences:

>> GRU cells have hidden state (h_t), but no cell state (C_t).

>> GRU cells have a reset gate instead of the input gate and an update gate instead of the forget gate.

>> GRU cells don't have any output gate mechanism.

The primary difference is that GRUs have two gates, called the reset gate and update gate, while LSTMs have three gates. The GRU's reset gate corresponds to the LSTM's input gate, and the GRU's update gate corresponds to the LSTM's forget gate. GRUs don't use a gate to restrict the cell's output. Figure 9-6 depicts a GRU cell and its gates.

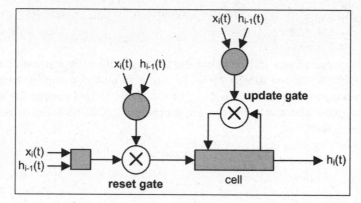

FIGURE 9-6: GRUs are similar to LSTMs, but they have two gates instead of three.

The GRU's lack of an output gate may seem like a superficial difference, but the simpler structure means that applications can train GRUs significantly faster than LSTMs.

Creating GRUs in code

The process of creating RNNs based on GRU cells is very similar to that of creating regular RNNs. The difference is that applications need to set the RNN's cell to an instance of the `tf.nn.rnn_cell.GRUCell` class. The class's constructor is given as follows:

```
GRUCell(num_units, activation=None, reuse=None,
    kernel_initializer=None, bias_initializer=None)
```

The third parameter is named `kernel_initializer`; it has no relationship with the image-filtering kernels discussed in Chapter 8. The `kernel_initializer` sets the cell's initial weights and `bias_initializer` sets its biases.

Predicting text with GRUs

The code in ch9/gru_lovecraft.py performs the same text prediction as the code in ch9/rnn_lovecraft.py and ch9/lstm_lovecraft.py. The only difference is that it creates an RNN using a GRUCell, as shown in the following code:

```
cell = tf.nn.rnn_cell.GRUCell(num_hidden)
outputs, _ = tf.nn.static_rnn(cell, [input_holder], dtype=tf.
    float32)
```

My experiments indicate that GRUs are significantly more efficient for training than LSTMs and vanilla RNNs. On my system, GRUs require an average of 29.17 seconds to reach 95 percent accuracy, while LSTMs require an average of 33.48 seconds and RNNs require an average of 35.54 seconds to reach 95 percent accuracy.

3

Simplifying and Accelerating TensorFlow

Chapter **10**

Accessing Data with Datasets and Iterators

When you start out in machine learning, your fondest wish is to have your application converge to a solution. But as you progress in the field, you become more and more concerned with performance. Performance is especially important when your training data occupies gigabytes or terabytes of memory.

This chapter and the following two chapters focus on ways to improve Tensor-Flow's performance — no more lengthy equations or geometric diagrams. Instead, I focus on capabilities that you can use to accelerate your applications. Two important capabilities are datasets and iterators, which make it easier to load and process input data.

Datasets

One effective method of improving an application's performance involves creating threads. Modern processors have multiple cores, and developers can take advantage of them by splitting an application's workload into threads. This multi-threading becomes particularly helpful when an application needs to load a great deal of data.

In the past, TensorFlow developers created threads by constructing instances of the QueueRunner class. But as of version 1.4, TensorFlow recommends using Datasets instead of QueueRunners. A Dataset is more than just a large chunk of data — it provides a high-performance pipeline for loading and processing data.

In general TensorFlow applications, the process of working with datasets consists of three steps:

1. **Create the dataset from data or a file.**

2. **Split the dataset into batches and preprocess the batches as needed.**

3. **Process the dataset's batches in a session.**

You can perform the first two steps by calling methods of the Dataset class. The following discussion explores these methods and shows how they can be used.

Creating datasets

In practice, a dataset is a container of training/testing data and its elements are the batches that an application uses to feed data to a session. Chapter 5 explains the topic of batching in detail.

You can create datasets from data, text files, or binary files. The following sections present these methods and explain how they can be performed in code.

Creating a dataset from data

You can create a dataset from data by calling one of the five Dataset methods listed in Table 10-1. All of these methods are static, so you'll need to call them through the tf.data.Dataset class.

The simplest of these methods is range, which returns a dataset containing values that make up a step-separated range of values. You can call this method with one, two, or three arguments:

>> range(a): Produces a range from 0 to a, not including a

>> range(a, b): Produces a range from a to b, not including b

>> range(a, b, c): Produces a range from a to b, not including b, in steps of c

TABLE 10-1   Functions That Create Datasets

Member	Description
range(*args)	Creates a dataset containing a range of values
from_tensors(tensors)	Creates a dataset that combines the input tensors into one element
from_tensor_slices(tensors)	Creates a dataset containing one element for each row of the input tensors
from_sparse_tensor_slices(sparse_tensor)	Creates a dataset containing one element for each row of the sparse tensor

from_generator(generator,
  output_types,
  output_shapes=None)
	Creates a dataset from the given generator

The following code demonstrates how you can use range in code:

```
ds1 = tf.data.Dataset.range(5)        # [1, 2, 3, 4]
ds2 = tf.data.Dataset.range(10, 13)   # [10, 11, 12]
ds3 = tf.data.Dataset.range(2, 8, 2)  # [2, 4, 6]
```

The from_tensors and from_tensor_slices are particularly useful, so it's important not to get them confused. from_tensors combines input tensors together and returns a dataset with one element. The following code demonstrates how from_tensors can be used:

```
t = tf.constant([[1, 2], [3, 4]])
ds = tf.data.Dataset.from_tensors(t)   # [[1, 2], [3, 4]]
```

In constrast, from_tensor_slices creates a separate element for each row of the argument. The following code demonstrates how from_tensor_slices can be used:

```
t = tf.constant([[1, 2], [3, 4]])
ds = tf.data.Dataset.from_tensor_slices(t)
# [1, 2], [3, 4]
```

This code creates an element from each row of the input tensor. Therefore, ds contains two elements that each contain two values. from_sparse_tensor_slices is similar to from_tensor_slices, but it returns a dataset containing one element for each row of a sparse tensor.

The `from_generator` method lets you create a dataset from values produced by a generator function. In Python, a *generator function* is a function that produces (or *yields*) a series of values. The process of using a generator consists of the following steps:

1. **In the generator function, use a `yield` statement to provide a value.**

2. **Obtain a generator object by invoking the function.**

   Proceed to either Step 3 or Step 4 depending on your version of Python.

3. **In Python 2.*x*, call the object's `next` method to invoke the generator function.**

4. **In Python 3.*x*, call the built-in `next` function with the generator object.**

For example, the following generator returns provides up to four integers:

```
def simple_gen():
    i = 0
    while i < 4:
        yield(i)
        i += 1
```

The following code obtains a generator object and calls `next` to access the generator's first three values:

```
simple_iter = simple_gen()
next(simple_iter)
next(simple_iter)
next(simple_iter)
```

The `from_generator` method creates a dataset containing an element for each value produced by a generator. An application must set the method's `generator` parameter to a generator function and the `output_types` parameter to a structure that identifies the type(s) of the generator's values.

For example, the following code creates a dataset from the `simple_gen` generator:

```
dset = tf.data.Dataset.from_generator(simple_gen, output_types=tf.int32)
```

The generator object returned by `simple_gen` produces four values. Therefore, `from_generator` returns a dataset containing four elements: one for each generated integer.

Creating a dataset from text

You can create a dataset containing the lines of text files by creating an instance of `TextLineDataset`, which is a subclass of `Dataset`. The class constructor is given as

```
TextLineDataset(filenames, compression_type=None, buffer_size=None)
```

To call this constructor, you need to assign `filenames` to a tensor containing one or more filenames. By default, the constructor assumes that the files contain uncompressed text. But if you set `compression_type` to `ZLIB` or `GZIP`, the constructor will decompress the archive before accessing its data.

The `TextLineDataset` will contain one string element for each line of the input files. For example, if `test1.txt` has three lines and `test2.txt` has four lines, the following code creates a dataset that contains seven strings:

```
ds = TextLineDataset(['test1.txt', 'test2.txt'])
```

After you read the strings into the dataset, you can loop through them using an `Iterator`. I explain what `Iterator`s are in the section "Iterators," later in the chapter.

Creating a dataset from binary files

In addition to text files, TensorFlow supports creating datasets from binary files if the files contain TFRecords. TFRecords are very useful when you need to access large amounts of data, but they're confusing and poorly documented. The overall process of storing TFRecord data to a file consists of three steps:

1. **Create a `tf.train.Example` that holds the data you want to store.**

2. **Store the `tf.train.Example` as a protocol buffer by calling its `SerializeToString` method.**

3. **Create a `tf.python_io.TFRecordWriter` and use it to write the protocol buffer to a TFRecord file.**

Like datasets, `Example`s store training and test data. Unlike datasets, they store their data in key-value pairs called *features*. Each feature is represented by a `tf.train.Feature`, and you can create an `Example` by calling its constructor with a `tf.train.Features` object that contains one or more `Features`. Working with these classes can be confusing, so I do my best to clarify:

>> In the `tf.train.Example` constructor, the `features` argument accepts a `tf.train.Features` instance.

» In the `tf.train.Features` constructor, the feature argument accepts a dict that associates names with `tf.train.Feature` instances.

» In the `tf.train.Feature` constructor, the `bytes_list` argument accepts a `tf.train.BytesList`, the `float_list` argument accepts a `tf.train.FloatList`, and the `int64_list` argument accepts a `tf.train.Int64List`.

The following code creates an `Example` made up of three features:

```
feat_a = tf.train.Feature(bytes_list = tf.train.BytesList(value=[ b'123' ]));
feat_b = tf.train.Feature(float_list = tf.train.FloatList(value=[ 1.0, 2.0,
         3.0 ]));
feat_c = tf.train.Feature(int64_list = tf.train.Int64List(value=[ 2, 3, 4 ]));
container = tf.train.Features(feature={'a' : feat_a, 'b' : feat_b, 'c' :
         feat_c})
example = tf.train.Example(features=container)
```

The constructors of the `BytesList`, `FloatList`, and `Int64List` classes all have a parameter named `value`. You can set a feature's data by assigning `value` to an array of the appropriate data type.

After you created an `Example`, you can call its `SerializeToString` method to store its data to a protocol buffer. Then you can write the buffer to a TFRecord file by accessing a `TFRecordWriter`. There are three points to know about this class:

» Its constructor accepts the name of the file to hold the TFRecord-formatted data and an optional compression method.

» Its `write` method accepts a protocol buffer and writes its data to the file given in the constructor.

» When you no longer need the writer, you can call its `close` method to close the file.

For example, if the name of your `Example` is `example`, the following code writes its data to the `example.tfrecord` file:

```
writer = tf.python_io.TFRecordWriter('example.tfrecord')
writer.write(example.SerializeToString())
writer.close()
```

After you've written one or more TFRecord files, you can load their data into a dataset by performing three operations:

1. Create a TFRecordDataset **containing the protocol buffers in the TFRecord files.**

2. **For each record, parse its features into a dict that associates feature names to tensors.**

3. **Assemble the tensors into a dataset.**

The TFRecordDataset constructor creates a dataset from one or more TFRecord files. The arguments for this constructor are the same as those for the TextLineDataset:

```
TFRecordDataset(filenames, compression_type=None, buffer_size=None)
```

After you call the constructor, the dataset will hold each protocol buffer as an element. Before you can access this data, you need to convert each of these elements into tensors. TensorFlow makes this possible by providing two functions:

» parseSingleExample(serialized, features, name=None, example_names=None): Converts an Example to a dict that matches feature keys to tensors

» parseExample(serialized, features, name=None, example_names=None): Converts one or more Examples to a dict that matches feature keys to tensors

For both functions, the serialized parameter accepts the protocol buffer or buffers containing Example data. The features parameter accepts a dict that matches a feature name to an instance of FixedLenFeature or VarLenFeature. The class to instantiate depends on the desired output tensor.

If you want to load a feature's data into a dense tensor, you should associate the feature's name with a FixedLenFeature. You can create a new FixedLenFeature by calling tf.FixedLenFeature:

```
tf.FixedLenFeature(shape, dtype, default_value=None)
```

The shape parameter sets the shape of the output tensor, and dtype sets the tensor's data type. To demonstrate how these parameters are used, the following code creates a TFRecordDataset from example.tfrecord. Then the dataset's map method calls a function that receives each element of the dataset. This function calls parseSingleExample to create a tensor with five elements from the feature named feat:

```
def parse_func(buff):
    features = {'feat': tf.FixedLenFeature(shape=[5], dtype=tf.float32)}
    tensor_dict = tf.parse_single_example(buff, features)
    return tensor_dict['feat']

dataset = tf.data.TFRecordDataset('example.tfrecord')
dataset = dataset.map(parse_func)
```

I discuss the map method later in the "Transforming Datasets" section. For now, it's important to know that map replaces dataset with a new Dataset that contains the return value of parse_func. In this code, parse_func returns a tensor containing the values of the feature named feat.

If a feature contains a significant number of zeros, you can load it into a sparse vector by associating the feature's name with a VarLenFeature. You can create a new VarLenFeature by calling tf.VarLenFeature:

```
tf.VarLenFeature(dtype)
```

I hope it's clear that the TFRecords API is unnecessarily complicated. I sincerely hope that a future version of TensorFlow will address this issue and simplify the usage of TFRecords.

Processing datasets

After you create a dataset, you can manipulate its elements by calling one of the many methods of the Dataset class. To present these methods, I split them into four categories:

>> Working with batches

>> Simple operations

>> Transformations

>> Creating Iterators

The following sections present the methods in the first three categories. I explore the topic of Iterators in the "Iterators" section, later in the chapter.

Working with batches

As discussed in Chapter 5, applications frequently divide datasets into batches. The Dataset class makes it easy to work with batches, and Table 10-2 lists two methods that perform batch-related operations.

TABLE 10-2   **Batch Operations**

Member	Description
batch(batch_size)	Split the dataset's content into batches
padded_batch(batch_size, padded_shapes, padding_values=None)	Split the dataset's content into batches and use padding to ensure that each batch has the desired shape

batch divides a dataset's values into batches of size batch_size. The following code divides the dataset into two batches of three elements each.

```
vals = tf.constant([1, 2, 3, 4, 5, 6], dtype=tf.int64)
ds1 = tf.data.Dataset.from_tensor_slices(vals)
ds2 = ds1.batch(3)   # contains [1, 2, 3], [4, 5, 6]
```

The padded_batch method pads each element (batch) of the dataset to the shape given by the padded_shapes parameter. Then the method combines the elements into one large element.

```
vals = tf.constant([[1., 2.], [3., 4.]])
ds1 = tf.data.Dataset.from_tensor_slices(vals)
ds2 = ds1.padded_batch(2, padded_shapes=[3]
            padding_values=1.)
# ds2 contains [[1., 2., 1.], [3., 4., 1.]]
```

This code creates batches of two elements each and pads each batch to a size of three. padded_batch sets the inserted values to 1.0 because of the method's padding_values parameter.

Simple operations

After dividing a dataset into batches, you can manipulate the batches by calling methods of the Dataset class. Table 10-3 lists nine methods that perform simple operations.

TABLE 10-3   **Simple Dataset Operations**

Member	Description
take(count)	Returns a dataset containing the first count elements
skip(count)	Returns a dataset that skips the first count elements
concatenate(dataset)	Appends the given dataset to the dataset
repeat(count=None)	Repeats the dataset count times
shuffle(buffer_size, seed=None)	Randomizes the order of a subset of the dataset's elements
shard(num_shards, index)	Returns a dataset with a subset of the dataset's elements
list_files(file_pattern)	Returns a dataset containing the names of the files that match the specified pattern
cache(filename='')	Caches elements of the dataset
prefetch(buffer_size)	Prefetches the given number of elements from the dataset

The first two methods, take and skip, are the simplest. They return datasets containing portions of other datasets.

```
ds1 = tf.data.Dataset.range(1, 8)    # [1 2 3 4 5 6 7]
ds2 = ds1.take(3)                    # [1 2 3]
ds3 = ds1.skip(3)                    # [4 5 6 7]
```

The concatenate method appends one dataset to another. repeat appends a dataset to itself.

```
ds1 = tf.data.Dataset.range(1, 3)    # [1 2]
ds2 = tf.data.Dataset.range(7, 10)   # [7 8 9]
ds3 = ds1.concatenate(ds2)           # [1 2 7 8 9]
ds4 = ds1.repeat(2)                  # [1 2 1 2]
```

shuffle creates a dataset by extracting and reordering elements of an existing dataset. The batch_size parameter identifies how many elements should be extracted.

```
ds1 = tf.data.Dataset.range(1, 8)    # [1 2 3 4 5 6 7]
ds2 = ds1.shuffle(4)                 # [2 3 6 4]
```

shard returns a dataset containing 1/num_shards of the elements in the original dataset. The index argument specifies the index of the subdataset to return.

To demonstrate this, the following code creates a dataset with eight elements (0...7) and calls shard to return a dataset that's one-fourth of the size.

```
dset = tf.data.Dataset.range(8)
dset_shard = dset.shard(4, 2)
```

As a result of this code, dset_shard will contain two elements instead of eight. The elements are [2, 6] because the subdataset contains the third value (index = 2) of every four values in the original. The list_files method creates a dataset from the names of the files on the developer's system. For example, if the working directory contains a.png and b.png, the following code creates a dataset containing only their names:

```
ds1 = tf.data.Dataset.list_files('./*.png')
            # ['a.png', 'b.png']
```

The cache method caches the dataset's elements so that you can retrieve them quickly. After you cache a dataset, you can launch an operation to retrieve its elements by calling prefetch. This method accepts a parameter that identifies the maximum number of elements to recover.

Transforming datasets

Table 10-4 lists four advanced routines for operating on datasets. These methods make it possible to perform sophisticated transformations of a dataset's elements.

TABLE 10-4   **Dataset Transformations**

Member	Description
filter(predicate)	Filters the dataset based on the predicate
map(map_func, num_threads=None, output_buffer_size=None)	Applies the function to the dataset's elements and provides a new element for each
flat_map(map_func)	Applies the function to the dataset's elements, produces a dataset for each, and concatenates the results
interleave(map_func, cycle_length, lock_length=1)	Applies the function to the dataset's elements, produces a dataset for each, and interleaves the results
zip(datasets)	Interleaves the datasets element-by-element

The first argument of filter, flat_map, and map is a function that receives each element of the dataset. If you can define your function in one line of code, you can set this argument to a *lambda*. A lambda definition consists of the lambda keyword, one or more arguments, a colon, and the return value. For example, the following lambda accepts two values and returns their sum:

```
lambda x, y: x + y
```

In the `filter` method, the function returns a Boolean that determines which elements should be kept in the dataset. In the following code, the dataset keeps only the elements whose sum exceeds 10.0:

```
vals = tf.constant([[2., 3.], [4., 5.], [6., 7.]])
ds1 = tf.data.Dataset.from_tensor_slices(vals)
ds1 = ds1.filter(lambda x: tf.reduce_sum(x) > 10.0)
# ds1 contains [6.0, 7.0]
```

In the `map` method, the function receives each element of the input dataset and produces an element to be inserted in the output dataset. In the following code, the lambda multiplies each element of the input dataset by 2 and inserts the resulting element into the output dataset.

```
vals = tf.constant([[2., 3.], [4., 5.], [6., 7.]])
ds1 = tf.data.Dataset.from_tensor_slices(vals)
ds2 = ds1.map(lambda x: x*2)
# ds2 contains [[4., 6.], [8., 10.], [12., 14.]]
```

`flat_map` is like `map`, but instead of returning an element of the output dataset, the function returns an entire dataset. `flat_map` concatenates the output datasets together and returns the flattened result.

```
vals = tf.constant([2, 3], dtype=tf.int64)
ds1 = tf.data.Dataset.from_tensor_slices(vals)
ds2 = ds1.flat_map(lambda x: tf.data.Dataset.range(x))
# ds2 contains [0, 1, 0, 1, 2]
```

As with `flat_map`, the function in `interleave` returns a dataset for each element of the input dataset. Unlike `flat_map`, it doesn't necessarily concatenate the resulting datasets. The `cycle_length` parameter identifies how many elements should be interleaved.

For example, if you set `cycle_length` to 2, the output dataset will contain the first elements of the first two datasets, then the next two elements of the first two datasets, and so on. The following code shows how `interleave` works.

```
vals = tf.constant([2, 3, 4], dtype=tf.int64)
ds1 = tf.data.Dataset.from_tensor_slices(vals)
```

```
ds2 = ds1.interleave(lambda x: tf.data.Dataset.range(x), cycle_length=3)
# ds2 contains [0, 0, 0, 1, 1, 1, 2, 2, 3]
```

This code provides three elements to the lambda and sets the `cycle_length` to 3. As a result, the output dataset contains the first three elements of the three datasets, then the next three elements of the three datasets, and so on.

The `zip` method also interleaves multiple datasets, but it doesn't accept a function or `cycle_length` parameter. This method always takes the first value from the first element, then the first value from the second element, and proceeds onward. The following code demonstrates how `zip` can be used.

```
ds1 = tf.data.Dataset.range(0, 3)
ds2 = tf.data.Dataset.range(10, 13)
ds3 = tf.data.Dataset.range(20, 23)
ds4 = tf.data.Dataset.zip((ds1, ds2, ds3))
# ds4 contains (0, 10, 20), (1, 11, 21), (2, 12, 22)
```

The `datasets` parameter of `zip` accepts the input datasets in a nested structure. An application can set this equal to a tuple, but not a list.

Iterators

An `Iterator` lets you iterate through the elements of one or more `Datasets`. TensorFlow provides four types of iterators:

>> **One-shot:** Iterates once through the dataset, can't be parameterized

>> **Initializable:** Requires special initialization, can be parameterized

>> **Reinitializable:** Can be associated with multiple datasets, must be initialized before each iteration

>> **Feedable:** Can be associated with multiple datasets, doesn't need to be initialized before each iteration

One-shot iterators

One-shot iterators are the simplest of the four, but they can iterate only once through a dataset's elements. An application can create a one-shot iterator for a dataset by calling a dataset's `make_one_shot_iterator` method.

After you create an iterator, you can access the next available element by calling get_next. This method resembles the next method of a regular Python iterator. To demonstrate how get_next is used, the following code creates a dataset with one element and calls get_next to print the element's value:

```
# Create the dataset and iterator
tensor = tf.constant([1, 2, 3])
dset = tf.data.Dataset.from_tensors(tensor)
iterator = dset.make_one_shot_iterator()

# Access the next element
next_elem = iterator.get_next()

# Print the element's value
with tf.Session() as sess:
    print('Element: ', sess.run(next_elem))

# Output: 'Element: [1 2 3]'
```

When a session evaluates a tensor returned by get_next, the tensor takes the value of the dataset's next element. To demonstrate, the following code creates a dataset with five elements and repeatedly evaluates the tensor returned by get_next:

```
# Create the dataset and iterator
dset = tf.data.Dataset.range(5)
iterator = dset.make_one_shot_iterator()

# Access the next element
next_elem = iterator.get_next()

# Print the values of the elements
with tf.Session() as sess:
    for i in range(5):
        print('Element: ', sess.run(next_elem))
```

In this code, Dataset.range creates a dataset with five elements. The iterator loops through the dataset, and the session prints the value of each. The resulting output is as follows:

```
Element: 0
Element: 1
Element: 2
Element: 3
Element: 4
```

A one-shot iterator can iterate through a dataset only once. If an application attempts to execute a second loop through the dataset, TensorFlow will raise an `OutOfRangeError: End of sequence`.

Initializable iterators

In addition to creating datasets from constant tensors, you can create datasets from placeholders. These kind of datasets are called *parameterized datasets*, and they receive their content when the application executes a session that feeds data to the placeholder.

One-shot iterators can't iterate through parameterized datasets, but initializable iterators can. To create an initializable iterator and iterate through a parameterized dataset, you need to perform six steps:

1. **Create a dataset from a placeholder by calling** `from_tensors` **or** `from_tensor_slices`.

2. **Create an iterator for the dataset by calling the dataset's** `make_initializable_iterator` **method.**

3. **Obtain the next element by calling the iterator's** `get_next` **method.**

4. **Initialize the iterator by running its initializer property in a session.**

5. **Associate the iterator's placeholder with data by setting the** `feed_dict` **parameter in the session's run method.**

6. **Access the iterators elements in a session by evaluating the result of the** `get_next` **method.**

This process may seem complicated, but parameterized datasets can be very helpful. To demonstrate how these datasets can be used, the following code creates a dataset from a placeholder that holds four floating-point values. Then it accesses the dataset using an initializable iterator:

```
# Create a placeholder and parameterized dataset
holder = tf.placeholder(tf.float32, shape=[4])
dset = tf.data.Dataset.from_tensor_slices(holder)

# Create the iterator and access its first element
iter = dset.make_initializable_iterator()
next_elem = iter.get_next()

with tf.Session() as sess:
```

```
    # Initialize the iterator
    sess.run(iter.initializer,
            feed_dict={holder: [0., 1., 2., 3.]})
    for _ in range(4):
        print('Element: ', sess.run(next_elem))
```

Looking at this code, it's important to see that the first call to sess.run initializes the iterator and feeds values to the parameterized dataset through the placeholder. After this initialization, the application can access the iterator's values through the value returned by get_next.

Reinitializable iterators

If you need to associate an iterator with multiple datasets, one-shot iterators and initializable iterators won't be sufficient. Instead, the application can create a *reinitializable iterator* by calling Iterator.from_structure:

```
Iterator.from_structure(output_types, output_shapes=None, shared_name=None)
```

A reinitializable iterator doesn't need to know about specific datasets in advance, but it needs to know about the types and shapes of their elements. An application can set output_types and output_shapes by accessing the identically named properties of a Dataset instance.

After creating the reinitializable iterator, you can associate it with multiple different datasets by creating a separate initializer for each dataset. The following code creates one iterator with two initializers. Then it uses the iterator to loop through two datasets:

```
# Create datasets with similar shapes
ds1 = tf.data.Dataset.range(8)
ds2 = tf.data.Dataset.range(3)

# Create iterator and get first element
iterator = tf.data.Iterator.from_structure(
    ds1.output_types, ds1.output_shapes)
next_elem = iterator.get_next()

# Create an initializer for each dataset
ds1_init = iterator.make_initializer(ds1)
ds2_init = iterator.make_initializer(ds2)

# Run both initializers in a session
with tf.Session() as sess:
```

```
# Associate the iterator with the first dataset
sess.run(ds1_init)
for _ in range(8):
    print('Element from ds1: ', sess.run(next_elem))

# Associate the iterator with the second dataset
sess.run(ds2_init)
for _ in range(3):
    print('Element from ds2: ', sess.run(next_elem))
```

This code calls `from_structure` with `ds1`'s shape and type. Then it associates the iterator with `ds1` and `ds2`. `ds1` and `ds2` don't have the same shape, but they're compatible because their shapes are similar.

Feedable iterators

If you'd like to switch between iterators without initializing from the start of the dataset, you can create a feedable iterator. The process of using a feedable iterator consists of six steps:

1. **Create a placeholder to contain a string.**

2. **Call `Iterator.from_string_handle` with the placeholder.**

3. **Create multiple iterators to iterate through datasets.**

4. **For each iterator, obtain a unique string tensor by calling `string_handle`.**

5. **Evaluate each unique string tensor in a session to obtain unique strings for the iterators.**

6. **To switch to a specific iterator, evaluate the result of `get_next` in a session and provide the iterator's string using the `feed_dict` parameter of `sess.run`.**

The following code demonstrates this process. It creates two datasets, a one-shot iterator for each dataset, and a feedable iterator that makes it possible to switch between the iterators.

```
# Create datasets
ds1 = tf.data.Dataset.range(8)
ds2 = tf.data.Dataset.range(10, 13)

# Create an iterator for each dataset
ds1_iterator = ds1.make_one_shot_iterator()
ds2_iterator = ds2.make_one_shot_iterator()
```

```
# Create a string placeholder and a feedable iterator
holder = tf.placeholder(tf.string, shape=[])
iterator = tf.data.Iterator.from_string_handle(
    holder, ds1.output_types, ds1.output_shapes)
next_element = iterator.get_next()

# Obtain a string tensor for each iterator
ds1_handle = ds1_iterator.string_handle()
ds2_handle = ds2_iterator.string_handle()

# Create the session
with tf.Session() as sess:

    # Obtain a string from each iterator
    ds1_string = sess.run(ds1_handle)
    ds2_string = sess.run(ds2_handle)

    # Iterate through the first four elements of ds1
    for _ in range(4):
        print('Element from ds1: ', sess.run(next_element,
            feed_dict={holder: ds1_string}))

    # Iterate through ds2
    for _ in range(3):
        print('Element from ds2: ', sess.run(next_element,
            feed_dict={holder: ds2_string}))

    # Iterate through the last four elements of ds1
    for _ in range(4):
        print('Element from ds1: ', sess.run(next_element,
            feed_dict={holder: ds1_string}))
```

This code prints the first four elements of ds1, the elements of ds2, and the last four elements of ds1. Because the iterator is feedable, the application doesn't need to reinitialize the ds1 iterator before the second iteration.

Putting Theory into Practice

The code in ch10/dataset.py demonstrates how you can create and process datasets. The module starts by creating an Example, writing the Example's data to a TFRecord file, and loading the file's data into a TFRecordDataset. Then it creates two more datasets, processes them using Dataset methods, and iterates through their elements. Listing 10-1 presents the code.

LISTING 10-1: **Creating and Processing Datasets**

```python
# Generator function
def generator():
    x = 20
    while x < 28:
        yield x
        x += 1


# Create an example containing floats
int_list = tf.train.Int64List(value=[0, 1, 2, 3])
feat = tf.train.Feature(int64_list=int_list)
container = tf.train.Features(feature={'feat' : feat})
example = tf.train.Example(features=container)


# Write the example to a GZIP file
opts = tf.python_io.TFRecordOptions(tf.python_io.TFRecordCompressionType.GZIP)
writer = tf.python_io.TFRecordWriter('ex.tfrecord', opts)
writer.write(example.SerializeToString())
writer.close()


# Function to parse TFRecords
def parse_func(buff):
    features = {'feat': tf.FixedLenFeature(shape=[4], dtype=tf.int64)}
    tensor_dict = tf.parse_single_example(buff, features)
    return tensor_dict['feat']


# Create a dataset from TFRecords
dset1 = tf.data.TFRecordDataset('ex.tfrecord', 'GZIP')
dset1 = dset1.map(parse_func)
iter1 = dset1.make_one_shot_iterator()
next1 = iter1.get_next()


# Create a parameterized dataset and reinitializable iterator
holder = tf.placeholder(tf.int64, shape=[2])
dset2 = tf.data.Dataset.from_tensor_slices(holder)
dset2 = dset2.concatenate(tf.data.Dataset.range(12, 14))


# Create the third dataset
dset3 = tf.data.Dataset.from_generator(generator, output_types=tf.int64)
dset3 = dset3.filter(lambda x: x < 24)


# Create a reinitializable iterator for the 2nd, 3rd datasets
iter2 = tf.data.Iterator.from_structure(
    dset2.output_types, dset2.output_shapes)
next2 = iter2.get_next()
```

(continued)

LISTING 10-1:   *(continued)*

```
# Create initializers for the 2nd, 3rd datasets
dset2_init = iter2.make_initializer(dset2)
dset3_init = iter2.make_initializer(dset3)

# Print the content of each dataset
with tf.Session() as sess:

    # Print the content of the first dataset
    print('Element from dset1: ', sess.run(next1))

    # Print the content of the second dataset
    sess.run(dset2_init, feed_dict={holder: [10, 11]})
    for _ in range(4):
        print('Element from dset2: ', sess.run(next2))

    # Print the content of the third dataset
    sess.run(dset3_init)
    for _ in range(4):
        print('Element from dset3: ', sess.run(next2))
```

This module creates, manipulates, and iterates through three datasets:

>> The first dataset, dset1, receives values stored in a TFRecord file. It has a single element with four values: 0, 1, 2, 3.

>> The second dataset, dset2, is parametric and receives values through a placeholder when the session executes. It has four elements with one value each: 10, 11, 12, 13.

>> The third dataset, dset3, receives eight values (20 through 27) from a generator function. The filter method removes every element with a value greater than 24, leaving it with four single-valued elements: 20, 21, 22, 23.

For the first dataset, the module writes a serialized Example to a file named ex.tfrecord. The module compresses the file's content using the gzip algorithm, and the following code shows how to configure the use of GZIP compression:

```
opts = tf.python_io.TFRecordOptions (tf.python_io.
         TFRecordCompressionType.GZIP)
writer = tf.python_io.TFRecordWriter('ex.tfrecord', opts)
```

After assembling the three datasets, the module creates two iterators. The first iterator is a one-shot iterator that displays the values of dset1 as the session runs.

The second iterator is a reinitializable iterator that displays the values in dset2 and dset3. The module creates two initializers for the reinitializable iterator. Within the session, the module runs both initializers and uses them to iterate through the values in dset2 and dset3.

Bizarro Datasets

In Chapter 6, I explain how to create a Dataset containing MNIST's handwriting samples by calling the read_data_sets method of the tf.contrib.learn. python.learn.datasets.mnist package. As strange as it may seem, that Dataset has nothing to do with the Dataset class discussed in this chapter. The tf.contrib.learn.python.learn.datasets package defines its own Dataset structure with the following code:

```
Dataset = collections.namedtuple('Dataset', ['data', 'target'])
```

I call this Dataset the *bizarro dataset* because it reminds me of Bizarro, Superman's ugly, less intelligent mirror-image. This Dataset doesn't have subclasses or interesting processing methods. It's just a named tuple with two elements: data contains data points, and target contains labels for the data points. For example, if an estimator's job is to classify points in space into categories, the Dataset will store the points' coordinates in its data element and the category IDs in its target element.

It irks me that TensorFlow provides two Dataset structures, but I have to admit that the functions of the tf.contrib.learn.python.learn.datasets package make it easy to load and access data. This simplicity explains why so many of TensorFlow's example applications rely on these functions. Table 10-5 lists five functions that create bizarro datasets and provides a description of each.

To explain these methods, I split them into two categories. Functions in the first category load data from comma-separated value (CSV) files. Functions in the second category load data from pre-existing machine learning datasets: the Iris dataset and the Boston dataset.

TABLE 10-5 **Creating Bizarro Datasets**

Member	Description
`load_csv_with_header(filename, target_dtype, features_dtype, target_column=-1)`	Loads a dataset from a CSV file with a header row
`load_csv_without_header(filename, target_dtype, features_dtype, target_column=-1)`	Loads a dataset from a CSV file without a header row
`shrink_csv(filename, ratio)`	Loads a minified dataset from the CSV file
`load_iris(data_path=None)`	Loads the Iris flower dataset from the training/test CSV files
`load_boston(data_path=None)`	Loads a dataset of Boston housing prices from the training/test CSV files

Loading data from CSV files

Many applications import and export data using comma-separated value (CSV) files. In a CSV file, each line provides a single record composed of values separated by commas. This format isn't particularly efficient, but humans and computers can read CSV files without difficulty.

The first three functions in the table load datasets from CSV files. `load_csv_with_header` loads a dataset from a CSV file containing a header, and `load_csv_without_header` loads a dataset from a CSV file without a header.

The `ratio` parameter of `shrink_csv` determines which lines of the CSV file should be stored in the dataset. If an application sets `ratio` to N, `shrink_csv` will store every Nth line to the dataset. By changing `ratio`, an application can select different assortments of CSV records for the dataset.

These functions will not create datasets from general CSV files. They expect CSV files to be formatted in a specific way:

>> If present, the file's header should start with the number of samples (the number of lines containing records) and the number of features (the number of fields per line).

>> Each data line should end with the desired category of the corresponding data point.

For example, the following text presents the first five lines of the CSV file containing training data for the Iris dataset:

```
30,4,setosa,versicolor,virginica
5.9,3.0,4.2,1.5,1
6.9,3.1,5.4,2.1,2
5.1,3.3,1.7,0.5,0
6.0,3.4,4.5,1.6,1
```

According to the header, this file provides 30 records, and each record has four fields. The last value in each line identifies the category, so the first data point belongs to Category 1.

In a regular CSV file, the header provides a name for each field in a record. But in this example, the header has three names, and each record has four fields preceding the category. As it turns out, the header names identify category names: `setosa` identifies Category 0, `versicolor` identifies Category 1, and `virginica` identifies Category 2.

Loading the Iris and Boston datasets

The TensorFlow website provides two popular datasets that make it easy to train and test machine learning applications. The first dataset, called the Iris dataset, associates physical traits of a flower with one of three types of irises. The second dataset, called the Boston dataset, associates characteristics of Boston properties with house prices.

For each dataset, TensorFlow provides two CSV files: one containing training data and one containing test data. For the Iris dataset, you can download the file containing training data from `http://download.tensorflow.org/data/iris_training.csv` and the test data from `http://download.tensorflow.org/data/iris_test.csv`.

After you download the files to your system, you can create a dataset by calling `load_iris` with the path of one of the Iris files. This function returns a `Dataset` whose `data` collection contains floating-point values (flower traits) and whose `target` collection contains integers (iris categories).

The Boston dataset identifies a number of statistics (from 1978) related to houses in the Boston area, including the per capita crime rate, the pupil-teacher ratio, and the average number of rooms in each house. You can download the Boston training data from `https://github.com/tensorflow/tensorflow/blob/master/tensorflow/examples/tutorials/input_fn/boston_train.csv` and the test data from `https://github.com/tensorflow/tensorflow/blob/master/tensorflow/examples/tutorials/input_fn/boston_test.csv`.

Like the MNIST dataset, the Iris and Boston datasets make it straightforward to test new machine learning algorithms. The next chapter explains how to test estimators using the Iris and Boston datasets.

Chapter **11**

Using Threads, Devices, and Clusters

feel the need ... the need for speed! If you've ever said this about machine learning, then this chapter is for you. In my experience, you can accelerate a TensorFlow application using four methods:

» Generate multiple threads of execution

» Access high-performance devices like graphics processor units (GPUs)

» Execute an application on a cluster of networked devices

» Deploy an application to the cloud

This chapter discusses the first three options and then demonstrates how to execute a TensorFlow application in a cluster. Chapter 13 explains how to run TensorFlow in the cloud.

Executing with Multiple Threads

A *thread* is a sequence of operations capable of executing independently from other threads. In a TensorFlow application, you can take advantage of threads in two main ways:

>> **Perform time-consuming operations, such as the loading and storing of data, in separate threads.** This approach lets your processing thread continue its work without interruption.

>> **Run a session with multiple threads.** In theory, this method will reduce the amount of time needed to process the session's operations.

For the first point, developers used to create QueueRunners, which store operations to be executed in separate threads. But as of version 1.4, TensorFlow's documentation recommends using datasets instead, which is why Chapter 10 discusses datasets and iterators instead of threads, queue runners, and coordinators.

To process a dataset in a multithreaded manner, you can set the num_parallel_calls argument of the Dataset's map method. For example, if you set this argument to 4, TensorFlow will perform the map operation with four threads. Chapter 10 discusses the Dataset class and its map method in glorious detail.

For the second point, you can execute a session with multiple threads by setting the right configuration parameters. You can set these parameters when you create a session or when you run the session.

Configuring a new session

All of the example code in Chapters 1 through 10 has called tf.Session without any arguments. But you can configure a session by setting the config parameter of tf.Session to a ConfigProto protocol buffer. The fields of this buffer determine the session's behavior, and Table 11-1 lists each of them.

This section focuses on the options that configure a session's threads. By default, a session executes one thread for each core on the target processor. If you run TensorFlow on an Intel Core i5 CPU, your session will execute with a maximum of four threads because the CPU has four cores.

It's important to see the difference between the intra_op_parallelism_threads and inter_op_parallelism_threads options. Many TensorFlow operations, such as matrix multiplication, can be accelerated using multiple threads. The intra_op_parallelism_threads option determines how many threads should be generated to execute a *single* operation. In contrast, if a graph has operations that can run in parallel, the `inter_op_parallelism_threads` option determines how many threads can be generated to execute them.

TABLE 11-1 **ConfigProto Fields**

Field	Type	Description
device_count	map<string, int32>	Identifies the number of devices of each type that can be accessed by the session
intra_op_parallelism_threads	int32	Uses multiple threads to perform a single operation
inter_op_parallelism_threads	int32	Uses multiple threads to perform separate operations
session_inter_op_thread_pool	ThreadPoolOptionProto	Configures session thread pools
placement_period	int32	Determines how often to assign nodes to devices
device_filters	string	Prevents named devices from being accessed by a session
gpu_options	GPUOptions	Configures any GPUs accessed by the session
allow_soft_placement	bool	Determines how operations are assigned to CPUs and GPUs
graph_options	GraphOptions	Configures options for the session's graph(s)
operation_timeout_in_ms	int64	Configures global timeout for the session's blocking operations
rpc_options	RPCOptions	Configures for the session's distributed runtime
cluster_def	ClusterDef	Lists workers to use in this session

To demonstrate how threads can be configured, the following code creates a `ConfigProto` that uses a maximum of six threads for single operations and a maximum of eight threads for parallel operations. Then it uses the `ConfigProto` to create a session:

```
conf = tf.ConfigProto(intra_op_parallelism_threads=6, inter_op_
        parallelism_threads=8)
with tf.Session(config=conf) as sess:
    ...
```

By default, a session will access threads from a global thread pool instead of creating threads of its own. You can change this behavior with the use_per_session_threads option. If you set this option to True, the session will create its own threads.

If you'd like a session to execute background tasks in addition to the main computation, you can configure it by setting session_inter_op_thread_pool to one or more ThreadPoolOptionProto buffers. Each ThreadPoolOptionProto identifies a separate pool of threads. This protocol buffer has two fields:

>> num_threads: The number of threads in the thread pool

>> global_name: A string identifier for the thread pool

When you want a session to execute with threads from a specific pool, you can identify the thread pool in the RunOptions accepted by the run method. The next section discusses the RunOptions buffer in full.

Configuring a running session

Just as you can set the config parameter of tf.Session to a ConfigProto, you can set the options parameter of a session's run method to a RunOptions. The fields of a RunOptions determine how the session will execute, and Table 11-2 lists these fields.

TABLE 11-2 **RunOptions Fields**

Field	Type	Description
trace_level	TraceLevel	Determines the type of tracing to be performed
timeout_in_ms	int64	Time to wait for the session operation to complete
inter_op_thread_pool	int32	Identifies the pool of threads to use for the operation
output_partition_graphs	bool	Identifies whether the session's partition graph(s) should be provided in the metadata
debug_options	DebugOptions	Sets configuration options for debugging the session operation

If you configure a Session to use multiple thread pools, you can tell the session to execute threads from a particular pool by setting the inter_op_thread_pool option in RunOptions. For example, if you set this option to 1, the session will execute threads in the second thread pool.

Configuring Devices

Modern processors can execute special instructions that perform math operations at high speed. For example, a special multiply instruction can multiply four pairs of values in the same time that a regular instruction can multiply a single pair of values. These special instructions operate on multiple values at once, and for this reason, they're called SIMD (single-instruction, multiple-data) instructions.

Unfortunately, when you install TensorFlow with a utility like pip, you get the basic, boring installation. This installation runs on new and old computers, but it won't take advantage of SIMD instructions, and it won't execute operations on a graphics processor unit (GPU), even if you've installed a compliant graphics card.

If you want TensorFlow to make the best use of your system's capabilities, you need to build TensorFlow specifically for your system.

Building TensorFlow from source

It takes time and effort to build TensorFlow from its source code, but if you execute a lot of machine learning applications, you'll save time in the long run. This section explains how to build TensorFlow for Windows, macOS, and Linux systems. But it's important to understand three topics: obtaining the TensorFlow source code, the Bazel build system, and GPU acceleration.

Downloading the TensorFlow source code

TensorFlow is an open-source project, and you can access the source code at https://github.com/tensorflow/tensorflow. If you know how to use git, you can clone the repository with the following command:

```
git clone https://github.com/tensorflow/tensorflow.git
```

If you don't know how to use git, click the green button entitled Clone or download. Then select the Download ZIP option to download a zip file containing the TensorFlow source code. Decompress the zip file when the download is complete.

Bazel and Java

Bazel is a Google tool that automates the process of building software. It operates by executing operations defined in a file named BUILD. The instructions in this file, called *rules,* are written in Skylark, a subset of Python.

If you look through the TensorFlow file hierarchy, you'll see a number of BUILD files and *.BUILD files. If you open the BUILD file in the tensorflow directory, you'll find a number of configuration settings, such as the following:

```
config_setting(
    name = "linux_x86_64",
    values = {"cpu": "k8"},
    visibility = ["//visibility:public"],
)
```

Each config_setting block identifies a supported platform for building TensorFlow.

Before you can install Bazel, you need to install Java on your system. Specifically, you need to install version 8.*x* of the Java Development Kit (JDK). If you don't have this version, you can download the installer for Windows and macOS at www. oracle.com/technetwork/java/javase/downloads/index.html.

If you're running a Debian-based system like Ubuntu, you can install the OpenJDK 8.*x* with the following command:

```
sudo apt-get install openjdk-8-jdk
```

After you install JDK 8.*x*, you're ready to install Bazel. The instructions for installing Bazel depend on your operating system.

Graphics Processor Unit (GPU) acceleration

While CPUs are designed for secure, general-purpose computing, GPUs are designed for high-speed graphical rendering, which involves a lot of math. For many machine learning applications, you can dramatically improve performance by running operations on a GPU instead of a CPU.

The two main languages for general-purpose GPU (GPGPU) development are OpenCL and CUDA. OpenCL is supported by multiple vendors and can run on many different types of devices, including CPUs, GPUs, and FPGAs. But TensorFlow supports OpenCL only on systems that have ComputeCpp installed. You can download ComputeCpp from www.codeplay.com/products/computesuite/computecpp.

The second GPGPU language, CUDA, runs only on Nvidia's GPUs. To install CUDA, visit https://developer.nvidia.com/cuda-downloads and click the buttons that identify your operating system, architecture, and OS version. Then download and launch the installer, which will walk you through the installation process.

Preparing the TensorFlow build on Windows

Building TensorFlow on Windows is hard because you need to set up a UNIX-like environment that supports Bash scripting, Python, and the GNU build tools, such as gcc and g++. To create this environment, most developers use Cygwin or MSYS2 (Minimal System 2). In this section, I explain how to build TensorFlow on Windows using MSYS2.

To install MSYS2, visit www.msys2.org and select the 32-bit (i686) or 64-bit (x86_64) executable. When the download is complete, launch the executable and proceed through the installation instructions.

Assuming that you chose the default options for 64-bit Windows, MSYS2 will place all of its files in a new directory named C:\msys64. Two folders are particularly important:

>> C:\msys64\mingw64\bin contains the utilities provided by MinGW (Minimalist GNU for Windows). When you install MSYS2, this folder will be empty.

>> C:\msys64\home\<name> is your home directory. When you launch MSYS2, it will be your initial directory.

To install TensorFlow, you need to be able to access build tools, such as gcc, g++, and ld, in the GNU toolchain. You can obtain these tools by downloading MinGW packages into the MSYS2 environment. The MSYS2 installer is called pacman, and you can install the necessary MinGW packages by launching MSYS2 and entering the following command:

```
pacman -S --needed mingw-w64-x86_64-python3-pip base-devel
        mingw-w64-x86_64-toolchain
```

This command adds a number of files and executables to the C:\msys64\mingw64\bin directory. To tell MSYS2 how to find these executables, you need to add this directory to your system's PATH variable.

If you run python --version on the MSYS2 command line, it may tell you that you're using Python 2.x. This version is a problem because TensorFlow on Windows requires Python 3.5. To fix this issue, I recommend four steps:

1. Open the C:\msys64\mingw64\bin **directory and rename** python.exe **to** old_python.exe.

2. In the same directory, copy python3.5.exe **and rename the copy** python.exe.

3. **In the same directory, copy** `pip3.exe` **and rename the copy** `pip.exe`.

4. **In the same directory, copy** `pip3-script.py` **and rename the copy**
   `pip-script.py`.

To verify that everything's working, run `python --version` in MSYS2 and make sure that the default Python version is 3.*x*. Then install TensorFlow's Python dependencies with the following command:

```
pip install six numpy wheel
```

Next, you need to install the Bazel tool. This process also requires four steps:

1. **If you've haven't done so already, install Java Development Kit (JDK) 8 for your system.**

   You can download the installer from www.oracle.com/technetwork/java/javase/downloads/index.html.

2. **Visit** `http://github.com/bazelbuild/bazel/releases` **and click the number of the latest release.**

3. **Scroll to the bottom of the page and find the Windows executable suitable for your system.**

4. **Download the executable, rename it to** `bazel.exe,` **and place it in the** `C:\msys64\mingw64\bin` **directory.**

After you install Bazel, copy the TensorFlow source code directory to the MSYS2 home directory (`C:\msys64\home\Part`). Then, inside the MSYS2 environment, change to the `tensorflow` directory. Now you're ready to build!

Preparing the TensorFlow build on macOS

Before you can build TensorFlow on a macOS system, you need to install Bazel and TensorFlow's dependencies. If you've already installed the Java JDK 8.*x*, then you can install Bazel using Homebrew.

You probably already have Homebrew installed on your system, but if you don't, you can install it with the following command:

```
/usr/bin/ruby -e "$(curl -fsSL https://raw.githubusercontent.
        com/Homebrew/install/master/install)"
```

With Homebrew installed, you can install Bazel with the following command:

```
brew install bazel
```

Before you can install TensorFlow, you need to install three of its dependencies: NumPy, six, and wheel. The following command installs all three:

```
sudo pip install six numpy wheel
```

If you'd like TensorFlow to access your system's GPU, you'll need to install GNU's core utilities. You can install them using Homebrew:

```
brew install coreutils
```

When you're done, you'll be all set to start configuring and building TensorFlow.

Preparing the TensorFlow build on Linux (Ubuntu)

Of the many Linux distributions available, TensorFlow supports only Ubuntu, specifically versions 14.04 and higher. If you've installed Python and Java JDK 8.*x*, installing TensorFlow on Ubuntu is easy.

The first step is to install the Bazel build tool, and you can add Bazel's distribution URI as a package source with the following commands:

```
echo "deb [arch=amd64] http://storage.googleapis.com/bazel-apt
        stable jdk1.8" | sudo tee /etc/apt/sources.list.d/
        bazel.list

curl https://bazel.build/bazel-release.pub.gpg | sudo apt-
        key add -
```

Afterward, you can install Bazel with the following command:

```
sudo apt-get update && sudo apt-get install bazel
```

Before you build TensorFlow, you need to install four dependency packages: NumPy, Python-Dev, pip, and wheel. If you're using Python 2.*x*, you can install these dependencies with the following command:

```
sudo apt-get install python-numpy python-dev python-pip python-wheel
```

If you're using Python 3.*x*, you can install TensorFlow's dependencies with the following command:

```
sudo apt-get install python3-numpy python3-dev python3-pip python3-wheel
```

If this installation completes successfully, you're ready to start building TensorFlow.

Building TensorFlow

After you have the TensorFlow source code downloaded to your system and have installed Bazel and TensorFlow's dependencies, you're ready to start building TensorFlow. To get started, change to the directory containing the source code and enter the following command:

```
./configure
```

This command executes the configure script, which asks a series of questions that configure the features of the TensorFlow package. In the following list, I cover the questions that I've encountered when installing on Linux. Each question ends with a default response in square brackets. You can select the default response by pressing Enter.

» **Python location:** The directory containing the Python interpreter

» **Python library path:** The directory containing Python libraries

» **jemalloc support:** Whether TensorFlow should allocate memory with the improved jemalloc function instead of malloc. I recommend choosing Yes (Y).

» **Google Cloud Platform support:** Whether TensorFlow should provide support for Google's cloud computingoffering, the Google Cloud Platform (GCP). Chapter 14 explains how to run TensorFlow on the GCP.

» **Hadoop File System support:** Whether TensorFlow should support the Hadoop File System

» **Amazon S3 File System support:** Whether TensorFlow should provide support for Amazon's distributed S3 file system

» **XLA JIT support:** Whether TensorFlow should use the experimental XLA (Accelerated Linear Algebra) compiler to accelerate math operations

» **GDR support:** Whether TensorFlow should enable CUDA's high-speed memory access, GPUDirect RDMA

» **VERBS support:** Whether TensorFlow should enable remote direct memory access (RDMA) through the VERBS package

» **OpenCL support:** Whether TensorFlow should enable GPU computing with OpenCL

» **CUDA support:** Whether TensorFlow should enable GPU computing with CUDA

» **MPI support:** Whether TensorFlow should enable cluster computing with the Message Passing Interface (MPI)

» **Optimization flags:** The optimization flags to use when building TensorFlow

The last option is particularly important. By default, the build process will include the flag `–march=native`. This flag tells the compiler to examine the target CPU and make sure that TensorFlow will use the most advanced capabilities supported by the processor. In general, I recommend staying with the default optimization option.

After you complete the questionnaire, the script stores your configuration choices in a file named `.tf_configure.bazelrc`. To continue the build, enter the following command:

```
bazel build --config=opt //tensorflow/tools/pip_package:build_pip_package
```

This command creates a script called `build_pip_package` in the `bazel-bin/tensorflow/tools/pip_package` directory. To build an installation package for TensorFlow, enter the following command:

```
bazel-bin/tensorflow/tools/pip_package/build_pip_package /tmp/tensorflow_pkg
```

This command creates a wheel file (`*.whl`) in your `/tmp/tensorflow_pkg` directory. You can install the new TensorFlow package by calling `pip install` with this wheel file. On my system, the wheel file is `tensorflow-1.4.0rc1-cp27mu-linux_x86_64.whl`. Therefore, I can install TensorFlow with the following command:

```
sudo pip install /tmp/tensorflow_pkg/tensorflow-1.4.0rc1-cp27mu-linux_x86_64.whl
```

When `pip install` finishes, the TensorFlow installation is complete. You can access the `tensorflow` package and its modules as if you'd installed the default TensorFlow installation.

Assigning operations to devices

If you've configured TensorFlow to execute on GPUs and you've installed the appropriate SDK, TensorFlow automatically assigns processing operations to the GPU.

For example, TensorFlow contains two versions of `matmul`: one that executes on CPUs and one that executes on GPUs. When an application executes `matmul`, TensorFlow executes the matrix multiplication on the GPU if it's available.

TensorFlow lets you assigns operations to devices manually, but first, it helps to know which devices are present.TensorFlow provides this information through an undocumented function named `list_local_devices` in the `tensorflow.python.client` package. This function returns a list of `DeviceAttribute` protocol buffers, and the following code calls `list_local_devices` to print a list of available devices:

```
from tensorflow.python.client import device_lib
devices = device_lib.list_local_devices()
for device in devices:
    print(device)
```

On my bargain-basement laptop, this code prints the following result:

```
name: "/device:CPU:0"
device_type: "CPU"
memory_limit: 268435456
locality {}
incarnation: 2086003163627480003
```

TensorFlow recognizes two types of devices: CPUs and GPUs. TensorFlow assigns a name to each device, and this name always has the same format:

```
/job:Part/replica:<replica>/task:<task>/device:<type>:<device_num>
```

Unless you're developing distributed applications, you can leave off the `job`, `replica`, and `task` fields and simply use `/device:<type>:<device_num>`. Here, `<type>` can be CPU or GPU, and `<device_num>` identifies the index of the device among the recognized devices of the given type. Therefore, the first CPU is `/device:CPU:0` and the second GPU is `/device:GPU:1`.

If you have multiple devices of a given type, you can configure a session to limit the number of devices it can access. The `device_count` parameter in the `ConfigProto` buffer makes it possible. As an example, the following code configures the session to use a maximum of two GPUs:

```
conf = tf.ConfigProto(device_count={'GPU': 2})
with tf.Session(config=conf) as sess:
    ...
```

If you'd like to execute operations on a specific device, you can call `tf.device` with the device's name. This function returns a context manager that assigns all operations in the context to the given device. For example, the following code specifies that subsequent operations should be assigned to the second GPU:

```
with tf.device('/device:GPU:1'):
    ...
```

Suppose that your application is executing a session and you'd like to know which device(s) the session is using. In this case, you can set the `log_device_placement` option to `True` in the session's constructor.

```
a = tf.constant(1.2, name='a_var')
b = tf.constant(3.4, name='b_var')
sum = a + b;
conf = tf.ConfigProto(log_device_placement=True)
with tf.Session(config=conf) as sess:
    print(sess.run(sum))
```

If a system has a single CPU, the printed output will look like the following:

```
4.6
Device mapping: no known devices.
add: (Add): /job:localhost/replica:0/task:0/device:CPU:0
b_var: (Const): /job:localhost/replica:0/task:0/device:CPU:0
a_var: (Const): /job:localhost/replica:0/task:0/device:CPU:0
```

Configuring GPU usage

If your TensorFlow installation can access GPUs and TensorFlow recognizes a compliant GPU, your sessions will assign math operations to the GPU by default. You can configure how the CPU interacts with the GPU by setting the `gpu_options` field in a session's `ConfigProto`. You must assign `gpu_options` to a `GPUOptions` buffer, and Table 11-3 lists its fields.

By default, TensorFlow pre-allocates all of a GPU's memory for its operations. But if you set `allow_growth` to `True`, TensorFlow won't allocate any memory in advance. Instead, it will allocate memory only as it becomes necessary.

If you set `per_process_gpu_memory_fraction` to a value less than 1, TensorFlow will pre-allocate that fraction of the GPU's visible memory. For example, the following code configures a session to pre-allocate 80 percent of the GPU's memory for its operations:

```
gpu_opts = tf.GPUOptions( per_process_gpu_memory_fraction=0.8)
conf = tf.ConfigProto(gpu_options=gpu_opts)
with tf.Session(config=conf) as sess:
    ...
```

TABLE 11-3   **GPUOptions Fields**

Field	Type	Description
per_process_gpu_memory_fraction	double	Configures the fraction of the GPU memory to allocate
allocator_type	string	Sets the GPU allocation strategy
deferred_deletion_bytes	int64	Delays deletion to reduce driver processing
allow_growth	bool	Enables/disables pre-allocation of GPU memory
visible_device_list	string	Determines how GPU devices are mapped
polling_active_delay_usecs	int32	Configures the number of milliseconds that should elapse between polling when active
polling_inactive_delay_msecs	int32	Sets the number of milliseconds between polling when inactive
force_gpu_compatible	bool	Forces tensors to be allocated in GPU's pinned memory

You can improve performance by reducing the number of commands that the CPU sends to the GPU. One frequent command involves deleting objects in GPU memory. By default, the CPU will tell the GPU to delete objects when they occupy more than several megabytes of storage. You can customize this behavior by setting the deferred_deletion_bytes field of a GPUOptions to a desired memory size.

Executing TensorFlow in a Cluster

In addition to running operations on GPUs, you can code distributed applications that execute on multiple computers. I found this topic very difficult to understand when I first encountered it, so I start by comparing it to a more familiar subject: web browsing.

When you browse the web, your browser (the client) sends a request to a remote machine called the *server*. To be precise, the server is a process on the remote machine (the server's host) that listens for requests on a specific port. When you send your request to a web server's host and port, the server sends a response containing a web page. A host can execute multiple servers, but each server always listens for messages from a specific port.

In a distributed TensorFlow application, a client accesses multiple servers, which may run on separate systems or the same system. Like a web server, each Tensor-Flow server listens for messages directed to a specific host and port.

Each server executes a single unit of work called a *task*. A group of related tasks form a *job*. The collection of servers associated with an application is called a *cluster*.

If you're comfortable with these terms (server, task, job, cluster), you'll have no trouble coding distributed TensorFlow applications. In general, the development process requires three steps:

1. **Define the application's jobs, tasks, and server hosts/ports in a ClusterSpec.**

2. **Create a tf.train.Server for each server in the cluster.**

3. **Define operations for each task.**

If your cluster executes on multiple computers, you don't have to rewrite the application for each computer. Just code the application once and pass different command-line arguments to each system. Alternatively, you can use a cluster manager like Kubernetes to manage the cluster and automatically define servers and tasks.

Creating a ClusterSpec

A cluster specification defines the application's jobs and tasks and associates each task with the network address of a server. Cluster specifications are represented by instances of tf.train.ClusterSpec. The class constructor accepts one argument that can take one of three forms:

>> A dict that associates job names with a list of network addresses

>> A dict that associates job names with dicts that associate task numbers with network addresses

>> An existing ClusterDef protocol buffer

This discussion focuses on the first two forms. For example, suppose that you want your cluster to execute tasks in two jobs. The first job, j1, has one task, and the second job, j2, has two tasks. You could define your cluster with the following ClusterSpec:

```
spec = tf.train.ClusterSpec({
        'j1': ['sys1.ex.com:121'],
        'j2': ['sys2.ex.com:122', 'sys3.ex.com:123']})
```

For each network address, you need to provide a host name, such as sys1.ex.com, and a port, such as 123. TensorFlow creates one task for each network address in the ClusterSpec and assigns each task a number corresponding to its order in the job's list. In the preceding example, TensorFlow assigns Task 0 to sys1.ex.com, Task 0 to sys2.ex.com, and Task 1 to sys3.ex.com.

You can assign your own task numbers by associating each job name with a dict that associates integers with addresses:

```
spec = tf.train.ClusterSpec({
                'j1': {3: 'sys1.ex.com:121'},
                'j2': {2: 'sys2.ex.com:122',
                       1: 'sys3.ex.com:123'}})
```

For the sake of simplicity, the ClusterSpecs in this book allow TensorFlow to set task indices automatically.

Creating a server

After you split your application's computation into tasks, you need to create servers to perform the tasks. You can create a server by calling the tf.train.Server constructor:

```
tf.train.Server(server_or_cluster_def, job_name=None, task_index=None,
                protocol=None, config=None, start=True)
```

You can set the first parameter to a ServerDef, which is a protocol buffer that defines a server's operating environment. But most applications assign the first parameter to a ClusterSpec. To tell the server which task it's intended to perform, you need to set the job_name and task_index parameters. As an example, the following code creates a server to perform Task 1 of the job named j2:

```
server = tf.train.Server(spec, job_name='j2', task_index=1)
```

The constructor's protocol parameter identifies the communication mechanism that the Server will use to receive tasks. At the time of this writing, the only accepted protocol is grpc, which identifies the gRPC protocol. This is Google's free implementation of remote procedure calls (RPC), and you can find out more about gRPC by visiting http://grpc.io.

The config parameter accepts a ConfigProto that configures all the sessions that run on the server. I present the ConfigProto and its many fields at the start of the chapter in the "Configuring a new session" section.

The `start` parameter identifies whether the server should start immediately after it's created. If you set this parameter to `True`, the server will start processing tasks after it's created. If you set it to `False`, you can start the server later by calling its `start` method.

Specifying jobs and tasks

After you define your cluster and create your servers, you need to provide code for the cluster's tasks. You don't need to write a separate program for each task. Instead, most developers write one program and partition its code so that different portions are executed by different tasks.

You can associate code with a specific task by calling the `tf.device` function discussed earlier in the "Assigning operations to devices" section. For example, the following code executes only on Task 0 of Job `j1`:

```
with tf.device('/job:j1/task:0'):
    const_a = tf.constant(3.6)
    const_b = tf.constant(1.2)
    total = const_a + const_b
```

You can also partition your code using `if` statements:

```
if job_name == 'j1' and task_num == 0:
    ...
elif job_name == 'j1' and task_num == 1:
    ...
```

When you define a cluster, you can create as many jobs and tasks as you like. But many distributed TensorFlow applications have only two jobs:

» **Parameter server (ps):** Stores the application's variables

» **Worker replica (worker):** Performs the application's computation, including the processing that updates the variables

You can define these jobs in a cluster specification with code like the following:

```
spec = tf.train.ClusterSpec({'ps': [..], 'worker': [..]})
```

This section introduces parameter servers and workers and shows you how to create them in code.

Parameter servers

In a distributed application, TensorFlow recognizes that variables with the same name on the same device represent the same data. That is, if Tasks X and Y both operate on a variable named `weight_var`, TensorFlow understands that they should access the same `weight_var` variable. These tasks run in different processes, so TensorFlow replicates the variables between the processes.

A *parameter server* (PS) serves as a central location for storing, saving, and retrieving variables. In many applications, a PS task will simply declare variables and then block until the application is complete. To demonstrate this, the following code defines a parameter server that declares two variables, `weights` and `biases`, and then blocks until the application is complete.

```
server = tf.train.Server(cluster, job_name='ps', task_index=0)
```

```
if job_name == 'ps':
    weights = tf.Variable(...)
    biases = tf.Variable(...)
    server.join()
```

After the parameter server declares the `weights` and `biases`, other tasks can access these variables and update them as needed. The `join` method tells the server to block indefinitely.

Workers

Generally speaking, any job that performs computation is considered a *worker job*. Each task in a worker job is called a *worker replica* or just a *worker*. To perform its computation, each worker needs to create and launch a session.

This requirement presents a problem: You can't create regular sessions in a distributed application. You need to run each session in the appropriate server process. To understand how to run a session in a server, you need to be familiar with server targets.

Just as web servers communicate using HTTP, TensorFlow servers communicate using gRPC. Each server has a gRPC address determined by its host and port. For example, if you configure a server to execute a task whose address is localhost:123, the server's gRPC address will be given as follows:

```
grpc://localhost:123
```

This gRPC address is called the server's *target*. You can access this target through the `target` property of the `Server` instance.

To create a session to run inside a server, you need to set the first parameter of `tf.Session` to the server's target. The following code creates a `Server` and then creates a session that connects to it:

```
server = tf.train.Server(spec, job_name='worker', task_index=1)
with tf.Session(server.target) as sess:
    ...
```

Here's a question: If workers in a distributed application need to access the same variable data, how can the variables be initialized? The parameter server can't initialize its variables because it doesn't run a session. But if every worker initializes the variables separately, TensorFlow won't be able to replicate the data between processes.

The answer is that one of the workers needs to handle initialization, and the other workers need to wait until the initialization is complete. The worker that handles initialization is called the *chief*. You can assign the chief's operations in a session by calling `tf.train.MonitoredTrainingSession`.

Workers and monitored sessions

Chapter 5 presents the fascinating topic of session hooks and explains how to associate hooks with a `MonitoredSession`. You can configure `MonitoredSession`s for distributed applications by calling a function called `tf.train.Monitored TrainingSession`:

```
MonitoredTrainingSession(master='', is_chief=True, checkpoint_dir=None,
    scaffold=None, hooks=None, chief_only_hooks=None, save_checkpoint_secs=600,
    save_summaries_steps=USE_DEFAULT, save_summaries_secs=USE_DEFAULT,
    config=None, stop_grace_period_secs=120, log_step_count_steps=100)
```

This function looks like a class constructor, but it returns a `MonitoredSession`, not a `MonitoredTrainingSession`. If a worker invokes this function with `is_chief` set to `True`, the `MonitoredSession` will perform the session's initialization when it's launched. Therefore, only one worker (the chief) should call this function with `is_chief` set to `True`. When other workers call this function, the returned `MonitoredSession` will wait until the chief's session has performed initialization.

The first argument, `master`, serves the same purpose as the `target` argument in the `Session` constructor. That is, it identifies the gRPC location of the worker intended to run the session, such as `grpc://localhost:123`.

The `MonitoredTrainingSession` function accepts general session hooks (`hooks`) and session hooks intended for the chief's session (`chief_only_hooks`). In addition, the function accepts parameters for setting checkpoints and generating summary data. By setting these parameters, you don't need to create `Checkpoint SaverHooks` or `SummarySaverHooks`.

Running a simple cluster

The code in the `ch11/cluster.py` module provides a simple example of a distributed TensorFlow application. The module doesn't perform any machine learning, but demonstrates how a set of worker tasks can combine their efforts to update a variable.

To be specific, the application creates four workers and uses them to approximate π. This approximation involves summing together the areas of the rectangles under the function $y = (1 + x^2)^{-1}$ as x runs from 0 to 1 and multiplying the sum by 4. In Figure 11-1, the graph divides the area under the function into 30 regions.

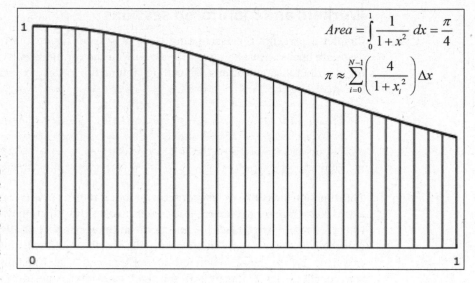

$$Area = \int_0^1 \frac{1}{1+x^2}\, dx = \frac{\pi}{4}$$

$$\pi \approx \sum_{i=0}^{N-1} \left(\frac{4}{1+x_i^2} \right) \Delta x$$

FIGURE 11-1: An application can approximate π by splitting the area under the function into rectangles and adding the areas together.

The `ch11/cluster.py` module generates four workers to perform the approximation. Listing 11-1 presents the code.

LISTING 11-1: **Approximating Pi in a Distributed Application**

```python
# Session hook to print output
class OutputHook(tf.train.SessionRunHook):

    def before_run(self, run_context):
        return tf.train.SessionRunArgs(pi_var)

    def after_run(self, run_context, run_values):
        print('Pi approximation:', run_values.results)

# Define a cluster with two jobs and five tasks
spec = tf.train.ClusterSpec({'worker':
    ['localhost:31415', 'localhost:31416', 'localhost:31417', 'localhost:31418']})

# Perform task-dependent operations
flags = tf.flags
flags.DEFINE_string('task', '', '')
if not flags.FLAGS.task:

    # Launch the worker processes
    subprocess.Popen('python cluster.py --task=0', stderr=subprocess.STDOUT)
    subprocess.Popen('python cluster.py --task=1', stderr=subprocess.STDOUT)
    subprocess.Popen('python cluster.py --task=2', stderr=subprocess.STDOUT)
    subprocess.Popen('python cluster.py --task=3', stderr=subprocess.STDOUT)

else:
    N = 10
    num_workers = float(spec.num_tasks('worker') - 1)
    delta_x = float(1)/float(N * num_workers)
    task_index = int(flags.FLAGS.task)

    # Create server
    server = tf.train.Server(spec, job_name='worker', task_index=task_index)

    with tf.device('/job:worker/task:0'):
        pi_var = tf.Variable(0., dtype=tf.float32)

    with tf.device('/job:worker/task:1'):
        for i in range(N):
            x_i = delta_x * (i * num_workers + 0.5)
            pi_var += 4 * delta_x/(1 + x_i * x_i)

    with tf.device('/job:worker/task:2'):
        for i in range(N):
            x_i = delta_x * (i * num_workers + 1.5)
            pi_var += 4 * delta_x/(1 + x_i * x_i)
```

(continued)

LISTING 11-1: *(continued)*

```
with tf.device('/job:worker/task:3'):
    for i in range(N):
        x_i = delta_x * (i * num_workers + 2.5)
        pi_var += 4 * delta_x/(1 + x_i * x_i)

# Launch session
output_hook = OutputHook()
with tf.train.MonitoredTrainingSession(master='grpc://localhost:31415',
        is_chief=(task_index == 0), chief_only_hooks=[output_hook]) as sess:
    sess.run(pi_var)
```

The module defines a ClusterSpec and launches four processes — one for each worker. Each worker process receives a different argument that identifies its task number. The workers use this task number to create and launch a server whose network address is determined by the ClusterSpec.

The module calls tf.device to assign code to the four workers. The first worker declares and initializes the pi_var variable. The rest of the workers update the value of pi_var by adding together the areas of ten of the rectangular regions underneath the function y = $(1 + x^2)^{-1}$.

Each worker calls tf.train.MonitoredTrainingSession and sets its target to the address of the first worker. The chief worker is the worker whose task index is 0, and this worker's session executes first and initializes the application's variables. After the initialization is complete, the other workers execute the session and update pi_var.

To display the output, the module associates the session with an OutputHook. This session hook prints the value of pi_var after the session completes its execution. The module associates the session hook with the function's chief_only_hooks parameter, so the hook applies only to the chief worker's session.

Chapter **12**

Developing Applications with Estimators

t a fundamental level, the process of using statistical regression for machine learning is a lot like the process of using neural networks (see Chapter 7): Load your data, train your model, and test the result. Unfortunately, the code needed to perform statistical regression in TensorFlow is quite different than the code needed to create neural networks.

To simplify development and testing, TensorFlow provides the Estimator framework. The `tf.estimator` package contains modules that analyze data through a common set of methods. For example, the estimator class that performs linear regression (`LinearRegressor`) has the same methods as the class that performs regression with deep neural networks (`DNNRegressor`).

You can take advantage of this commonality by coding your own estimators. That is, if you package your custom machine learning algorithm as an estimator, other developers will have no trouble training and testing your application.

Introducing Estimators

The tf.estimator package provides an assortment of classes that analyze data, including LinearClassifier and DNNClassifier. These classes all extend the Estimator class, whose methods make it possible to perform machine learning in an algorithm-agnostic manner.

Throughout this book, I use the term *estimator* to refer to instances of the Estimator class and its subclasses. In general, the process of working with estimators consists of six steps:

1. Load data into a dataset.

2. Create feature columns that associate the dataset's fields with names and data types.

3. Create an instance of the estimator's class with the feature columns.

4. Train the estimator with training data.

5. Evaluate the estimator's performance with test data and examine the results.

6. Use the estimator for real-world prediction or classification.

Step 3 depends on the type of estimator you're interested in. You can perform Steps 4, 5, and 6 by calling the three fundamental methods of the Estimator class: train, evaluate, and predict. Once you understand these methods, you'll have a solid grasp of what estimators are all about.

Training an Estimator

After you load data into a dataset and create an estimator, the next step is to start training. Every estimator supports the train method:

```
train(input_fn, hooks=None, steps=None, max_steps=None)
```

The input_fn parameter identifies a function that provides training data as a tuple. This tuple contains two data elements: features and labels. A feature identifies a single, complete observation, such as the N coordinates of a point in N-dimensional space. A label identifies the category of the corresponding feature, such as a 1 if the point represents success or a 0 if the point represents failure.

To identify features, input_fn provides a dictionary that associates strings with tensors. Each string identifies the data in the tensor. To demonstrate how you can set input_fn, the following function provides three features — one for each point dimension.

```
def train_func():
    features = {
        'x-coords': tf.constant([[0.1], [0.2]]),
        'y-coords': tf.constant([[0.5], [0.6]]),
        'z-coords': tf.constant([[1.0], [1.1]])
    }
    labels = tf.constant([[0], [1]])
    return features, labels
```

This set of features consists of two points: (0.1, 0.5, 1.0) and (0.2, 0.6, 1.1). But the code may seem confusing because of how the data is structured. Instead of returning one point at a time, the function provides all the x-coordinates in the first feature, all the y-coordinates in the second feature, and all the z-coordinates in the third feature.

The second part of the tuple returned by input_fn is a tensor containing labels. If the estimator's purpose is to classify, the labels represent categories. In the preceding example code, the first point has a label of 0, and the second point has a label of 1.

Looking at this code, you may wonder where the names x-coords, y-coords, and z-coords came from. When you call an estimator's constructor, you need to provide a *feature column* for each feature. A feature column associates a name, such as x-coords, with the type of data provided in the feature. I discuss the fascinating topic of feature columns in the upcoming section "Using Feature Columns."

By default, estimators continue training until the loss approaches zero. But you can control the number of training steps by setting the steps parameter or the max_steps parameter. The difference is that the steps parameter is incremental, so if you want to perform 30 training steps now and 20 training steps later, you can start by calling train with steps equal to 30. Later on, you can call train with steps equal to 20.

You can monitor the training process by setting the hooks parameter to a list of session hooks. Chapter 5 explains how session hooks make it possible to monitor a session's execution.

Testing an Estimator

After you create and train your estimator, you should make sure that it works properly. Testing your estimator is the purpose of the `evaluate` method:

```
evaluate(input_fn, steps=None, hooks=None, checkpoint_path=None, name=None)
```

The parameters of `evaluate` are similar to those of `train`. As with `train`, the `input_fn` function provides a tuple containing features and labels. The only difference is that these features and labels represent test data instead of training data.

The `checkpoint_path` parameter identifies the directory where the method should store its outputs. If you set this parameter to None, the method will use the `model_dir` parameter of the estimator's constructor. If you don't set this parameter, the method will store its outputs in a temporary directory.

`evaluate` returns the test results in a dict whose content depends on the estimator's model. TensorFlow's documentation doesn't list any required keys for this dict, but every estimator I've used has provided the following:

>> `accuracy`: The percentage of correct predictions

>> `loss`: Difference between the model's prediction and actual result

>> `average_loss`: Average of the loss

In addition to these metrics, the dict returned by `evaluate` also contains the value of the global step. An application can access this value through the `global_step` key.

Running an Estimator

After you train and test your estimator and you're happy with the test results, it's showtime! You can execute your estimator with real-world data points by calling `predict`:

```
predict(input_fn, predict_keys=None, hooks=None, checkpoint_path=None)
```

Like `train` and `evaluate`, `predict` accepts a function as its first parameter. But instead of providing a tuple containing features and labels, this function only returns features. That is, `input_fn` returns a dictionary that matches strings (names of feature columns) to tensors. These tensors contain the data points for your real-world application.

`predict` returns the estimator's prediction in a dict that matches names to values. If `checkpoint_path` is set, the method will store its output files in the given directory.

Creating Input Functions

The `train`, `evaluate`, and `predict` methods require an input function as their first parameter. Two functions in `tf.estimator.inputs` simplify the process of coding this input function:

>> `numpy_input_fn`: Accepts NumPy arrays and returns a function that provides a features/target tuple

>> `pandas_input_fn`: Accepts a pandas `DataFrame` and returns a function that provides a features/target tuple

The signature of `numpy_input_fn` is given as follows:

```
numpy_input_fn(x, y=None, batch_size=128, num_epochs=1, shuffle=None,
    queue_capacity=1000, num_threads=1)
```

The `x` parameter identifies features and the `y` parameter provides a label for each feature. The `shuffle` parameter identifies whether the features and labels should be shuffled. When calling this function, you must set `shuffle` to `True` or `False`.

You must set the `x` and `y` parameters to NumPy arrays, and you can load these arrays from a CSV file by calling the `load_csv_with_header` or `load_csv_without_header` functions discussed in Chapter 10. The following code passes feature data from `load_csv_with_header` to `numpy_input_fn`:

```
dataset = tf.contrib.learn.datasets.base.
    load_csv_with_header(filename='example.csv', target_dtype=np.int32,
    features_dtype=np.float32)
...
input_fn = tf.estimator.inputs.numpy_input_fn( x={'column': np.array(dataset.
    data)}, y=np.array(dataset.target), shuffle=True, num_epochs=1000)
```

The num_epochs parameter is particularly important for training because it defines how many epochs the session will execute. For evaluation and prediction, you should set num_epochs to 1.

The pandas toolset stores data in DataFrames. You can create an input function from a DataFrame by calling pandas_input_fn:

```
pandas_input_fn(x, y=None, batch_size=128, num_epochs=1, shuffle=None, queue_
    capacity=1000, num_threads=1, target_column='target')
```

The arguments of this function are nearly identical to those of numpy_input_fn. The only difference is the target_column argument, which identifies the column containing target (label) data.

Configuring an Estimator

The constructor of every estimator class accepts an argument named config. By setting this to a tf.contrib.learn.RunConfig, you can configure many aspects of the estimator's operation, such as when it saves variables and generates summary data.

You can create a RunConfig by calling its constructor. Table 12-1 lists the constructor's parameters.

As discussed in Chapter 11, distributed applications rely on gRPC to execute sessions on remote servers. The master parameter identifies the estimator's gRPC target and the evaluation_master parameter identifies the evaluation target. If you don't set these parameters, the estimator will run locally. If you leave num_cores at 0, the system will use every core on the target processor.

model_dir identifies the location where the estimator should save its data. Most of the other fields specify how often the data should be saved. To specify when checkpoint data should be saved, you can set save_checkpoint_steps or save_checkpoint_secs, but not both.

The session_config parameter defines properties of the estimator's underlying session. To configure the session, you need to assign this parameter to a ConfigProto buffer, and Chapter 11 presents its fields.

TABLE 12-1 **Parameters of the RunConfig Constructor**

Parameter	Default	Description
master	None	Target for running the estimator
num_cores	0	Number of cores to use
log_device_placement	False	Bool that identifiers whether the estimator should print which device(s) it runs on
gpu_memory_fraction	1	Fraction of GPU memory to be used by the estimator
tf_random_seed	None	Random seed for initializers
save_summary_steps	100	Number of steps to wait before saving summaries
save_checkpoints_secs	600	Number of seconds to wait before saving checkpoints
save_checkpoints_steps	--	Number of steps to wait before saving checkpoints
keep_checkpoint_max	5	Maximum number of checkpoint files to store
keep_checkpoint_every_n_hours	10000	Number of hours between each checkpoint to be saved
log_step_count_steps	100	Number of steps between logging of the global step per second
evaluation_master	' '	The gRPC target for evaluating the estimator
model_dir	None	Directory to save graph and model parameters
session_config	None	The ConfigProto used to configure the estimator's session

Using Feature Columns

Applications provide features to estimators using structures that resemble database tables. In a database table, each column identifies a specific field (First name, Age, and so on) and each value in a column has the same data type. Each row contains all the information for a single record.

In a TensorFlow application, a feature column serves the same role as a column header in a database table. That is, it provides a name for the column's data and indicates the data type of the column's values. Feature columns play an important role in this discussion because the constructor of every estimator class requires one or more feature columns.

The tf.feature_column package provides an assortment of classes that represent feature columns. Each of them extends the _FeatureColumn class, and Figure 12-1 illustrates the class hierarchy.

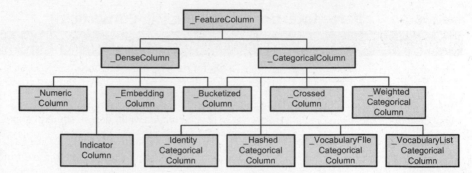

FIGURE 12-1:
TensorFlow's
feature column
classes determine
the data type of
the values in the
column.

A _DenseColumn identifies data from a dense tensor, and a _CategoricalColumn identifies data that can be expressed categorically. That is, if a column needs to store values that can be expressed as an enumerated type, such as a direction (NORTH, SOUTH, EAST, WEST), you should create a subclass of _CategoricalColumn. For all other types of data, you should create a subclass of _DenseColumn.

The tf.estimator package contains the classes in Figure 12-1, but the functions needed to create instances are in the tf.feature_column package. Table 12-2 lists eight of these functions and describes the content of the feature column created by the function.

Each of these functions accepts a key that identifies the column's data. You can think of this key as the name of the column in a database table. An estimator receives the column's data through the input function of train, evaluate, and predict. As discussed in the "Introducing Estimators" section, the first part of the function's tensor is a dict that associates the names of feature columns with tensors.

Numeric columns are almost trivially easy to work with. The default data type is tf.float32, and the default shape is (1). Therefore, the following code returns a _NumericColumn that contains single floating-point values:

```
temp = numeric_column('temp')
```

Of the categorical columns, the simplest is the _IdentityCategoricalColumn, which can be created by calling categorical_column_with_identity. This column contains integers that represent categories. The num_buckets parameter determines the number of categories, so the following code creates an _Identity CategoricalColumn whose elements can take any value between 0 and 11:

```
month = categorical_column_with_identity('month', num_buckets=12)
```

TABLE 12-2 **Functions that Create Feature Columns**

Function	Column Content
`numeric_column(key, shape=(1,), default_value=None, dtype=tf.float32, normalizer_fn=None)`	Real values and other numbers
`categorical_column_with_identity(key, num_buckets, default_value=None)`	Categories represented by unique integers
`categorical_column_with_hash_bucket(key, hash_bucket_size, dtype=tf.string)`	Categories represented by hashed integers or strings
`categorical_column_with_vocabulary_list(key, vocabulary_list, dtype=None, default_value=-1, num_oov_buckets=0)`	Categories accessed through a list of integer IDs associated with strings or integers
`categorical_column_with_vocabulary_file(key, vocabulary_file, vocabulary_size, num_oov_buckets=0, default_value=None, dtype=tf.string)`	Categories accessed through a file that associates integer IDs with strings or integers
`bucketized_column(source_column, boundaries)`	Values from a numeric column discretized according to different ranges
`indicator_column(categorical_column)`	Convert a categorical column to a dense column
`embedding_column( categorical_column, dimension, combiner='mean', initializer=None, ckpt_to_load_from=None, tensor_name_in_ckpt=None, max_norm=None, trainable=True)`	Convert a sparse categorical column to a dense column

If your application identifies categories with strings, you may find it inconvenient to provide a unique integer for every category. In this case, you can call `categorical_column_with_hash_bucket`, which uses a hash function to generate ID values for string or integer data. The following code creates a _HashedCategoricalColumn with 195 categories:

```
nation = categorical_column_with_hash_bucket('nation', num_buckets=195)
```

Rather than use a hash function, you may find it simpler to list the different values of the categories. Then the feature column will determine its own IDs for the categories. You can do this by calling `categorical_column_with_vocabulary_list`. For example, the following code creates a _VocabularyListCategorical Column that creates a category for each of the seven strings in the `vocabulary_list` parameter:

```
day_of_the_week = categorical_column_with_vocabulary_list (key='day',
    vocabulary_list=('Monday', 'Tuesday', 'Wednesday', 'Thursday', 'Friday',
    'Saturday', 'Sunday'))
```

The `categorical_column_with_vocabulary_file` function is like `categorical_column_with_vocabulary_list`, but you provide the elements of the vocabulary in a file. If you assign a field to an undefined value, the function will assign the field to the `default_value` if the parameter is defined. If `default_value` isn't defined and the application assigns a value to `num_oov_buckets`, the function will create additional categories as needed.

If you need to place numbers into categories according to their range, you can call `bucketized_column`. This function accepts a `_NumericColumn` and a list/tuple of ranges. As an example, the following code categorizes values of `temp_column` according to a list of temperature ranges:

```
boundaries = [-273.15, 0., 100.]
temp_state = bucketized_column(temp_column, boundaries)
```

If the `boundaries` parameter contains N values, `bucketized_column` will create N+1 value ranges. In the example, the first range runs from negative infinity to -273.15, the second range runs from -273.15 to 0.0, the third range runs from 0.0 to 100.0, and the fourth range runs from 100.0 to infinity.

Many operations, like DNN analysis, can be performed only on data in dense columns. For this reason, TensorFlow provides `indicator_column` and `embedding_column`, which convert categorical columns to dense columns. `indicator_column` is simpler and converts category values to multihot values. For example, if a column's category values run from 0 to 3 and a feature has a value of 2, `indicator_column` will convert this value to [0, 0, 1, 0].

`embedding_column` gives you more flexibility in creating dense columns. If your category IDs contain multiple values, the `combiner` parameter of `embedding_column` determines how the values should be combined. Currently, you can set this to `mean`, `sqrtn`, and `sum`. The default combiner is `mean`, which indicates that the function computes dense values by finding the average of the categorical values.

Creating and Using Estimators

The `tf.estimator` package provides six concrete estimator classes that you can instantiate in your applications:

>> `LinearClassifier`: Classifies data points using a linear model

>> `LinearRegressor`: Makes predictions using a linear model

>> `DNNClassifier`: Classifies data points using a deep neural network

» `DNNRegressor`: Makes predictions using a deep neural network

» `DNNLinearCombinedClassifier`: Classifies data points using a linear model and a deep neural network

» `DNNLinearCombinedRegressor`: Makes predictions using a linear model and a deep neural network

Each estimator performs a specific type of task using a specific methodology. Regressors make predictions, and classifiers place data points into categories. Some estimators use linear modeling, some use deep neural networks, and the last two estimators use both.

If you're unclear about the difference between regressors and classifiers, remember the Iris and Boston datasets from Chapter 10. The Iris dataset associates physical traits with a type of iris, so a problem involving this dataset requires a classifier. The Boston dataset associates location characteristics with housing prices, so a problem involving this dataset requires a regressor.

I don't explore all six of these classes in detail. Instead, I focus on three: the `LinearRegressor`, `DNNClassifier`, and `DNNLinearCombinedClassifier`. In each case, I explain how to create and train the estimator and then use it to make a prediction.

TECHNICAL STUFF

TensorFlow provides more estimator classes than just the six I list. The `tf.contrib. learn` package provides a handful of estimator classes, including `DynamicRnn Estimator`, `LogisticRegressor`, and `SVM`.

The Estimator API makes it straightforward to code your own estimators. In addition to implementing the `train`, `evaluate`, and `predict` methods, you'll need to set the estimator's model and the method it uses to compute loss.

Linear regressors

Chapter 6 explains how statisticians use linear regression to analyze data trends by fitting a line to a group of data points. Mathematically, linear regression sets $mx + b$ as its model and computes loss using mean-squared error. The goal of training is to determine which values of m and b minimize the distance between the line and the observed data.

The simplest of TensorFlow's estimator classes, LinearRegressor, performs the same operation. Its constructor is given as follows:

```
LinearRegressor(feature_columns, model_dir=None, label_dimension=1, weight_
    column=None, optimizer='Ftrl', config=None, partitioner=None)
```

The only required parameter is feature_columns, which accepts a list of _Feature Columns that identify the estimator's data. The model_dir parameter tells the estimator where it should store its outputs, such as event files and checkpoints. If you don't set model_dir, the estimator will use a temporary directory instead.

An estimator's train function expects a function that returns a tuple of features and labels. In most applications, a label consists of a single value, such as a category number. But if your estimator needs multivalued targets, you can configure this by setting the label_dimension parameter.

If you set the weight_column parameter, the estimator creates an additional column that assigns a weight to each feature. The input functions of train and evaluate must provide values for this column. The estimator multiplies the feature's loss by this weight, so a high weight means a high loss, which means the estimator will take larger steps during the optimization process.

If you look in the ch12 folder in this book's example code, you'll see that it contains two files named lin_reg.csv and lin_reg.py. The first file defines a series of two-dimensional points. Its first five lines are given as follows:

```
20,1
0.5,0.25
1.0,0.2
1 4,0.25
0.75,0.5
```

This header states that the file contains 20 features and that each feature consists of a single value. Each feature value identifies a point's x-coordinate, and the target identifies the point's y-coordinate. Figure 12-2 illustrates these points graphically. The dashed line is the line that best fits the data, and its equation is $y = 0.76x - 0.22$.

To analyze the points in ch12/lin_reg.csv, the ch12/lin_reg.py code creates a dataset and a feeds its data to a LinearRegressor. Listing 12-1 presents the code.

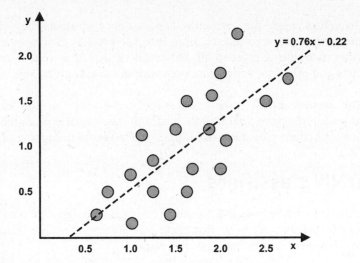

FIGURE 12-2:
A Linear
Regressor finds
the slope and
y-intercept of the
line that best fits
a set of points.

| LISTING 12-1: | **Using an Estimator for Linear Regression** |

```
# Read dataset from CSV file
dataset = tf.contrib.learn.datasets.base.load_csv_with_header(
    filename='lin_reg.csv', target_dtype=np.float32,
    features_dtype=np.float32, target_column=1)


# Create feature column containing x-coordinates
column = tf.feature_column.numeric_column('x', shape=[1])


# Create the LinearRegressor
lin_reg = tf.estimator.LinearRegressor([column])


# Train the estimator
train_input = tf.estimator.inputs.numpy_input_fn(
    x={'x': np.array(dataset.data)},
    y=np.array(dataset.target), shuffle=True, num_epochs=50000)
lin_reg.train(train_input)


# Make two predictions
predict_input = tf.estimator.inputs.numpy_input_fn(
    x={'x': np.array([1.9, 1.4], dtype=np.float32)},
    num_epochs=1, shuffle=False)
results = lin_reg.predict(predict_input)


# Display the results
for value in results:
    print(value['predictions'])
```

Given how simple the problem is, I decided not to evaluate the estimator. Instead, the module proceeds directly from `train` to `predict`. The `predict` method provides its results in a generator that produces dicts. This code iterates through the dicts and prints the value associated with the `predictions` key.

The results of the `LinearRegressor` come close to the expected results. At x = 1.9, the correct value of y is 1.22, and the estimator produced a result of 1.20. At x = 1.4, the correct value of y is 0.84, and the estimator produced a result of 0.86.

DNN classifiers

A `DNNClassifier` uses a deep neural network to assign data points to categories. Its constructor is a lot like that of the `LinearRegressor`, but includes parameters that define the neural network's structure:

```
DNNClassifier(hidden_units, feature_columns, model_dir=None, n_classes=2,
    weight_column=None, label_vocabulary=None, optimizer='Adagrad', activation_
    fn=tf.nn.relu, dropout=None, input_layer_partitioner=None, config=None)
```

The `hidden_units` parameter sets the size and shape of the neural network. For each element of the tensor, the constructor creates a hidden layer for the network. The value of each element in the tensor sets the number of nodes in the corresponding hidden layer.

For example, if you set `hidden_units` to [16, 32], the network will contain two hidden layers. The first layer will contain 16 nodes, and the second layer will contain 32 nodes. These nodes are fully connected, so the network connects the output of each node to each node of the next layer.

The `n_classes` and `label_vocabulary` parameters tell the classifier about the application's categories, and you'll find these parameters in all classifiers. `n_classes` sets the number of categories, and `label_vocabulary` provides a set of names for the categories. If you set `label_vocabulary`, be sure to use the category names in the input functions of `train` and `evaluate`.

The `ch12/dnn_class.py` module demonstrates how to create a `DNNClassifier` and use it to classify data points. It loads MNIST training data from `mnist_train.tfrecords` and loads test data from `mnist_test.tfrecords`. Listing 12-2 presents the code.

LISTING 12-2: **Classifying MNIST Images with a DNN Classifier**

```python
# Constants
image_dim = 28
num_labels = 10
batch_size = 80
num_steps = 8000
hidden_layers = [128, 32]

# Function to parse MNIST TFRecords
def parser(record):
    features = tf.parse_single_example(record,
        features={
            'images': tf.FixedLenFeature([], tf.string),
            'labels': tf.FixedLenFeature([], tf.int64),
        })
    image = tf.decode_raw(features['images'], tf.uint8)
    image.set_shape([image_dim * image_dim])
    image = tf.cast(image, tf.float32) * (1. / 255) - 0.5
    label = features['labels']
    return image, label

# Create the DNNClassifier
column = tf.feature_column.numeric_column('pixels',
    shape=[image_dim * image_dim])
dnn_class = tf.estimator.DNNClassifier(hidden_layers, [column],
    model_dir='dnn_output', n_classes=num_labels)

# Train the estimator
def train_func():
    dataset = tf.data.TFRecordDataset('mnist_train.tfrecords')
    dataset = dataset.map(parser).repeat().batch(batch_size)
    image, label = dataset.make_one_shot_iterator().get_next()
    return {'pixels': image}, label
dnn_class.train(train_func, steps=num_steps)

# Test the estimator
def test_func():
    dataset = tf.data.TFRecordDataset('mnist_test.tfrecords')
    dataset = dataset.map(parser).batch(batch_size)
    image, label = dataset.make_one_shot_iterator().get_next()
    return {'pixels': image}, label
metrics = dnn_class.evaluate(test_func)

# Display metrics
print('\nEvaluation metrics:')
for key, value in metrics.items():
    print(key, ': ', value)
```

This module creates a feature column and uses it to construct a `DNNClassifier`. It sets the estimator's `hidden_units` parameter to [128, 32], which means the classifier has two hidden layers with 128, and 32 hidden units, respectively. It sets the `n_classes` parameter to 10 because each MNIST image can fall into one of ten categories. The `label_vocabulary` parameter isn't set, so the classifier assumes that the labels will be provided as integers from 0 to 9.

After training and evaluation, the module prints the keys and values of dict returned by `evaluate`. On my system, these results are given as follows:

```
Evaluation metrics:
accuracy      :   0.9595
average_loss  :   0.129958
loss          :   10.3966
global_step   :   8000
```

Combined linear-DNN classifiers

If the linear estimators and DNN estimators don't meet your requirements, you can create an estimator that uses both learning methods. TensorFlow provides two such estimators: the `DNNLinearCombinedRegressor` and the `DNNLinearCombined Classifier`. This discussion focuses on the `DNNLinearCombinedClassifier`.

Before proceeding, I'd like to clarify some terminology. This estimator's name includes "Linear," but it doesn't perform line fitting. Despite its name, a linear classifier relies on logistic regression, not linear regression, to do its job. Chapter 6 fearlessly explores the topics of linear and logistic regression.

To determine which category a point belongs to, a TensorFlow linear classifier relies on the softmax function. If j is one of N categories, this function is given as follows:

$$\sigma\big(f(x)\big)_j = \frac{e^{f(x)_j}}{\sum_{i=0}^{N-1} e^{f(x)_i}}$$

A classifier is linear if f(x) is a linear combination of x, as in mx + b. To determine loss, a linear classifier computes cross entropy.

A `DNNLinearCombinedClassifier` combines a linear classifier and a DNN classifier. You can create an instance of this classifier by calling its constructor:

```
DNNLinearCombinedClassifier(model_dir=None, linear_feature_columns=None,
    linear_optimizer='Ftrl', dnn_feature_columns=None, dnn_optimizer='Adagrad',
    dnn_hidden_units=None, dnn_activation_fn=tf.nn.relu, dnn_dropout=None,
    n_classes=2, weight_column=None, label_vocabulary=None, input_layer_
    partitioner=None, config=None)
```

It's important to see that the constructor accepts separate feature columns for linear classification (`linear_feature_columns`) and DNN classification (`dnn_feature_columns`). This separation indicates that the linear classifier and DNN classifier process different features.

Google Research has given a special name to the process of combining linear classification and DNN classification: *wide and deep learning*.

Wide and deep learning

The ultimate goal of deep learning is to derive general principles from a body of data. I want my stock-picking application to derive general principles that will pick tomorrow's stocks based on yesterday's results. I want my medical application to derive general principles that will accurately classify health conditions in new patients based on records of existing patients.

But there's a problem. In many cases, the desire for generality and accuracy conflict. Consider the following generalization:

Statement 1: Vampires have sharp teeth and usually hunt in the evening.

Statement 2: Werewolves have sharp teeth and usually hunt in the evening.

Generalization: All vampires are werewolves.

Humans can look at these statements and immediately spot the problem with this reasoning. But deep neural networks can't. A DNN may base its generalizations on trivial features (sharp teeth) instead of important features (lycanthropy, aversion to sunlight, and thirst for blood).

To improve on deep learning, Google updated their Google Play recommendation system to augment DNN classification with linear classification. To train the linear classifier, Google provides input features and *cross products* of input features. A cross product determines how features interact by multiplying the features together:

$$\phi_k(x) = \prod_{i=1}^{d} x_i^{c_{ki}} \quad c_{ki} \in \{0,1\}$$

In a TensorFlow application, you can combine features into a cross product by calling `tf.feature.crossed_column`. In essence, this combines multiple categorical columns into a single hashed categorical column. Its signature is given as follows:

```
crossed_column(keys, hash_bucket_size, hash_key=None)
```

The first parameter, `keys`, accepts one or more categorical columns to be examined together. `hash_bucket_size` sets the maximum number of unique values in the new categorical column.

Cross products may not seem exciting, but linear classifiers can use them to arrive at conclusions that DNN classifiers would find difficult to obtain. Linear classifiers are particularly effective when problems have many categorical features that may or may not interact on one another. For this reason, Google Research refers to the use of linear classifiers as *wide learning*. According to Heng-Tze Cheng and other Google researchers, "Online experiment results show that Wide & Deep significantly increased app acquisitions compared with wide-only and deep-only models."

Analyzing census data

Wide learning is helpful for problems with many categorical features. This requirement makes the usual datasets — MNIST, CIFAR, Iris, and Boston — unsuitable for demonstration. For this reason, the `ch12/combined.py` module analyzes census data. To be precise, the module creates a `DNNLinearCombined Classifier` that examines data from the 1994 Census to determine whether a person will make more or less than $50,000 per year.

I provide the census data in two CSV files: `ch12/adult.data` contains training data and `ch12/adult.test` contains test data. The University of California, Irvine (UCI) provides these files for free at their site `https://archive.ics.uci.edu/ml/machine-learning-databases/adult`.

Each record of census data provides 14 statistics about a person:

» age: The person's age in years

» workclass: Work status (Private, Self-emp-not-inc, self-emp-inc, Federal-gov, Local-gov, State-gov, Without-pay, Never-worked)

» fnlwgt: A weighting value (final weight) computed by the Census Bureau

» education: Highest level of education (Preschool, 1st-4th, 5th-6th, 7th-8th, 9th, 10th, 11th, 12th, HS-grad, Some-college, Prof-school, Assoc-acdm, Assoc-voc, Bachelors, Masters, Doctorate)

» education-num: Number of years in education

» marital-status: Marital status (Never-married, Divorced, Separated, Widowed, Married-civ-spouse, Married-AF-spouse, Married-spouse-absent)

» occupation: Place of work (Tech-support, Craft-repair, Other-service, Sales, Exec-managerial, Prof-specialty, Handlers-cleaners, Machine-op-inspct, Adm-clerical, Farming-fishing, Transport-moving, Priv-house-serv, Protective-serv, Armed-Forces)

» relationship: Marital status (Wife, Own-child, Husband, Not-in-family, Other-relative, Unmarried)

» race: Self-identified race (White, Asian-Pac-Islander, Amer-Indian-Eskimo, Other, Black)

» sex: Gender (Female, Male)

» capital-gain: Profit from buying/selling capital assets

» capital-loss: Loss from buying/selling capital assets

» hours-per-week: Number of hours worked per week

» native-country: Country of origin (United-States, Cambodia, England, Puerto-Rico, Canada, Germany, Outlying-US(Guam-USVI-etc), India, Japan, Greece, South Korea, China, Cuba, Iran, Honduras, Philippines, Italy, Poland, Jamaica, Vietnam, Mexico, Portugal, Ireland, France, Dominican-Republic, Laos, Ecuador, Taiwan, Haiti, Columbia, Hungary, Guatemala, Nicaragua, Scotland, Thailand, Yugoslavia, El-Salvador, Trinadad&Tobago, Peru, Hong Kong, Holand-Netherlands)

As an example, the adult.test file contains the following record:

```
36, Local-gov, 403681, Bachelors, 13, Married-civ-spouse, Prof-specialty,
    Husband, White, Male, 0, 0, 40, United-States, >50K
```

The last column provides the classification label as a string. The label >50K indicates that the person makes more than $50,000 per year, and <=50K indicates that the person makes less than or equal to $50,000 per year.

Unfortunately, you can't load this census data with load_csv_with_header or load_csv_without_header. Instead, I recommend using the pandas data analysis library. If you have pip available, you can install pandas with the following command:

```
pip install pandas
```

After you install the toolset, you can read CSV data by calling read_csv. This function accepts quite a few parameters, and seven of them are particularly important:

>> filepath_or_buffer: Handle of the file containing CSV data

>> header: Row number(s) containing column names

>> names: Names of the CSV fields

>> dtype: Data type or list of data types for columns

>> engine: Parser engine

>> skipinitialspace: Boolean that specifies whether to ignore spaces after the delimiter (default: False)

>> skiprows: Number of rows to skip after the start of the file

read_csv returns a DataFrame that holds data from the CSV file. For example, the following code obtains a handle to adult.data and calls read_csv to read its data into a DataFrame:

```
columns = ['age', 'workclass', 'fnlwgt', 'education', 'education_num',
    'marital_status', 'occupation', 'relationship', 'race', 'gender',
    'capital_gain', 'capital_loss', 'hours_per_week', 'native_country',
    'income_bracket']
train_file = open('adult.data', 'r')
train_frame = pd.read_csv(train_file, names=columns, engine='python',
    skipinitialspace=True, skiprows=1)
```

After you create a DataFrame, you can call pandas_input_fn to convert the DataFrame into a function that can be passed to an estimator's train or evaluate method. The ch12/combined.py module demonstrates how an application can read data from a CSV file with pandas, and Listing 12-3 presents the code.

LISTING 12-3: **Analyzing Census Data with Wide and Deep Learning**

```
# Define column headings
columns = ['age', 'workclass', 'fnlwgt', 'education', 'education_num',
    'marital_status', 'occupation', 'relationship', 'race', 'gender',
    'capital_gain', 'capital_loss', 'hours_per_week', 'native_country',
    'income_bracket']

# Create feature columns
age = tf.feature_column.numeric_column('age')
workclass = tf.feature_column.categorical_column_with_vocabulary_list(
    'workclass', ['Private', 'Self-emp-not-inc', 'self-emp-inc', 'Federal-gov',
        'Local-gov', 'State-gov', 'Without-pay', 'Never-worked'])
```

```python
fnlwgt = tf.feature_column.numeric_column('fnlwgt')
education = tf.feature_column.categorical_column_with_vocabulary_list(
    'education', [...])
education_num = tf.feature_column.numeric_column('education_num')
marital_status = tf.feature_column.categorical_column_with_vocabulary_list(
    'marital_status', ['Never-married', 'Divorced', 'Separated', 'Widowed',
        'Married-civ-spouse', 'Married-AF-spouse', 'Married-spouse-absent'])
occupation = tf.feature_column.categorical_column_with_vocabulary_list(
    'occupation', [...])
relationship = tf.feature_column.categorical_column_with_vocabulary_list(
    'relationship', ['Wife', 'Own-child', 'Husband', 'Not-in-family',
        'Other-relative', 'Unmarried'])
race = tf.feature_column.categorical_column_with_vocabulary_list(
    'race', ['White', 'Asian-Pac-Islander', 'Amer-Indian-Eskimo',
    'Other', 'Black'])
gender = tf.feature_column.categorical_column_with_vocabulary_list(
    'gender', ['Female', 'Male'])
capital_gain = tf.feature_column.numeric_column('capital_gain')
capital_loss = tf.feature_column.numeric_column('capital_loss')
hours_per_week = tf.feature_column.numeric_column('hours_per_week')
native_country = tf.feature_column.categorical_column_with_vocabulary_list(
    'native_country', [...])

# Create groups of columns
linear_columns = [
    tf.feature_column.crossed_column(
        ['education', 'occupation'], hash_bucket_size=1000),
    tf.feature_column.crossed_column(
        ['native_country', 'occupation'], hash_bucket_size=1000),
    tf.feature_column.crossed_column(
        ['workclass', 'occupation'], hash_bucket_size=1000)]

dnn_columns = [
    tf.feature_column.indicator_column(workclass),
    tf.feature_column.indicator_column(education),
    tf.feature_column.indicator_column(gender),
    tf.feature_column.indicator_column(relationship),
    tf.feature_column.indicator_column(native_country),
    tf.feature_column.indicator_column(occupation),
    age, education_num, capital_gain, capital_loss,
    hours_per_week, fnlwgt]

# Create classifier
classifier =
tf.estimator.DNNLinearCombinedClassifier(linear_feature_columns=linear_columns,
    dnn_feature_columns=dnn_columns, dnn_hidden_units=[120, 60])
```

(continued)

LISTING 12-3: *(continued)*

```
# Train the classifier
train_file = open('adult.data', 'r')
train_frame = pd.read_csv(train_file,
    names=columns, engine='python',
    skipinitialspace=True, skiprows=1)
train_labels = train_frame['income_bracket'].apply(lambda x: '>50K' in x)
train_fn = tf.estimator.inputs.pandas_input_fn(
    x=train_frame, y=train_labels,
    batch_size=100, num_epochs=600,
    shuffle=True)
classifier.train(train_fn)

# Test the estimator
test_file = open('adult.test', 'r')
test_frame = pd.read_csv(test_file,
    names=columns, engine='python',
    skipinitialspace=True, skiprows=1)
test_labels = test_frame['income_bracket'].apply(lambda x: '>50K' in x)
test_fn = tf.estimator.inputs.pandas_input_fn(
    x=test_frame, y=test_labels,
    num_epochs=1, shuffle=False)
metrics = classifier.evaluate(test_fn)

# Display metrics
print('\nEvaluation metrics:')
for key, value in metrics.items():
    print(key, ': ', value)
```

Before you can execute this module, you need to place the adult.data and adult.test files in the current directory. You also need to install the pandas data analysis package.

The module starts by creating a feature column for each field in the census data. Then it creates three crossed columns: one that combines the education and occupation columns, one that combines the native_country and occupation columns, and one that combines the workclass and occupation columns.

After creating the crossed columns, the module creates a set of feature columns intended for the DNN classifier. You can't feed categorical columns to a neural network, so the module converts categorical columns into dense columns by calling tf.feature_column.indicator_column.

Next, the module creates a DNNCombinedLinearClassifier and provides it with the two sets of feature columns. That is, it directs the crossed columns to the linear classifier and the dense columns to the DNN. The dnn_hidden_units parameter configures the neural network to have two hidden layers: one with 120 nodes and one with 60 nodes.

After creating the classifier, the module calls its `train` and `evaluate` methods. To train the classifier, the module reads the fields from `adult.data` and converts the `DataFrame` to a dataset. The training process consists of 500 epochs, with each training step operating on shuffled batches containing 100 data points each.

To test the classifier, the module reads the fields from `adult.test` into a `DataFrame` and converts the `DataFrame` to a dataset. Then it prints each metric contained in the dict returned by `evaluate`. On my system, the module displays the following results:

```
accuracy              :  0.802285
accuracy_baseline     :  0.763774
auc                   :  0.87448
auc_precision_recall  :  0.710498
average_loss          :  0.511923
label/mean            :  0.236226
loss                  :  65.1142
prediction/mean       :  0.336511
global_step           :  195360
```

In this list, `auc` stands for "area under the curve." This metric is common for classifiers, as it measures the likelihood of a classifier making successful predictions compared to unsuccessful predictions.

Running Estimators in a Cluster

Chapter 11 introduces distributed TensorFlow applications, which involve jobs, tasks, and servers. You can run estimators in distributed applications, but you need to tell TensorFlow about the cluster and the task assigned to the server running the estimator.

You can provide this information by setting a `TF_CONFIG` variable that describes the cluster and the server's task. To be specific, you need to set `TF_CONFIG` to a JSON (JavaScript Object Notation) object that contains three fields:

» `cluster`: A description of the cluster

» `task`: The node's task

» `job`: Parameters of the job

You can set the first field by providing the argument of the ClusterSpec instance. If you have an existing ClusterSpec, you can obtain a suitable description by calling its as_cluster_def method.

The task field identifies the task assigned to the node on which TF_CONFIG is set. This field has three fields of its own:

>> type: the type of task (worker, master, or ps)

>> index: the index of the task within the job

>> trial: string identifier of the trial to be run, starts with '1'

The job field of TF_CONFIG describes the node's job. A distributed application usually receives this information through command-line arguments, so you can ignore this field. The following code gives you an idea how you can set this variable:

```
TF_CONFIG = {
    'cluster': {'ps': ['host1:123'],
                'worker': ['host2:456']},
    'task': {
        'type': 'worker',
        'index': 0,
        'trial': '1'
    }
}
```

In this case, the cluster has two jobs and two tasks. The task assigned to the node with this TF_CONFIG variable has an index of 0 and a type of worker. In this case, the cluster has a job with the task's type, but this isn't always the case. You can assign any name to a job, but a task's type must be worker, master, or ps.

Accessing Experiments

To simplify the process of executing estimators in a distributed environment, TensorFlow provides the Experiment class. To use an Experiment in code, you need to perform three steps:

1. **Create an estimator.**

2. **Construct an instance of tf.contrib.learn.Experiment with the estimator created in Step 1.**

3. **Launch the experiment by calling tf.contrib.learn.learn_runner.run.**

This discussion presents these steps and demonstrates how an experiment can be used to classify MNIST images. Chapter 13 presents an application that launches an experiment in the cloud.

Creating an experiment

Every experiment requires an estimator and functions for training and evaluation. You can create a `tf.contrib.learn.Experiment` by calling its constructor, whose arguments are listed in Table 12-3.

The most important parameter of the constructor is the first, which identifies the estimator to be executed by the experiment. The second and third parameters identify the functions that the experiment should use to train and evaluate the estimator.

TABLE 12-3   **Parameters of the Experiment Constructor**

Parameter	Default	Description
estimator	--	Estimator to be launched by the experiment
train_input_fn	--	Function that returns training features and labels
eval_input_fn	--	Function that returns evaluation features and labels
eval_metrics	None	Evaluation metrics to monitor
train_steps	None	Number of training steps
eval_steps	None	Number of evaluation steps
eval_hooks	None	Session hooks to pass to the estimator
eval_delay_secs	120	Number of seconds to wait before evaluating
continuous_eval_throttle_secs	60	Number of seconds to wait after the start of evaluation before re-evaluating
min_eval_frequency	None	Minimum number of steps between evaluations
delay_workers_by_global_step	False	Bool that specifies whether to delay training workers by global step instead of time
export_strategies	None	Export strategies
train_steps_per_iteration	None	Number of training steps in each training-evaluation iteration
checkpoint_and_export	False	Bool that specifies whether to save checkpoints and exports during training

The train_steps parameter identifies the number of steps to be performed during the training process. If you don't set this parameter, the estimator's training will continue indefinitely. The eval_steps parameter specifies how many steps should be performed during testing. If you don't set this parameter, the test will continue as long as input data is available.

Methods of the experiment class

After you create an Experiment, you can access its methods. Table 12-4 lists these methods and provides a description of each.

The first four methods are straightforward to use and understand. The train method will continue forever unless you've set the train_steps parameter in the constructor. evaluate will continue testing until its input is exhausted or until it reaches the eval_steps parameter. In both methods, you can specify how long the experiment should wait by setting the delay_secs parameter.

TABLE 12-4   **Methods of the Experiment Class**

Method	Description
train(delay_secs=None)	Train the estimator with training data
evaluate(delay_secs=None, name=None)	Evaluate the estimator with test data
train_and_evaluate()	Train and evaluate the estimator
test()	Train, evaluate, and export for one step
continuous_eval(delay_secs=None, throttle_delay_secs=None, evaluate_checkpoint_only_once=True, continuous_eval_predicate_fn=None, name='continuous')	Evaluate estimator continuously
continuous_eval_on_train_data(delay_secs=None, throttle_delay_secs=None, continuous_eval_predicate_fn=None, name='continuous_on_train_data')	Evaluate estimator continuously with training data
continuous_train_and_eval(*args, **kwargs)	Interleave training and evaluation
extend_train_hooks(additional_hooks)	Associate additional session hooks for training
reset_export_strategies(new_export_strategies=None)	Associate new export strategies
run_std_server()	Start a TensorFlow server and joins the serving thread

The `continuous_eval` and `continuous_eval_on_train_data` methods both perform repeated evaluation. You can control whether the evaluation continues by assigning the `continuous_eval_predicate_fn` to a suitable function. This function receives the results of the preceding evaluation and determines whether evaluation should continue.

The `continuous_train_and_eval` method is experimental and may change at any time. This iterates through training and evaluation, and you can set the number of training steps with the constructor's `train_steps_per_iteration` parameter.

Running an experiment

You can train and/or evaluate experiments by calling `tf.contrib.learn.learn_runner.run`. This function accepts four arguments:

- » `experiment_fn`: Function that returns an experiment

- » `schedule`: The method of the experiment to invoke

- » `run_config`: A RunConfig that provides configuration settings

- » `hparams`: An HParams that provides additional data for the experiment

To call this function, you need to assign the first parameter to a function that receives two arguments: a `RunConfig` and an `HParams`. The function must return an `Experiment`.

Every estimator constructor has a `config` parameter that accepts a `tf.contrib.learn.RunConfig` instance. The `run_config` parameter of the `run` method accepts the same type of `RunConfig`. Remember that the `model_dir` field tells the experiment where to store its outputs.

You can pass data to the `experiment_fn` function using an instance of `tf.contrib.training.HParams`. The constructor accepts one or more key-value pairs separated by commas. The following code shows how you can create an `HParams` instance:

```
hparams = tf.contrib.training.HParams(learning_rate=0.01, hidden_units=[10, 20])
```

The `schedule` parameter identifies which experiment method should be invoked. You can control where the method's return value should be stored by setting the `model_dir` field of the `RunConfig`.

Putting theory into practice

The code in the ch12/experiment.py module demonstrates how experiments can be created and launched. The experiment analyzes MNIST data using a DNNClassifier similar to the estimator from ch12/dnn_class.py. Listing 12-4 presents the code.

LISTING 12-4: **Classifying MNIST Images with an Experiment**

```
# Set parameters
batch_size = 80
image_dim = 28
hparams = tf.contrib.training.HParams(
    num_labels=10,
    batch_size=80,
    num_steps=8000,
    hidden_layers=[128, 32])


# Function to parse MNIST TFRecords
def parser(record):
    features = tf.parse_single_example(record,
        features={
            'images': tf.FixedLenFeature([], tf.string),
            'labels': tf.FixedLenFeature([], tf.int64),
        })
    image = tf.decode_raw(features['images'], tf.uint8)
    image.set_shape([image_dim * image_dim])
    image = tf.cast(image, tf.float32) * (1. / 255) - 0.5
    label = features['labels']
    return image, label


# Create the DNNClassifier
def create_estimator(hidden_layers, num_labels, conf):
    column = tf.feature_column.numeric_column('pixels',
        shape=[image_dim * image_dim])
    return tf.estimator.DNNClassifier(hidden_layers, [column],
        n_classes=num_labels, config=conf)


# Train the estimator
def train_func():
    dataset = tf.data.TFRecordDataset('mnist_train.tfrecords')
    dataset = dataset.map(parser).repeat().batch(batch_size)
    image, label = dataset.make_one_shot_iterator().get_next()
    return {'pixels': image}, label
```

```
# Test the estimator
def test_func():
    dataset = tf.data.TFRecordDataset('mnist_test.tfrecords')
    dataset = dataset.map(parser).batch(batch_size)
    image, label = dataset.make_one_shot_iterator().get_next()
    return {'pixels': image}, label

# Create experiment
def create_experiment(conf, params):
    return tf.contrib.learn.Experiment(
        estimator=create_estimator(params.hidden_layers,
            params.num_labels, conf),
        train_input_fn=train_func,
        eval_input_fn=test_func,
        train_steps=params.num_steps)

# Run experiment
run_config = tf.contrib.learn.RunConfig(model_dir='experiment_output')
tf.contrib.learn.learn_runner.run(
    experiment_fn=create_experiment,
    run_config=run_config,
    schedule='train_and_evaluate',
    hparams=hparams
)
```

This module starts by creating an HParams that contains the batch size, number of labels, number of training steps, and the number of hidden layers. The module also creates a RunConfig that identfies the directory where the experiment's output should be stored.

When the module calls tf.contrib.learn.learn_runner.run, it provides the HParams instance, the RunConfig instance, and a function that returns an Experiment. This function calls the Experiment constructor with three functions:

> ❯❯ create_estimator: Creates a DNNClassifier with the experiment's configuration settings

> ❯❯ train_func: Provides training data and labels for the DNNClassifier

> ❯❯ test_func: Provides test data and labels for the DNNClassifier

The module sets the schedule parameter of tf.contrib.learn.learn_runner. run to train_and_evaluate. This calls the experiment's train_and_evaluate function, which trains and tests the experiment's estimator.

Chapter **13**

Running Applications on the Google Cloud Platform (GCP)

O f all the success stories in the world of technology, none are more spectacular than the rise of Google. Since its initial public offering in 2004, Google has constructed a vast computational architecture that spans the globe. Everyone with an Internet connection knows how to search for information on google.com and view media on youtube.com. Google's technology has become so popular that the verb google has entered the Merrian-Webster Dictionary.

While Google's technology is famous across the world, the Google Compute Platform (GCP) isn't as well-known. This is a shame, because the GCP lets developers like you and me take advantage of Google's vast resources, which include terabytes of distributed storage and clusters of high-speed processors.

I love using the GCP because my applications can access Google's technologies, which include Google Maps, Gmail, YouTube, and AdSense. This chapter focuses on Google's Machine Learning (ML) Engine, which lets you execute TensorFlow applications in the Google Cloud Platform.

Overview

The good news is that you can dramatically reduce the time required for machine learning by deploying applications to Google's Machine Learning (ML) Engine. The bad news is that the process of configuring and deploying applications isn't easy. Five steps are involved:

1. **Create a project for the Google Cloud Platform (GCP) and configure it to use the Cloud Machine Learning API.**

2. **Install the Cloud Software Development Kit (SDK).**

3. **Structure your TensorFlow application as a package.**

4. **Upload your package and processing data to Google Cloud Storage.**

5. **Use the Cloud SDK to execute a training or prediction job.**

In writing this chapter, I assume that you've never heard of the GCP. Therefore, before I explain how to deploy applications, I introduce the Cloud Software Development Kit (SDK) and Cloud Storage and explain how to create a GCP project.

Working with GCP Projects

If you want to take advantage of the GCP's features, the first step is to create a project. This project serves as the central container of your development effort and includes all your metadata and configuration files. Before you can execute code or launch a web application, you need to upload the files to your project. Similarly, if you'd like access to special features, you need to make requests through the project.

To build a GCP project that can access the ML Engine, you need to perform three steps:

1. **Create a project in the Google Developer Console.**

2. **Enable billing for the project.**

3. **Enable the project to access the Machine Learning Engine.**

TIP

The ch13 directory in this book's example code contains two folders: cloud_mnist and cluster_mnist. These folders contain packages that can be deployed to the ML Engine, but they are not GCP projects. A GCP project resides in the cloud, so if you want to follow the development in this chapter, you need to create and configure a GCP project on your own.

Creating a new project

Anyone with a valid email address can create a GCP project without any fees or obligations. The process involves five steps:

1. Visit the Cloud Console at `https://console.cloud.google.com`.

2. If this is your first time visiting the console, provide a contact email address and a password.

3. In the upper horizontal bar, click Select a Project.

4. In the Select dialog box, click the plus button on the right.

5. In the New Project page, enter a project name and click the Create button.

When working with the GCP, you need to understand the difference between a project's name and ID. A project's name is chosen by the developer, and the console uses it to display the current project.

In contrast, a project's ID is chosen by the GCP based on the project's name, and it uniquely identifies the project across all projects in the GCP. If you want to upload code or change a project's configuration, you'll need to access your project by its ID. Therefore, it's a good idea to know the IDs of your projects.

Billing

Machine learning is a powerful capability, but unlike TensorFlow, it's not free. Google's fees for machine learning depend on three factors: the type of operation (training or prediction), the length of time, and your location:

» Training: $0.49 per hour per training unit in the U.S., $0.54 in Europe and Asia

» Prediction: $0.10 per thousand predictions plus $0.40 per hour in the U.S., $0.11 per thousand predictions plus $0.44 per hour in Europe and Asia

Google charges money after you use the ML Engine, not in advance. But you need to identify a means of payment before you use the engine, and you can configure this by associating your project with a billing account:

1. Visit your project page in the Cloud Console.

2. Open the menu (three horizontal bars) in the upper-left and select the Billing option.

3. Click the button entitled Add billing account.

4. Enter your contact information and billing information.

At the bottom of the page, a button lets you set up automatic payment, which authorizes Google to withdraw funds from the account as resources are used.

Accessing the machine learning engine

After you set up a billing account for your project, you can access paid features like the ML Engine. To enable this feature, open the menu in the upper-left of the project page and select APIs & Services. This opens the APIs & Services page, which identifies the features that the project can access.

The left side of the page displays three links: Dashboard, Library, and Credentials. The Library link opens a page that lists the APIs available for your project. To enable access to the ML Engine, you need to perform five steps:

1. **From the APIs & Services page, click the Library link to the left.**

2. **Find the Machine Learning group and click the View All link to the right.**

3. **Click the link entitled Google Cloud Machine Learning Engine.**

4. **Click the Enable link at the top of the page.**

5. **Wait until the GCP grants access to the new capability.**

After performing these steps, you can verify that your project can access the ML Engine by visiting the APIs & Services dashboard. The lower part of the page lists the different APIs your project can access, and this should include Google Cloud Storage and the Google Cloud Machine Learning Engine.

The Cloud Software Development Kit (SDK)

After you understand how to create a GCP project and configure it to access the ML Engine, you're ready to interact with your project. Google makes this possible through the Google SDK.

You can download the SDK from `http://cloud.google.com/sdk`. Clicking the Install button opens a page that provides instructions for downloading the SDK installer on your development system. I recommend installing all of the available components.

When you launch the installer, it asks you to log in to your account and grant privileges so that the SDK can access your GCP account. It also asks you to choose a cloud project to serve as the SDK's default project. After you select this, all further SDK commands affect the default project.

After you install the SDK, you're able to access two command-line utilities:

>> **gcloud:** Provides general project interaction and accesses Google's App Engine, Datastore, DNS, and ML Engine

>> **gsutil:** Accesses Google Cloud Storage

If you're running Windows, you can access these utilities through gcloud.cmd and gsutil.cmd. If you're running Linux or Mac OS, you can access them through the gcloud and gsutil executables.

Before you start using the SDK, you should make sure that you can access gcloud and gsutil from a command prompt. If you enter gcloud version and you don't see any version information, add the google-cloud-sdk/bin folder to your PATH environment variable.

The gcloud Utility

After you install the SDK, you can execute gcloud commands on a command line. All gcloud commands have the same format:

```
gcloud [optional flags] <group | command>
```

For example, you can check the version of gcloud by entering the following:

```
gcloud version
```

This command identifies the SDK's version and the versions of its components. You can install the latest components by entering the following command:

```
gcloud components update
```

In this example, components is a *group name* because it requires additional commands, such as update. You can think of a group like a submenu in a graphical user interface. In contrast, version is a *command name* because it doesn't accept further commands.

If you enter gcloud help, you see a long list of gcloud's groups and commands. gcloud's groups make it possible to manage web applications, access databases, and configure DNS settings. Table 13-1 lists ten of these groups.

TABLE 13-1

gcloud Groups

Group	Operation
app	Manage App Engine deployments
auth	Manage oauth2 credentials
components	Install, update, and remove SDK components
compute	Access resources related to the Compute Engine
config	View and edit SDK configuration
domains	Manage domains associated with the project
ml	Access machine learning capabilities
ml-engine	Manage machine learning jobs and models
projects	Create and manage project access
services	List, enable, and disable APIs and services

The ml-engine group plays a central role in this chapter because it lets you upload and execute TensorFlow applications in the cloud. Figure 13-1 displays many, but not all, of the groups and commands associated with ml-engine.

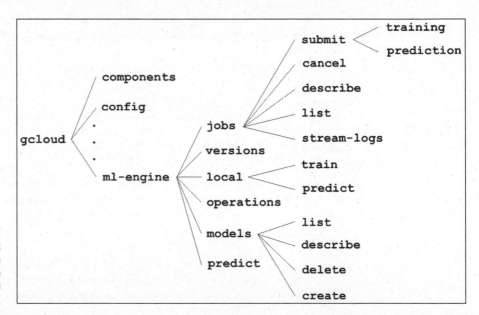

FIGURE 13-1: Commands in the Cloud SDK have many levels and options.

To deploy and run an application in the cloud, you need to be familiar with the commands in the `jobs` subgroup of `gcloud ml-engine`. To the ML Engine, a job refers to a processing task, which could be training or prediction. For example, the following command tells the engine that you want it to launch a training job:

```
gcloud ml-engine jobs submit training
```

To tell the GCP where to find your code, you need to follow the command with configuration flags. Three flags are particularly important:

>> `--package-path`: The local directory containing the training source code

>> `--module-name`: The name of the package's main module

>> `--staging-bucket`: The Cloud Storage bucket where the package and its dependencies should be stored

Before I explain how to submit jobs to the cloud, I explain in the next section how Cloud Storage works so that you can set the `--staging-bucket` flag. Then I explain how to prepare an application so that you can set the `--package-path` flag.

Google Cloud Storage

The GCP provides many options for storing data in the cloud, including the Datastore, BigTable, and Spanner. But if you want to store and access data for machine learning, you have to use Google Cloud Storage. That is, the ML Engine requires that you upload all your source files, dependencies, and data to Cloud Storage.

Thankfully, Cloud Storage is easy to work with. It stores data in containers called *buckets*, and you can think of a bucket as a directory in the cloud. Each data item in a bucket is called an *object*.

Buckets

The filesystem on your computer stores data in files and organizes files using directories. Cloud Storage stores data in objects and collects objects inside buckets. Buckets have a lot in common with directories, but there's one major difference: Buckets can't be nested. That is, you can't organize buckets into a hierarchy in the way that you can organize directories.

When working with buckets, you should be familiar with three points:

>> All load/store/delete operations involving Cloud Storage must identify at least one target bucket.

>> Every bucket has a globally unique name, a storage class, and a geographic location.

>> A project can create/delete buckets at most once every two seconds.

This last point is important. Creating and deleting buckets takes a significant amount of time, so Google recommends creating a small number of persistent buckets and reusing them as needed.

Bucket names

When you access a bucket, you need to identify it through its Uniform Resource Identifier (URI), which starts with `gs://`. A bucket's name must be unique across all GCP projects, not just your own projects. Therefore, it's a good idea to prepend your project ID to your bucket name, as in `gs://myproject3712_tfbook`.

The GCP sets the following criteria for bucket names:

>> A bucket's name must have more than two characters and fewer than 64.

>> The characters in a bucket's name are limited to letters, numbers, dashes, underscores, and dots.

>> A bucket's name can't start with "goog", and it can't contain "google" or misspellings of "google."

If you create a bucket whose name contains dots, Cloud Storage assumes that you've named your bucket after a domain, as in `www.evilrobot.com`. The good news is that Cloud Storage extends the maximum name length of domain-named buckets to 222 characters. The bad news is that you need to convince Google that you own the domain.

Storage classes and locations

Every bucket has a storage class that determines its availability, pricing, and storage characteristics. Table 13-2 lists the four different storage classes and their characteristics.

For example, suppose that you want a bucket to contain video that will be displayed across the world. In this case, you'd create a bucket and set its storage class to `multi_regional`. You can set a multi-regional bucket's location to one of three values: `eu`, `us`, and `asia`.

TABLE 13-2   ## Storage Classes of Cloud Storage Buckets

Storage Class	ID	Description
Multi-Regional	`multi_regional`	Data frequently accessed across a wide area (Price: $0.026 per GB per month)
Regional	`regional`	Data frequently accessed in a limited region (Price: $0.02 per GB per month)
Nearline	`nearline`	Data accessed no more than once per month (Price: $0.01 per GB per month)
Coldline	`coldline`	Data accessed no more than once per year (Price: $0.007 per GB per month)

If your data needs to be accessed only in a specific region, you should set the bucket's storage class to Regional. You can associate a Regional bucket with one of 13 different locations, and Table 13-3 lists them all.

TABLE 13-3   ## Location Codes of Regional Buckets

us–east1	us–east4	us–central1	us–west1
asia–east1	asia–northeast1	asia–southeast1	asia–south
australia–southeast1	europe–west1	europe–west2	europe–west3
southamerica–east1			

Google's list of supported regions increases regularly. For up-to-date information on storage classes, visit the GCP documentation at `http://cloud.google.com/storage/docs/storage-classes`. For up-to-date information on bucket locations, visit `http://cloud.google.com/storage/docs/bucket-locations`.

Objects and virtual hierarchy

Each piece of data in a Cloud Storage bucket is an object. A bucket may contain an unlimited number of objects, but each object must be 5 TB in size or less.

Every object has data and metadata. When you upload a file to a bucket, the file's content becomes the object's data. An object's metadata holds name-value pairs that describe the object.

The criteria for object names is much less restrictive than the criteria for bucket names:

>> An object's name can contain any sequence of valid Unicode characters.

>> An object's name can't contain any Carriage Return or Line Feed characters.

>> Google recommends against using #, [,], *, or ? in object names, as gsutil interprets these characters as wildcards.

A bucket's name must start and end with a letter, but an object's name can start and end with a slash (/). Therefore, you can construct a virtual hierarchy of objects by starting an object's name with a slash.

For example, suppose that you create a bucket named gs://dummies-tfbook. You can create an object in the bucket named gs://dummies-tfbook/data and another object named gs://dummies-tfbook/data/images. Cloud Storage won't recognize any relationship between these objects, but humans will understand that the objects form a virtual hierarchy.

The gsutil utility

The gsutil utility lets you create, access, and modify buckets and objects. For the most part, gsutil commands have the same names and purposes as common *nix commands.

Table 13-4 lists 13 of gsutil's commands. For a more thorough discussion, visit Google's documentation at https://cloud.google.com/storage/docs/gsutil.

Many of these commands are straightforward, but a few of them deserve explanation. This discussion explores the mb, cp/mv, ls/stat, and cat/compose commands.

Creating buckets (mb)

Before you upload data to Cloud Storage, you need to create one or more buckets. The command to know is mb:

```
gsutil mb [-c class] [-l location] [-p project_id] url...
```

TABLE 13-4 **gsutil Commands**

Command	Description
`mb [-c class] [-l location]` `. [-p proj_id] url...`	Make a new bucket
`rb [-f] url...`	Remove buckets

`cp [OPTION]... src_url dst_url`
`cp [OPTION]... src_url... dst_url`
`cp [OPTION]... -I dst_url`
	Copy files and objects

`mv [-p] src_url dst_url`
`mv [-p] src_url... dst_url`
`mv [-p] -I dst_url`
	Move objects and/or subdirectories

`rm [-f] [-r] url...` `rm [-f] [-r] -I`	Remove objects
`ls [-a] [-b] [-d] [-l] [-L] [-r]` `[-p proj_id] url...`	List buckets and objects
`stat url...`	Display object status
`rewrite -k [-f] [-r] url...` `rewrite -k [-f] [-r] -I`	Rewrite objects
`du url...`	Display object size usage
`cat [-h] url...`	Concatenate object to standard output

`compose gs://bucket/obj1`
`[gs://bucket/obj2 ...]`
`. gs://bucket/composite`
	Concatenate multiple objects into one

`[-D] config [-a] [-b] [-e] [-f] [-n]` `. [-o <file>] [-r] [-s <scope] [-w]`	Obtain credentials and create a configuration file

`web set [-m main_page_suffix]`
`. [-e error_page] bucket_url...`
`. web get bucket_url`
	Associate one or more buckets with a web page

The `-c`, `-l`, and `-p` flags are particularly important:

>> `-c`: The bucket's storage class: `multi_regional`, `regional`, `nearline`, and `coldline`. (Default: `multi_regional` or `regional`).

>> `-l`: The bucket's multi-regional location or regional location. (Default: us).

>> `-p`: The project's ID. (Default: the ID in the gsutil configuration file).

For example, the following command creates a regional bucket named `gs://dummies123-tfbook/example` and associates it with the `us-central1` region.

```
gsutil mb -c regional -l us-central1 gs://dummies123-tfbook/example
```

Copying (cp) and moving (mv)

After you create a bucket, you can upload files to it, thereby adding objects to the bucket. Similarly, you can download an object to your system as a file. Google makes these operations possible through the `cp` (copy) and `mv` (move) commands. Both commands transfer a source entity to a destination, but `cp` leaves the source entity in place while `mv` removes the source entity.

The best way to understand these commands is to look at some examples. The following command uploads a local file, `hello.txt`, to a bucket in Cloud Storage named `gs://newbucket`:

```
gsutil cp hello.txt gs://newbucket
```

Similarly, the following command moves `hello.txt` from `gs://newbucket` to the current directory on your development system. Note that `mv` removes `hello.txt` from the bucket:

```
gs mv gs://newbucket/hello.txt .
```

`cp` and `mv` accept many of the same flags as their counterparts in Linux and Unix. These flags include the following:

>> -r: Copy/move a directory and its contents

>> -L: Outputs a log file for each source entity of the copy/move

>> -e: Excludes symbolic links from the copy/move

For example, the following command moves the local `mydir` directory and its contents to `firstbucket`.

```
gsutil mv -r mydir gs://firstbucket
```

This command copies `mydir` and its contents from `firstbucket` to `secondbucket`:

```
gsutil cp -re gs://firstbucket/mydir gs://secondbucket
```

Because of the `-e` flag, `gsutil` won't copy any symbolic links from `mydir` to `secondbucket`.

Reading information (ls and stat)

The `ls` and `stat` commands provide information about buckets and objects in Cloud Storage. The simplest usage of `ls` is `gsutil ls`, which lists all of the buckets associated with the current GCP project.

One interesting feature of `ls` is that it recognizes the virtual hierarchy of objects. For example, suppose that `gs://mybucket` contains `/mydir/a.txt`, `/mydir/b.txt`, and `/newdir/c.txt`. The command `gsutil ls gs://mybucket` prints `/mydir` and `/newdir`, but none of the underlying objects. But if you set the `-r` flag, the entire contents of a bucket will be displayed. The following command demonstrates this:

```
gsutil ls -r gs://mybucket
```

Another useful flag is `-l`, which tells `ls` to print detailed output for each object of interest. These details include object sizes, creation sizes, and ownership. The `-L` flag prints even more information, including the content type, storage class, and update time of each object of interest.

If you want detailed information about one object, `stat` is more efficient than `ls -L`. As an example, the following command prints detailed information about the `training.dat` object in `mybucket/mydir`:

```
gsutil stat gs://mybucket/mydir/training.dat
```

The exit code of this command will equal 1 if the object exists and 0 if it doesn't. One important difference between `stat` and `ls` is that `stat` only provides information about objects.

Concatenation (cat and compose)

`cat` directs an object's text to standard output. For example, the following command prints the text contained in `gs://mybucket/a.txt`:

```
gsutil cat gs://mybucket/a.txt
```

Despite its name, you can't concatenate objects with `cat`, but you can concatenate objects with `compose`. That is, the following command concatenates the content of `a.txt` and `b.txt` in `gs://mybucket` and stores the combined result to `c.txt`:

```
gsutil compose gs://mybucket/a.txt gs://mybucket/b.txt gs://mybucket/c.txt
```

When you use compose, keep three points in mind:

>> A project can perform at most 200 compose operations per second.

>> A compose operation can combine a maximum of 32 entities.

>> A given object can be appended to at most 1,023 times.

TIP

compose is particularly helpful if you have to upload very large files to Cloud Storage. Rather than upload an entire file from one computer, you can upload portions of the file from separate computers and use compose to combine the portions.

Preparing for Deployment

Before you submit an application for training or prediction, you should prepare it in two ways:

>> Configure the application to receive command-line arguments from the ML Engine

>> Structure the application's files in a package

Receiving arguments

When the ML Engine executes your application, it passes arguments that provide information about the operating environment. Table 13-5 lists the possible arguments.

TABLE 13-5

Machine Learning Arguments

Argument	Operation
--job-dir	Location of the application's data
--train_batch_size	Batch size for training
--train_steps	Number of steps for each training epoch
--eval_batch_size	Batch size for evaluation
--eval_steps	Number of steps to run evaluation at each checkpoint
--eval_delay_secs	Time to wait before first evaluation
--min_eval_frequency	Minimum number of training steps between evaluations

`--job-dir` is particularly important because it tells the application where it should store its output files. The following code demonstrates how you can access this using an `ArgumentParser`:

```
if __name__ == '__main__':
    parser = argparse.ArgumentParser()
    parser.add_argument(
        '--job-dir',
        help='Checkpoint/output location',
        required=True
    )
    args = parser.parse_args()
```

In addition to the built-in arguments, you can provide arguments of your own. When you submit a job, the ML Engine will pass your arguments to the application. But keep two points in mind:

>> User-defined flags must follow all of the built-in flags.

>> Two dashes (--) must separate the built-in flags from the user-defined flags.

For example, suppose that you want to pass two arguments to your application named `data_dir` and `num_epochs`. When you execute a command, you need to set the `--data_dir` and `--num_epochs` flags at the end of the command and separate them from the command's normal flags with `--`.

Packaging TensorFlow code

You can launch a training operation with the command `gcloud ml-engine jobs submit training`. When you execute this, you can identify your source code with the `--package-path` and `--module-name` flags. The `--package-path` flag identifies the directory that contains your code, and this directory must meet the following requirements:

>> The directory must contain the module identified by `--module-name`.

>> The parent directory must have a file named `setup.py`.

>> Every directory under the parent directory must have a file named `__init__.py`. This file is usually empty.

>> The development system must have `setuptools` installed.

This last point is important. Before uploading a package, the ML Engine uses setuptools to zip the parent directory into a *.tar.gz file. If you've installed pip, you can install setuptools with pip install setuptools.

setup.py

In a Python package, setup.py contains instructions for building and installing the package. If you want the ML Engine to install your package, setup.py must perform two operations:

>> Import setuptools.setup.

>> Call the setup function of the setuptools module.

The setup function accepts a great deal of information about the package, including its name, version, and dependencies. Table 13-6 lists nine of the parameters that you can set.

TABLE 13-6 **Parameters of the setup Function**

Parameter	Description
name	Package name
version	Release version
packages	Dependency packages
install_requires	Packages that need to be installed when the package is installed
author	Name of the package's author
author_email	Author's email address
url	Package's home page
description	Short description of the package
license	The package's license

Rather than list your package's dependencies, you can call the find_packages provided by setuptools. Listing 13-1 presents the content of the setup.py file in the ch13/cloud_mnist folder:

```
from setuptools import find_packages
from setuptools import setup

REQUIRED_PACKAGES = ['tensorflow>=1.3']

setup(
    name='trainer',
    version='0.1',
    install_requires=REQUIRED_PACKAGES,
    packages=find_packages(),
    include_package_data=True,
    author='Matthew Scarpino'
    description='Running MNIST classification in the cloud'
)
```

Sadly, the ML Engine doesn't always have the latest versions of the packages installed. At the time of this writing, the current TensorFlow version is 1.4, but the default version supported by the ML Engine is 1.2.

You can request a specific version of a package by setting the `install_requires` field. In Listing 13-1, this field requests a version of TensorFlow greater than or equal to 1.3. For more information on supported versions, visit the site `http://cloud.google.com/ml-engine/docs/runtime-version-list`.

Executing Applications with the Cloud SDK

If you understand how to use the Cloud SDK, transfer data to Cloud Storage, and structure your application in a package, you're ready to start launching jobs with the Cloud SDK.

The ML Engine supports two types of jobs: training and prediction. Despite the names, training jobs don't necessarily train and prediction jobs don't necessarily predict. The difference between them involves the nature of the input. A training job expects a Python package as input and a prediction job expects a machine learning model stored as a `SavedModel`. Chapter 5 introduces `SavedModel`s and the methods available for accessing them.

Local execution

This chapter focuses on cloud computing, so it may seem strange to use the Cloud SDK to launch jobs locally. But the ML Engine is neither simple nor free, so I recommend that you test your applications locally before deploying them to the cloud. Another reason to execute your code locally is that you can view printed text on the command line instead of having to download and read logs.

You can launch a job on your development system by entering one of the following commands:

>> `gcloud ml-engine local train`: run a training job locally

>> `gcloud ml-engine local predict`: run a prediction job locally

These commands accomplish different results and accept different configuration flags.

Running a local training job

A GCP training job executes a Python package and produces output in the directory specified by the `--job-dir` flag. Table 13-7 lists `--job-dir` and other flags you can set for local training jobs.

TABLE 13-7   **Flags for Local Training**

Flag	Description
`--module-name=MODULE_NAME`	Identifies the module to execute
`--package-path=PACKAGE_PATH`	Path to the Python package containing the module to execute
`--job-dir=JOB_DIR`	Path to store training outputs
`--distributed`	Runs code in distributed mode
`--parameter-server-count=PARAMETER_SERVER_COUNT`	Number of parameter servers to run
`--start-port=START_PORT`	Start of the range of ports reserved by the local cluster
`--worker-count=WORKER_COUNT`	Number of workers to run

The `--package-path` flag identifies the top-level directory of your package. This is the directory that contains your package's `setup.py` file. The `--module-name` flag identifies the module to execute inside the package.

If you'd like to try this for yourself, copy the `mnist_train.tfrecords` and `mnist_test.tfrecords` files from the `ch12` directory to the `ch13` directory. Then go to the `ch13/cloud_mnist` directory and enter the following command:

```
gcloud ml-engine local train --module-name trainer.task--
    package-path trainer --job-dir output ----data_dir ../images
```

In this command, `--package-path` indicates that the `trainer` directory represents a package, and `--module-name` indicates that the name of the package's module is `trainer.task`. The `--job-dir` flag tells the application to store its results in a directory named `output`.

Two dashes (`--`) separate `--job-dir` from `--data_dir`. This indicates that `--data_dir` and any following flags are defined by the user.

Running a local prediction job

After training is complete, you can launch a local prediction job by executing `gcloud ml-engine local predict`. Table 13-8 lists the different flags you can set.

TABLE 13-8

Flags for Local Prediction

Flag	Description
`--model-dir=MODEL_DIR`	Path of the model
`--json-instances=JSON_INSTANCES`	Path to a local file containing prediction data in JSON format
`--text-instances=TEXT_INSTANCES`	Path to a local file containing prediction data in plain text

You should assign the `--model-dir` flag to the directory that contains the output of the training operation. Also, you need to identify prediction parameters using the `--json-instances` or `--text-instances` flags.

Deploying to the cloud

If you succeeded in launching jobs locally, deploying your applications to the cloud shouldn't present any difficulty. But be mindful of two issues:

>> You need to upload training/evaluation data to Cloud Storage.

>> The ML Engine may not support the versions of the packages you need.

Before you execute either of the applications in the ch13 directory, you'll need to upload the mnist_test.tfrecords and mnist_train.tfrecords files to a Cloud Storage bucket. For example, if your project's ID is $(PROJECT_ID), you can create a bucket named $(PROJECT_ID)_mnist in the central United States with the following command:

```
gsutil mb -c regional -l us-central1 gs://$(PROJECT_ID)_mnist
```

After you create the bucket, you can upload the two MNIST files to the bucket with the following command:

```
gsutil cp mnist_test.tfrecords mnist_train.tfrecords gs://$(PROJECT_ID)_mnist
```

After the command executes, it's a good idea to check that Cloud Storage created objects for the two files. You can verify this by running the command gsutil ls gs://$(PROJECT_ID)_mnist.

Running a remote training job

After you upload your test/evaluation data, you can launch a training job with the following command:

```
gcloud ml-engine jobs submit training $(JOB_ID)
```

$(JOB_ID) provides a unique identifier for the training job. After you launch the job, you can use this ID to check on the job's status.

In addition to identifying the job, you need to tell the ML Engine where to find your package and your input data. You also need to tell the engine where it should store output files. You can provide this information by following the command with flags, and Table 13-9 lists each of them.

The --module-name, --package-path, and --job-dir flags serve the same purposes as the similarly named flags for local training jobs. The --staging-bucket flag identifies the bucket to hold the deployed package. The --region flag accepts one of the regions listed in Table 13-3.

By default, deployed applications run on the latest stable version of the ML Engine. You can configure this by setting the --runtime-version flag. You can get the list of versions at cloud.google.com/ml-engine/docs/runtime-version-list.

I prefer to set the --stream-logs flag because it forces the command to block until the job completes. As the job runs, the console prints messages from the remote log. Aborting the command (Ctrl-C) doesn't affect the remote job.

TABLE 13-9   **Flags for Cloud Training Jobs**

Flag	Description
--module-name=MODULE_NAME	Identifies the module to execute
--package-path=PACKAGE_PATH	Path to the Python package containing the module to execute
--job-dir=JOB_DIR	Path to store output files
--staging-bucket=STAGING_BUCKET	Bucket to hold package during operation
--region=REGION	The region of the machine learning job
--runtime-version=RUNTIME_VERSION	The version of the ML Engine for the job
--stream-logs	Block until the job completes and stream the logs
--scale-tier=SCALE_TIER	The job's operating environment
--config=CONFIG	Path to a job configuration file

By default, applications uploaded to the ML Engine can run only on a single CPU. You can configure the execution environment by setting the --scale-tier flag to one of the values listed in Table 13-10.

TABLE 13-10   **Scale Tier Values**

Value	Description
basic	A single worker on a CPU
basic-gpu	A single worker with a GPU
basic-tpu	A single worker instance with a Cloud TPU
standard-1	Many workers and a few parameter servers
premium-1	A large number of workers and many parameter servers
custom	Define a cluster

If you set --scale-tier to basic-gpu, you can execute your code on an Nvidia Tesla K80 GPU. This has 4,992 CUDA cores and 24 GB of GDDR5 memory. If you set --scale-tier to basic-tpu, you can execute your code on one or more of Google's Tensor Processing Units (TPUs). At the time of this writing, Google restricts TPU access to developers in its Cloud TPU program, and you can learn more about this program at http://cloud.google.com/tpu.

If you set --scale-tier to standard-1 or premium-1, you can run your job on a cluster of processors. If you set --scale-tier to custom, you can configure the cluster by assigning the --config flag to the name of a configuration file.

Running a remote prediction job

Chapter 5 introduces SavedModels, and if you upload a SavedModel to a Cloud Storage bucket, you can launch a prediction job with the following command:

```
gcloud ml-engine jobs submit prediction $(JOB_ID)
```

This command accepts flags that specify where the prediction job should read its input and write its output. Table 13-11 lists each of these flags.

TABLE 13-11   **Flags for Cloud Prediction Jobs**

Flag	Description
--model-dir=MODEL_DIR	Path of the bucket containing the saved model
--model=MODEL	Name of the model to use for prediction
--input-paths=INPUT_PATH, [INPUT_PATH,...]	Path to the input data to use for prediction
--data-format=DATA_FORMAT	Format of the input data
--output-path=OUTPUT_PATH	Path to store the prediction results
--region=REGION	The region of the machine learning job
--batch-size=BATCH_SIZE	Number of records per batch
--max-worker-count=MAX_WORKER_COUNT	The maximum number of workers to employ for parallel processing
--runtime-version=RUNTIME_VERSION	The version of the ML Engine for the job
--version=VERSION	Version of the model to be used

When you launch a remote prediction job, you must identify the model's name with --model or the bucket containing the model files with --model-dir. You also need to identify the location of the input files with --input-paths.

The ML Engine accepts prediction input data in one of three formats. You can identify the format of your data by setting --data-format to one of the following values:

>> `text`: Text files with one line per instance

>> `tf-record`: TFRecord files

>> `tf-record-gzip`: GZIP-compressed TFRecord files

The last required flag is `--output-path`. This tells the ML Engine which Cloud Storage bucket should contain the prediction results.

Viewing a job's status

After you launch a job, you can view the job's status in two ways. First, you can use `gcloud` commands, such as the following:

>> `gcloud ml-engine jobs list`: List the jobs associated with the default project along with their statuses and creation times

>> `gcloud ml-engine jobs describe $(JOB_ID) --summarize`: Provide detailed information about a specific job in human-readable format

When I want to check on a job, I prefer to visit the Google Cloud Console. If you click the menu bars in the upper left and scroll down, you see an entry entitled ML Engine. This entry leads to two options: Jobs and Models.

If you click the ML Engine ⇨ Jobs option, the page lists all the jobs associated with the project. If you click on a job name, a new page provides detailed information about the job's execution, including its status and any log messages.

Configuring a Cluster in the Cloud

By default, GCP jobs execute on a single CPU. But if you set `--scale-tier` to `custom`, you can launch a job to execute on a cluster of processors. You can configure the cluster and the nature of its processing by following the `--config` flag with the name of a configuration file.

You can format the configuration file using YAML (YAML Ain't Markup Language) or JSON (JavaScript Object Notation). If a setting in your configuration file conflicts with a command flag, the job uses the file's setting. Table 13-12 lists the four fields that configure training and prediction.

TABLE 13-12 **Training/Prediction Configuration Fields**

Field	Type	Description
trainingInput	TrainingInput	Input parameters to create a training job
trainingOutput	TrainingOutput	Result of the current training job
predictionInput	PredictionInput	Input parameters to create a prediction job
predictionOutput	PredictionOutput	Result of the current prediction job

A configuration file can provide at most one input object and at most one output object. If you're launching a training job, you may want to set the trainingInput field to a TrainingInput and/or the trainingOutput field to a TrainingOutput. If you're launching a prediction job, you may want to set the predictionInput field to a PredictionInput and/or the predictionOutput field to a Prediction Output.

Setting the training input

A TrainingInput provides information about the training you want to perform and configures the cluster to execute the training job. Table 13-13 lists the fields that you can set.

The scaleTier field specifies the desired execution environment for the cluster, and it accepts the same values as the --scale-tier flag. The masterType, serverType, and parameterServerType fields get more specific, and identify the type of virtual machine that should be used to serve the given role. You can set each of these fields to one of ten strings:

>> standard: Basic configuration for small to moderate datasets

>> large_model: High-memory configuration for models with large datasets and many hidden layers

>> complex_model_s: Provides greater computation than standard configuration

>> complex_model_m: Twice as many cores and twice as much memory as the complex_model_s configuration

>> complex_model_l: Twice as many cores and twice as much memory as the complex_model_m configuration

>> standard_gpu: Similar to the standard configuration, but provides access to an Nvidia Tesla K80 GPU

>> `complex_model_m_gpu`: Similar to the `standard` configuration, but provides access to four Nvidia Tesla K80 GPUs

>> `complex_model_l_gpu`: Similar to the `standard` configuration, but provides access to four Nvidia Tesla K80 GPUs

>> `standard_p100`: Similar to the `standard` configuration, but provides access to an Nvidia Tesla P100 GPU

>> `complex_model_m_p100`: Similar to the `standard` configuration, but provides access to four Nvidia Tesla P100 GPUs

TABLE 13-13   **TrainingInput Fields**

Field	Type	Description
scaleTier	ScaleTier	The job's execution platform
masterType	string	Machine type for the master
workerType	string	Machine type for workers
parameterServerType	string	Machine type for parameter servers
workerCount	string	Number of workers in the cluster
parameterServerCount	string	Number of parameter servers in the cluster
packageUris	string	The locations of the application's packages and dependencies
pythonModule	string	The module ro run after installing the package
args	[string]	Command-line arguments to pass to the module
hyperpameters	HyperparameterSpec	Specifies which parameters to optimize during training
region	string	The target region for running the job
jobDir	string	Cloud storage path to contain training outputs
runtimeVersion	string	The version of the Cloud ML Engine to use for training

You can identify specific parameters for training by setting the hyperparameters field to an array of HyperparameterSpecs. Each HyperparameterSpec has four fields:

>> goal: Nature of the optimization (MAXIMIZE or MINIMIZE)

>> params: Array of ParameterSpecs that identify the parameters to optimize during training

>> maxParallelTrials: Maximum number of training runs to execute in parallel

>> hyperparameterMetricTag: Identifier for the optimization. TensorBoard uses this tag to label the optimization process

A HyperparameterSpec identifies one or more parameters for the training job to optimize. You can identify the parameters of interest by setting the params field to a list of ParameterSpecs. Each ParameterSpec has seven fields:

>> parameterName: The parameter's name, which must be unique among all parameters in the HyperparameterSpec

>> type: The parameter's data type, which can be INTEGER, DOUBLE, DISCRETE, CATEGORICAL, or PARAMETER_TYPE_UNSPECIFIED

>> minValue: Minimum value of the parameter (required for INTEGER or DOUBLE parameters)

>> maxValue: Maximum value of the parameter (required for INTEGER or DOUBLE parameters)

>> categoricalValues: A list of strings that identify the different categories (required for CATEGORICAL parameters)

>> discreteValues: A list of numbers that identify the different discrete values of the parameter (required for DISCRETE parameters)

>> scaleType: Nature of the scaling that should be applied (can be NONE, UNIT_LINEAR_SCALE, UNIT_LOG_SCALE, or UNIT_REVERSE_LOG_SCALE)

The ch13/cluster_mnist package is similar to the ch13/cloud_mnist package. The only difference is that it uses a configuration file to define a custom cluster. Listing 13-2 presents the content of ch13/cluster_mnist/config.yaml.

LISTING 13-2: **Configuration File for Custom Cluster Execution**

```
trainingInput:
  scaleTier: CUSTOM
  masterType: standard
  workerType: standard
  parameterServerType: standard
  workerCount: 4
  parameterServerCount: 2
```

This configuration file tells the ML Engine to execute the job with four workers and two parameter servers. It also states that the workers and parameter servers should be executed on standard systems.

Obtaining the training output

You can configure how a training job produces output by setting the training Output field of your configuration file to a TrainingOutput. Table 13-14 lists the possible fields.

TABLE 13-14 **TrainingOutput Fields**

Field	Type	Description
completedTrialCount	string	The number of hyperparameter trials that completed successfully
trials	[{ HyperParameterOutput }]	Results of hyperparameter trials
consumedMlUnits	number	The number of units of the Machine Learning Engine consumed during the job's execution
isHyperparameterTuningJob	boolean	Whether the job tuned hyperparameters

If you set the hyperparameters field of the TrainingInput, you can access the results in the trials field of the TrainingOutput. This is a list of Hyperparameter Outputs, and each HyperparameterOutput has four fields:

>> trialId: A string that identifies the trial

>> hyperparameters: A dictionary that associates parameter names with the trained values

>> `finalMetric`: A `HyperparameterMetric` that identifies the trial's final objective metric

>> `allMetrics`: A list of `HyperparameterMetrics` that contain all recorded object metrics for the trial

The ML engine provides training metrics as `HyperparameterMetrics`, and each `HyperparmeterMetric` has two fields: `trainingStep` and `objectiveValue`. The `trainingStep` field identifies the global training step, and `objectiveValue` identifies the objective value at the given step.

Setting the prediction input

You can configure the input to a prediction job by setting the file's `prediction Input` field to a `PredictionInput`. Table 13-15 lists the fields that you can set in a `PredictionInput`.

TABLE 13-15 **PredictionInput Fields**

Field	Type	Description
dataFormat	DataFormat	Format of the data files
inputPaths	[string]	Cloud storage buckets containing the data files
outputPath	string	Cloud Storage location for storing output files
maxWorkerCount	string	Maximum number of workers to be used for parallel processing
region	string	Region in which to launch the prediction job
runtimeVersion	string	The version of the Cloud ML Engine to use for training
batchSize	string	Number of records to process per batch
modelName	string	Complete name of the model
versionName	string	Version of the model to use for prediction
uri	string	Cloud storage location for the mdoel

To perform a prediction job, you need to provide a `SavedModel` and files containing input data. You can identify the format and location of your input data by setting the first two fields, `dataFormat` and `inputPaths`. To specify the format of your data, you need to set `dataFormat` to `TEXT`, `JSON`, `TF_RECORD`, `TF_RECORD_GZIP`, or `DATA_FORMAT_UNSPECIFIED`.

The last three entries form a union called model_version, so you can set only one of the three in a PredictionInput. You can identify your model by setting modelName to a string with the following format:

```
projects/<var>[YOUR_PROJECT]</var>/models/<var>[YOUR_MODEL]</var>
```

If you identify your model with versionName, you need to provide a slightly-different string:

```
projects/<var>[YOUR_PROJECT]</var>/models/<var>YOUR_MODEL/
    versions/<var>[YOUR_VERSION]</var>
```

If the Cloud Storage bucket only contains one model, you can simply set the uri field to the bucket's location.

Obtaining the prediction output

You can configure the output of a prediction job by setting the file's prediction Output field to a PredictionOutput. Table 13-16 lists the fields you can set.

TABLE 13-16 **PredictionOutput Fields**

Field	Type	Description
outputPath	string	The Cloud Storage location for storing the prediction output
predictionCount	string	The number of generated predictions
errorCount	string	The number of data instances that produced errors
nodeHours	number	The number of node hours consumed by the prediction job

These fields are straightforward to understand and use. The nodeHours field provides the product of the number of nodes used by the job and the number of hours required to complete the job.

4

The Part of Tens

Chapter **14**

The Ten Most Important Classes

The TensorFlow API is immense, comprising hundreds of packages and thousands of modules. Given its size, newcomers may find it hard to know which classes to study closely. To remedy this confusion, I selected TensorFlow's ten most important classes and explain what the class accomplishes and why it's so important.

Tensor

Tensors play a central role in TensorFlow development and serve as the primary objects for storing and manipulating data. Optimizers only accept data contained in tensors, and image-processing functions require images to be provided as tensors. All neural network layers, from dense layers to dropout layers, accept tensors as input and return tensors as output.

A tensor serves as an N-dimensional array, where N can be zero or more. A tensor's number of dimensions is called the tensor's *rank,* and the size of each dimension is called the tensor's *shape.* For example, a 3-x-5 matrix has shape [3, 5], and an RGB image whose size is 200 x 200 would be represented by a tensor with size [200, 200, 3].

TensorFlow provides hundreds of functions for creating, transforming, and processing tensors (see Chapter 3). You can create a tensor with constant values by calling tf.constant or create a tensor with random values by calling tf.random_normal or tf.random_uniform. You can reshape a tensor with tf.reshape and extract part of a tensor with tf.slice.

Operation

When the Python interpreter reaches a function that operates on tensors, it doesn't execute the operation immediately. Instead, it creates an instance of the Operation class that represents the operation. Every Operation has a property called inputs that contains its input tensors and a property called outputs that contains its output tensors.

Every Operation has a property called type that is usually set to the function that created it. For example, if you call tf.add, the corresponding operation will have its type set to add.

Other math operations include tf.divide, tf.round, and tf.sqrt. TensorFlow also supports traditional matrix operations, including tf.matmul, tf.diag, and tf.matrix_solve.

Graph

TensorFlow creates a Tensor instance for each tensor in your application and an Operation for each operation involving tensors. It stores these Tensors and Operations in a data structure called a Graph. Only one Graph can be active at a time, and you can make a new Graph active by calling as_default.

The Graph class provides a number of methods for accessing the data contained in the graph. You can access a particular tensor with get_tensor_by_name or access all of the graph's operations by calling get_operations.

Each Graph stores data in a series of containers called *collections*. Every collection can be accessed through a particular key, and get_all_collection_keys provides the full list of keys. For example, a graph stores its global variables in the collection whose key is tf.GraphKeys.GLOBAL_VARIABLES.

Session

After you add tensors and operations to a graph, you can execute the graph's operations by creating and running a session. You can create a session by calling tf.Session and then launch the session by calling its run method.

The first argument of the run method tells the session what processing to perform. If this argument contains tensors, the session will compute the elements of each tensor and return the elements in a NumPy array. If this argument contains Operations, the session will perform each operation and return the appropriate result.

If the questions on StackOverflow are any indication, run's feed_dict confuses many developers. This parameter accepts a dictionary that associates values with tensors (usually *placeholders*) in the graph. But the dictionary's values can't be tensors. For this reason, it's generally a good idea to store and process input data using NumPy arrays before executing a session.

Variable

Variables resemble tensors in many respects. They store values in N-dimensional arrays and can be operated upon using regular TensorFlow operations. But during training operations, applications rely on variables to store the state of the model. For example, if an application consists of a neural network, the network's weights and biases will be stored as variables.

Another difference is that variables require a different set of methods than tensors. For example, after you create a Variable, you need to initialize its value by running a special operation in the session. If your application has many variables, you can obtain a combined initialization operation by calling tf.global_variables_initializer.

At a low level, the goal of training is to set the application's variables to values that will bring the model in line with observed data. These variables are critically important, so it's a good idea to store them to checkpoint files with Savers. Chapter 5 explains how to create, initialize, and save variables in a TensorFlow application.

Optimizer

The disparity between an application's model and the observed data is called *loss*. A TensorFlow application reduces loss using an optimizer. In code, you can create an optimizer by instantiating a subclass of the `Optimizer` class. Every optimizer has a `minimize` method that returns an operation that can be executed in a session.

TensorFlow supports a number of different optimization algorithms, and each is represented by a different subclass of `Optimizer`. As an example, the simplest optimization algorithm, the gradient descent method, is represented by the `GradientDescentOptimizer`. But the simplest algorithm is rarely the most effective, and I recommend optimizing your applications with the `AdamOptimizer` or `AdagradOptimizer` instead.

Estimator

As discussed in Chapter 12, estimators dramatically simplify the process of developing and deploying machine learning algorithms. When you use an estimator, you don't have to worry about sessions and graphs. You simply need to know three methods of the `Estimator` class: `train`, `evaluate`, and `predict`.

Another advantage of using estimators is that TensorFlow provides many subclasses of `Estimator`. These canned estimators, such as `LinearRegressor` and `DNNClassifier`, make it easy to train and test machine learning. The `DNNLinearCombinedClassifier` is particularly helpful because it lets you take advantage of wide and deep learning.

Dataset

One of the most recent changes to the TensorFlow API is the promotion of the `tf.contrib.data` package to `tf.data`. This package provides the all-important `Dataset` class, which TensorFlow recommends for loading and processing data. This class provides many powerful methods for batching and transforming data, and in many cases, you can perform these operations in a multithreaded manner.

The `Dataset` class is also important because it's the superclass of `TextLineDataset` and `TFRecordDataset`. These two classes make it straightforward to read data from text files and TFRecord files. Chapter 10 provides a lengthy discussion of these classes and their usage.

Iterator

The Dataset class provides many powerful capabilities, but it doesn't let you access its data directly. To extract tensors from a dataset, you need to create an instance of the Iterator class.

TensorFlow provides four different ways to iterate through a dataset's content. The simplest is the one-shot iterator, which can iterate through a dataset only once. You can reuse initializable and reinitializable iterators, but you'll need to run special initialization operations first. Feedable iterators are the most complicated, but you can associate them with multiple datasets and you don't need to initialize them before each iteration.

Saver

The goal of training is to determine which variables produce the least possible loss. Training can take hours or days, so it's crucial to store the variable's values during and after training. TensorFlow makes this possible by providing the Saver class.

Using this class is easy. After you create a Saver instance, you can call save to store the model's state in numbered checkpoint files. You can load the model's variables from the checkpoint files by calling the restore method.

Chapter **15**

Ten Recommendations for Training Neural Networks

I n most software development efforts, an application will always do its job if you code it correctly. But when you work with neural networks, this isn't the case. You can write flawless code and still end up with lousy results. No matter what the academics say, neural network development is not an exact science — there's still a lot of art involved.

In this chapter, I present ten recommendations that can help you improve the accuracy and performance of your neural networks. These general rules are based on my experience and what I've learned from other developers and researchers. But keep in mind that neural networks are never completely reliable: Even a perfectly coded neural network can fail from time to time.

Select a Representative Dataset

This recommendation is the simplest because it doesn't involve any math or software development. When it comes to training samples, more is better, but size isn't the only priority. You need to make sure that your training dataset resembles the real world. Also, if your application classifies samples into categories, you need to make sure that you have a large number of samples for each category.

When it comes to image classification, you never know what bizarre features the neural network will focus on. For this reason, many developers add low levels of random noise to their input samples. This noise shouldn't obfuscate the image, but should force the neural network to pay attention to relevant characteristics.

Standardize Your Data

When you test a machine learning application or use it for practical prediction, you should make sure that the test data statistically resembles the training data. That is, the test/prediction data should have the same mean and standard deviation as the training data.

As discussed in Chapter 7, the process of setting the mean and standard deviation of a dataset is called standardization. Many applications standardize their data by setting the mean to 0 and setting the standard deviation to 1. In a TensorFlow application, you can accomplish this by calling `tf.nn.moments` and `tf.nn.batch_normalization`.

Use Proper Weight Initialization

Researchers have devised a number of mathematical procedures for initializing the weights of a neural network. One of the most popular methods is called the Glorot method or Xavier method. You can use this method in your applications by calling `tf.contrib.layers.xavier_initializer`.

Start with a Small Number of Layers

For complex problems, you probably won't know how many hidden layers to create. Some developers assume that larger is better, and construct neural networks with many (more than 10) hidden layers. But this increases the likelihood of overfitting, in which the neural network becomes focused on your specific training data and fails to analyze general data.

To avoid overfitting, it's a good idea to start small. If the accuracy is unacceptable, increase the network's depth until the accuracy reaches a suitable value. In addition to reducing the likelihood of overfitting, the start-small method guarantees faster execution than the start-large method.

Add Dropout Layers

In addition to dense layers, I recommend that you add dropout layers to your neural networks. A dropout layer sets a percentage of its inputs to 0 before passing the signals as output. This reduces the likelihood of overfitting by reducing the codependency of the inputs entering the dropout layer.

In TensorFlow, you can create a dropout layer by calling `tf.nn.dropout`. This layer accepts a tensor whose values identify the probability that the corresponding input should be discarded.

Train with Small, Random Batches

After you preprocess your data, initialize your weights, and determine the initial structure of your neural network, you're ready to start training. Rather than train with the entire dataset at once, you should split your data into batches. The neural network will update its gradients and weights with each batch processed.

Reducing the batch size increases the training time, but it also decreases the likelihood that the optimizer will settle into a local minimum instead of finding the global minimum. It also reduces the dependence of the analysis on the order of the samples. You can reduce this dependence further by shuffling batches as training proceeds.

Normalize Batch Data

Even if you standardize the samples entering your neural network, the mean and variance of your data will change as it moves from one hidden layer to the next. For this reason, developers normalize the data as it leaves each layer.

This normalization involves setting the mean to zero and the standard deviation to one. But the process is slightly more complicated because you need to approximate the mean and variance of the entire batch. Rather than do the math yourself, I recommend calling `tf.contrib.layers.batch_norm`.

Try Different Optimization Algorithms

Your choice of optimizer will play a critical role in determining the accuracy and performance of your application. While writing this book, I searched many online forums for the answer to the question "Which optimization method is best?" But despite decades of analysis, researchers haven't reached a consensus.

Personally, I like to start with the Adam and Adagrad optimizers, but if you're not getting the performance and accuracy you want, it's a good idea to try other methods. In a TensorFlow application, you set the optimization method by creating an instance of an optimizer class, such as `tf.train.AdamOptimizer`, calling its `minimize` method, and running the returned operation in a session.

Set the Right Learning Rate

An optimizer's learning rate determines how an optimizer updates its weights with each training step. If you set the learning rate too high, the optimizer will make dramatic changes to the weights, and it may never converge to a solution. If you set the learning rate too low, the optimizer will proceed slowly, and it may converge to a local minimum instead of a global minimum.

Typical learning rates vary from 0.0001 to 0.5, but the best learning rate varies from application to application. I recommend starting with a high value and repeatedly reducing the learning rate until you're satisfied with the application's accuracy and performance.

Check Weights and Gradients

Machine learning applications frequently fail because the weights drop to zero (the vanishing gradient problem) or grow very large (the exploding gradient problem). In both cases, you may need to adjust the number of layers in your network and/or the activation function of each layer.

Thankfully, TensorFlow lets you save a layer's weights and visualize the weights with TensorBoard. Chapter 4 introduces TensorBoard and explains how to generate and print summary data for visualization. Chapter 5 explains how to visualize training results with TensorBoard.

Index

K

keep_checkpoint_every_n_hours parameter, 253

keep_checkpoint_max parameter, 253

keep_dims parameter, 134

keep_prob parameter, 140

Keras framework, 15

kernel_initializer parameter, 157, 197

kernel_regularizer parameter, 157

kernel_size parameter, 157, 158

kernels. *See* filtering images

key parameter, 142

keys, 48, 254, 310

L

–l flag, 287, 289

–L flag, 288, 289

l1_regularizer function, 140–141

l2_regularizer function, 140–141

label_dimension parameter, 258

label_vocabulary parameter, 260, 262

labels, CIFAR-10 images, 161

labels argument, 115

labels function, 112

lambda definition, 211–212

Lamblin, Pascal, 126

latest_filename parameter, 83

layers, neural network

  batch normalization, 137

  number of, 316–317

  overview, 127–129

  tuned, creating, 144–147

learn_runner.run function, 273, 275

learning rate, 73, 74, 75, 77, 318

lecun_uniform function, 136

LeCunn, Yann, 12

license parameter, 292

life-cycle methods, 91–92

likelihood, 107–108, 114

linear classifiers, 262–263, 264

linear interpolation, 173

linear regression, 10, 100–102, 257–260

LinearClassifier class, 256

LinearRegressor class, 256, 258–260

linspace function, 28, 31

Linux, TensorFlow on, 20, 233

list command, 18

list_files method, 210, 211

list_local_devices function, 235–236

load function, 86

load_boston function, 222

load_csv_with_header function, 222–223, 251

load_csv_without_header function, 222–223

load_iris function, 222, 223

local execution, with Cloud SDK, 294–295

local minimum of loss, 74–75, 80

local_variables_initializer function, 68

location codes, Cloud Storage, 284–285

log function, 39, 55

log likelihood method, 108

log_device_placement parameter, 237, 253

log_every_n function, 55, 56

log_first_n function, 55, 56

log_if function, 55, 56

log_step_count_steps parameter, 253

logarithmic operations, 38–39

--logdir DIR flag, 57

logdir parameter, 60

logging, 54–56

LoggingTensorHook class, 93

logistic (sigmoid) function, 106–107, 124, 126

logistic regression

  binary, 100, 105–110

  multinomial, 100, 110–116

  overview, 106

logits argument, 115

logp1 function, 39

long short-term memory (LSTM) cells, 183, 192–196

loss

  cross entropy, 114–115

  defined, 312

  determining, 69

  example code, 86–88

  in gradient descent algorithm, 73

  L1/L2 regularization, 140–141

  maximum likelihood estimation, 107–108

  mean-squared error, 100–101, 103

  neural networks, 129–130

  optimization, 70–78

multiple graphs in multiple sessions, 62–64

`multiply` function, 35, 36

`MultiRNNCell` class, 190–191

multithreading, 201–202, 226–228. *See also* datasets

mv (move) command, 287, 288

N

`n_classes` parameter, 260, 262

name parameter
  for functions creating tensors, 29
  `get_variable`, 142
  image, 178
  `max_pooling2d`, 159
  setup, 292
  `tf.layers.conv2d`, 157
  `variable_scope`, 142

`name_scope` function, 143

names parameter, 266

NanTensorHook class, 93

nearest-neighbor interpolation, 172

`negative` function, 36

Nesterov Accelerated Gradient (NAG) descent algorithm, 76

Netflix, 13

neural networks. *See also* convolutional neural networks; recurrent neural networks
  activation functions, 123–127
  batch normalization, 136–139, 317
  bias, 122–123
  deep learning, implementing, 131–133
  deep learning, improving, 143–147
  deep learning, overview, 129
  dropout layers, 317
  input standardization, 134–135
  layers, 127–129, 316–317
  loss, determining, 69
  mathematical modeling, 67
  neurons, 118–119
  optimization, 318
  overview, 2, 10–11, 117–118
  perceptrons, 119–120
  regularization, 139–141
  representative dataset for, 315–316
  standardization, 134–135, 316
  versus statistical regression, 118
  training, tips for, 315–318

training with backpropagation, 129–131
  tuning, 133–141
  variable scope, 141–143
  weight initialization, 135–136, 316
  weights, overview of, 121–122

neurons, 118–119

next method, 204

`next_batch` method, 112, 113

node element, `GraphDef`, 49, 50

nodeHours field, 305

nodes. *See also* activation functions
  graphs, 46
  neural networks, 121–122, 123, 139–141
  recurrent neural networks, 181–182

noise, image, 151–152

norm function, 40

normalization, batch, 134, 136–139, 317

`normalizer_fn` parameter, 144, 145

`normalizer_params` parameter, 144, 145

num parameter, 35

`num_cores` parameter, 252, 253

`num_epochs` parameter, 252

`num_examples` function, 112

`num_outputs` parameter, 144, 145

`num_parallel_calls` argument, 226

`num_proj` parameter, 195

`num_threads` field, 228

`num_units` parameter, 185

numeric columns, 254

NumPy, 165

`numpy_input_fn` function, 251–252

O

objects, Google Cloud Storage, 283, 285–286

Office of Naval Research, 10

`offset` parameter, 135

one-hot vectors, 113

ones function, 28, 30

one-shot iterators, 213–215, 221

OpenCL, 230

`operation_timeout_in_ms` option, 227

operations (`Operation` class)
  assigning to devices, 235–237
  basic math, 35–37
  exponents and logarithms, 38–39

WholeFileReader function, 168
wide and deep learning, 263–269
Windows, TensorFlow on, 20–21, 231–232
workerCount field, 301
--worker-count flag, 294
workers, in clusters, 241, 242–244, 246
WorkerSessionCreator subclass, 94
write method, 206
write_graph function, 51

X

x parameter, 134, 140, 251
xavier_initializer function, 136

Y

y parameter, 251

Z

zero_debias_moving_mean parameter, 138
zero_state method, 185
zeros function, 28, 30
zip method, 211, 213

Notes

Notes

Notes

Notes

About the Author

Matthew Scarpino has been a programmer and engineer for nearly 20 years. In addition to developing neural networks for image recognition, he's designed circuitry to model human cognition for the Defense Advanced Research Projects Agency (DARPA). He's currently the lead developer at plutocracy.com, which uses machine learning to analyze financial trends.

Matthew became a Google Certified Data Engineer in 2018. In his spare time, he programs robots and writes a blog on TensorFlow, tfblog.com.

Dedication

This book is dedicated to the AI pioneer, Frank Rosenblatt. Though his contemporaries dismissed him as a starry-eyed academic, modern accomplishments have not only vindicated his wildest predictions but surpassed them.

Author's Acknowledgments

In the late 1990s, I came across *C For Dummies* in a college bookstore and fell madly in love. Dan Gookin didn't just make C programming approachable — he made it *funny*. I spent many happy hours reading his silly explanations and working through his whimsical programming examples.

I'm not half the author Dan Gookin is, but I'd like to thank Executive Editor Katie Mohr for giving me the chance to write a *For Dummies* book. As a newcomer, I had millions of asinine questions, ranging from chapter structure to table fonts to equation formatting. Katie replied to every question, and her pleasant disposition never flagged for a moment.

The book's Project Editor, Kelly Ewing, did an excellent job. She worked tirelessly to improve the clarity and quality of the text, and the book benefitted greatly from her careful attention. Also, it took me some time to acclimate myself to the *For Dummies* editing criteria, and I'm deeply grateful for Kelly's patience and assistance.

The prolific author Guy Hart-Davis reviewed the book from a technical perspective and provided comments and support. Thanks to his feedback, I reworded many passages to better explain TensorFlow's approach to machine learning. Also, Guy caught many more technical errors than I'd care to admit. Thanks, Guy!

I'd like to extend my deep gratitude to the entire Wiley production team. In particular, I'd like to thank Lisa Stiers for her work in proofreading the text and Tamilmani Varadharaj for his work as the production editor.

Last but not least, I'd like to thank Matt Wagner, literary agent extraordinaire. From my initial proposal to the published book, he has served as agent, editor, coach, and diplomat. Despite working on many projects at once, he always made the time to address my questions and concerns.

Publisher's Acknowledgments

Senior Acquisitions Editor: Amy Fandrei
Project Editor: Kelly Ewing
Copy Editor: Kelly Ewing
Editorial Assistant: Serena Novosel
Sr. Editorial Assistant: Cherie Case
Reviewer: Guy Hart-Davis

Production Editor: Tamilmani Varadharaj
Cover Image: © Funny Drew/Shutterstock

Take dummies with you everywhere you go!

Whether you are excited about e-books, want more from the web, must have your mobile apps, or are swept up in social media, dummies makes everything easier.

Find us online!

dummies.com

dummies
A Wiley Brand

Leverage the power

Dummies is the global leader in the reference category and one of the most trusted and highly regarded brands in the world. No longer just focused on books, customers now have access to the dummies content they need in the format they want. Together we'll craft a solution that engages your customers, stands out from the competition, and helps you meet your goals.

Advertising & Sponsorships

Connect with an engaged audience on a powerful multimedia site, and position your message alongside expert how-to content. Dummies.com is a one-stop shop for free, online information and know-how curated by a team of experts.

- Targeted ads
- Video
- Email Marketing
- Microsites
- Sweepstakes sponsorship

20 **MILLION**
PAGE VIEWS
EVERY SINGLE MONTH

15
MILLION
UNIQUE
VISITORS PER MONTH

43%
OF ALL VISITORS
ACCESS THE SITE
VIA THEIR MOBILE DEVICES

700,000 NEWSLETTER
SUBSCRIPTIONS
TO THE INBOXES OF
300,000 UNIQUE INDIVIDUALS
EVERY WEEK

# of dummies

Custom Publishing

Reach a global audience in any language by creating a solution that will differentiate you from competitors, amplify your message, and encourage customers to make a buying decision.

- Apps
- Books
- eBooks
- Video
- Audio
- Webinars

Brand Licensing & Content

Leverage the strength of the world's most popular reference brand to reach new audiences and channels of distribution.

For more information, visit dummies.com/biz

PERSONAL ENRICHMENT

Staying Sharp

9781119187790
USA $26.00
CAN $31.99
UK £19.99

Facebook

9781119179030
USA $21.99
CAN $25.99
UK £16.99

Guitar

9781119293354
USA $24.99
CAN $29.99
UK £17.99

Investing

9781119293347
USA $22.99
CAN $27.99
UK £16.99

Beekeeping

9781119310068
USA $22.99
CAN $27.99
UK £16.99

Digital Photography

9781119235606
USA $24.99
CAN $29.99
UK £17.99

Meditation

9781119251163
USA $24.99
CAN $29.99
UK £17.99

Pregnancy

9781119235491
USA $26.99
CAN $31.99
UK £19.99

Samsung Galaxy S7

9781119279952
USA $24.99
CAN $29.99
UK £17.99

iPhone

9781119283133
USA $24.99
CAN $29.99
UK £17.99

Crocheting

9781119287117
USA $24.99
CAN $29.99
UK £16.99

Nutrition

9781119130246
USA $22.99
CAN $27.99
UK £16.99

PROFESSIONAL DEVELOPMENT

Windows 10

9781119311041
USA $24.99
CAN $29.99
UK £17.99

AutoCAD

9781119255796
USA $39.99
CAN $47.99
UK £27.99

Excel 2016

9781119293439
USA $26.99
CAN $31.99
UK £19.99

QuickBooks 2017

9781119281467
USA $26.99
CAN $31.99
UK £19.99

macOS Sierra

9781119280651
USA $29.99
CAN $35.99
UK £21.99

LinkedIn

9781119251132
USA $24.99
CAN $29.99
UK £17.99

Windows 10

9781119310563
USA $34.00
CAN $41.99
UK £24.99

SharePoint 2016

9781119181705
USA $29.99
CAN $35.99
UK £21.99

Fundamental Analysis

9781119263593
USA $26.99
CAN $31.99
UK £19.99

Networking

9781119257769
USA $29.99
CAN $35.99
UK £21.99

Office 2016

9781119293477
USA $26.99
CAN $31.99
UK £19.99

Office 365

9781119265313
USA $24.99
CAN $29.99
UK £17.99

Salesforce.com

9781119239314
USA $29.99
CAN $35.99
UK £21.99

Coding

9781119293323
USA $29.99
CAN $35.99
UK £21.99